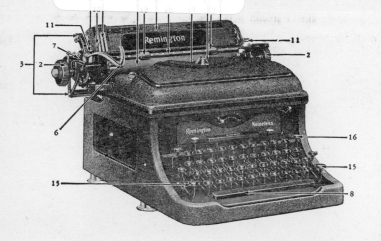

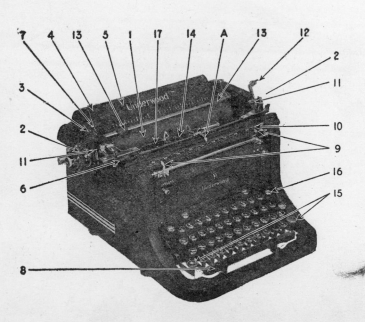

Reference List of Operating Parts and Their Uses

1. **Cylinder**—the hard rubber roll around which the paper is fed and held in position for typing. (Also called the *platen*.)

2. **Cylinder Knobs**—the small rubber rollers at the two ends of the cylinder; used to feed the paper into the cylinder.

3. **Carriage**—that part of the typewriter which is movable from side to side. (The cylinder moves with the carriage.)

4. **Paper Guide**—a strip of metal, which may be moved to the right or left, and which serves to guide the left edge of the paper as it is fed into the machine.

5. **Paper Rest**—the wide metal piece on which the name of the machine appears and against which the paper rests when it has been put into the machine.

6. **Carriage Return Lever**—used to throw back the carriage and space the lines of writing. (Also called the *Line Space Lever*.)

7. **Line Space Regulator**—a device used to adjust the machine for single-spaced, double-spaced, or triple-spaced writing.

8. **Space Bar**—the black bar just below the lower or bottom row of keys; operated by the right thumb and used to space between words.

9. **Margin Stops**—metal catches used to secure the length of writing line and the width of side margins desired.

10. **Margin Scale**—the scale showing stroke-spaces across the sheet; used as a guide in setting the margin stops.

11. **Carriage Release Lever**—levers at each end of the cylinder which release the carriage and enable the operator to move it quickly to any point.

12. **Paper Release Lever**—a metal lever which releases the pressure on the paper; used when straightening or removing the paper.

13. **Paper Holders**—small movable rubber rollers which hold the paper firmly against the cylinder.

14. **Type Guide**—the part between the two small metal pieces where the type strikes the paper.

15. **Shift Keys**—used in writing capitals and certain symbols.

16. **Margin Release Key**—used to release the margin stop. When the stop for the right margin is released, the operator can continue the writing.

17. **Line Scale**—the scale on the metal pieces to the right and left of the type guide.

Reference List of Operating Parts and Their Uses

1. **Cylinder**—the hard rubber roll around which the paper is fed and held in position for typing. (Also called the *platen*.)

2. **Cylinder Knobs**—the small rubber rollers at the two ends of the cylinder; used to feed the paper into the cylinder.

3. **Carriage**—that part of the typewriter which is movable from side to side. (The cylinder moves with the carriage.)

4. **Paper Guide**—a strip of metal, which may be moved to the right or left, and which serves to guide the left edge of the paper as it is fed into the machine.

5. **Paper Rest**—the wide metal piece on which the name of the machine appears and against which the paper rests when it has been put into the machine.

6. **Carriage Return Lever**—used to throw back the carriage and space the lines of writing. (Also called the *Line Space Lever*.)

7. **Line Space Regulator**—a device used to adjust the machine for single-spaced, double-spaced, or triple-spaced writing.

8. **Space Bar**—the black bar just below the lower or bottom row of keys; operated by the right thumb and used to space between words.

9. **Margin Stops**—metal catches used to secure the length of writing line and the width of side margins desired.

10. **Margin Scale**—the scale showing stroke-spaces across the sheet; used as a guide in setting the margin stops.

11. **Carriage Release Lever**—levers at each end of the cylinder which release the carriage and enable the operator to move it quickly to any point.

12. **Paper Release Lever**—a metal lever which releases the pressure on the paper; used when straightening or removing the paper.

13. **Paper Holders**—small movable rubber rollers which hold the paper firmly against the cylinder.

14. **Type Guide**—the part between the two small metal pieces where the type strikes the paper.

15. **Shift Keys**—used in writing capitals and certain symbols.

16. **Margin Release Key**—used to release the margin stop. When the stop for the right margin is released, the operator can continue the writing.

17. **Line Scale**—the scale on the metal pieces to the right and left of the type guide.

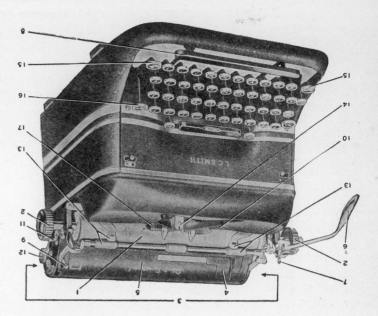

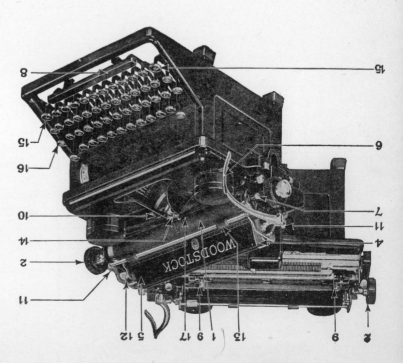

COLLEGE TYPING

by Ray Wall Fisher
Walter T. White
Charles G. Reigner

REVISED

THE H. M. ROWE COMPANY
BALTIMORE   CHICAGO

FOREWORD

COLLEGE
TYPING

BY RAY WALL FISHER
WALTER J. WHITE
CHARLIE G. RIDGWAY

REVISED

THE H. M. ROWE COMPANY

Manufactured in the United States of America

List No. 145

The H. M. Rowe Company, Baltimore, Md.

FOREWORD . . .

THE primary emphasis in COLLEGE TYPING is on the vocational aspects of typewriting. The major objective, therefore, in the construction of the book has been to provide material which will, in the shortest possible time, develop those skills and techniques which are required in the business and professional man's office. The content of the text has been carefully arranged for ease of learning, simplicity of teaching, and effectiveness of results. All non-essentials have been eliminated, and discussion has been reduced to the minimum. Typing skills are developed through action, not through reading.

Division 1 consists of nine lessons which cover the keyboard, including the figures. The approach used establishes the guide position at the outset, with the result that control of the reach keys is quickly mastered. Beginning with Lesson 2, the Contrast Method is employed. By this method, letter-stroke confusion (*i* for *e*, *g* for *h*, *b* for *n*, etc.) which often arises from like-finger reaches is lessened. Those factors that tend to create hesitation in the initial learning stage—difficult combinations, infrequent words, and complex sentences—have been studiously avoided. Reading control, too, is obtained by the careful arrangement of the content of the exercises and by the inclusion of lines of random letter drill in the early lessons. Such drill forces the student to adopt a slow reading rate in the initial stages and encourages concentration on the copy as well as on the feel of each stroke in the finger.

Throughout the book the lessons have been arranged for ease of administration and definiteness of assignment. In Division 1, each lesson is a complete unit and consists of four parts: (1) Warming-up Drill, (2) New Stroke Control, (3) Practice Exercise, and (4) Lesson Summary. Special instructions and explanations are given at the time and place at which the student needs them.

Each Warming-up Drill constitutes a review of the preceding lessons. The drill may be practiced individually by the students, or it may be used by the teacher as material for class unison drill. The arrangement and content of these drills are such that, when they are used as class unison drills, each student may type the drill which accompanies the particular lesson on which he is working at the time.

The New Stroke Control introduces the particular strokes taken up in the lesson. These drills are also so constructed that they may be used as class unison drills if desired. Each student confines himself to the lesson on which he is working at the time. In this way each individual is permitted to progress at his own rate and on his own level.

The Practice Exercise establishes the new stroke responses. The Lesson Summary provides material by which the student himself, as well as the teacher, may determine his degree of mastery of the work covered up to that point.

Division 2 develops those stroke controls which involve the shift of the figure row keys, so that the quotation, apostrophe, and other characters used in straight copy may be automatized. Thorough training is also given on the typing of special characters. Short, common words make up the Warming-up Drills. Acceleration is secured through the writing of phrases and short sentences. Controlled writing is developed through concentration exercises. Finally, the student is stimulated to secure practical writing skill through the typing of short paragraphs of low stroke intensity. These paragraphs may be used as straight copy matter or as one-minute, two-minute, or three-minute Timed Writings.

Division 3 continues with longer Timed Writings of greater stroke intensity than those given in Division 2. In this Division the student is also given training in the centering of headings and articles. Heading and paragraph styles are developed.

Division 4 consists of a compendium of drills of various kinds which can be used as independent assignments or in connection with the Divisions that follow. These special drills enable the teacher to give attention to the individual needs of students.

Division 5 takes up letter styles on a new and original plan. The parts of the business letter have been grouped in two classes—the Major Parts, or those which are essential to every business letter, and the Minor Parts, or those which may be and often are included in a letter. Each Style Letter is so written that it explains the particular style in which it is typed. The letter placement chart enables the student to set up the problem letters according to mechanical principles. By the time the ten Assignments are completed, he will have obtained a wide variety of experience and practice in the arrangement of letters.

Division 6 is devoted wholly to tabulation and billing. In many offices a large share of the work of typists involves tabulating. In this Division the student learns that the essential feature of attractive tabulating work is the preliminary planning. A graphic representation or working plan which can be applied to any problem in tabulating is presented. When the student once understands the procedure and can set up a working plan, tabulation becomes merely a matter of adeptness in the use of the tabular key, in writing figures, and in centering. Billing is merely tabulating applied to special forms.

Rough Drafts are taken up in Division 7. Practical problem material consisting of handwriting in various styles is included. The typing of rough drafts is a valuable aid to the student in learning to proof-read his own work.

Division 8, "Secretarial Typing," contains problems on a wide variety of typewriting representing the everyday work of the office typist, other than letter writing, tabulating, and rough draft work. The instructions are brief and to the point. The Division contains a number of attractive and helpful models and illustrations.

Division 9 is devoted to legal typing. The typing of legal papers and documents gives a training in accuracy that can hardly be obtained through any other kind of work. This Division enforces close attention to details. A valuable phase of the work is the typing of all the papers that are prepared in connection with an actual suit at law.

In Division 10 the student prepares a Correspondence Guide. This Division is in the nature of a summary of all the training provided in the text. Students should save their work on this Division and bind the sheets as instructed in the text. When they do so, they will have a useful Guide containing various letter styles, envelope address styles, and brief summaries of English, punctuation, and correct word division.

COLLEGE TYPING is the final outcome of extensive studies of typewriting teaching problems, as well as of wide classroom experience on the college level. The problem work of the book reflects also the results of an extensive investigation of the kind of work actually done by typists in business offices. The entire text is so organized that the teacher's work is reduced to the minimum, and the students may progress as rapidly as their individual industry and aptitudes permit.

The Authors

About the Authors

Ray Wall Fisher holds the degrees of Bachelor of Science from the University of California and Master of Commercial Education from Armstrong College, Berkeley, California. Mr. Fisher was formerly Director of the School of Secretarial Science, Armstrong College. He is now Chairman of the Typewriting Department of Merritt Business School, Oakland, California. He has been instructor in Methods of Teaching Typewriting at Armstrong College, at Bowling Green Business University, Bowling Green, Kentucky, and at the University of California.

Walter J. White is a graduate of Stanford University, from which institution he holds the degree of Bachelor of Arts. For a number of years he conducted summer courses in Methods of Teaching Typewriting in various colleges. Mr. White is the author of TYPING FOR ACCURACY, a widely used supplementary book based on an extensive study of the cause and cure of errors in typewriting. He is also co-author, with Mr. Reigner, of ROWE TYPING. As a member of the staff of The H. M. Rowe Company, Mr. White has had opportunities to observe the teaching of typewriting in leading business schools and collegiate institutions.

Charles G. Reigner has been an undergraduate and graduate student at Princeton University, University of Pennsylvania, New York University, and the University of Pittsburgh, from which institution he holds the degree of Bachelor of Arts and the Bachelor's Diploma in Education. He has had wide teaching experience in various types of schools, and is the author of more than a score of well-known textbooks. His books in the English, secretarial, and typewriting fields are widely used in business schools and collegiate institutions throughout the country. As President of The H. M. Rowe Company, he is in constant touch with all phases of commercial education.

CONTEST RULES

(Adapted from the International Contest Rules)

1. Papers should be written with double spacing. Charge one error for each line written with single or irregular spacing—in addition to any other errors in the same line.

2. Each 8½ x 11 sheet except the last one must have at least 29 lines of writing. Charge one error only for a short page—not one error for each line that the page is short.

3. Except at the end of a paragraph or in the last line of writing, charge one error for each line having fewer than 61 or more than 76 characters. Other errors in such short or long lines are also to be counted.

4. Paragraphs should be indented exactly five stroke-spaces. Charge one error for each wrong indentation—in addition to any other errors in the same line.

5. Charge one error for each violation of the spacing rules governing punctuation marks. (See page 210.) Any mark incorrectly made, inserted, omitted, or in any way changed constitutes an error, unless the preceding word contains an error.

6. Charge one error for any letter struck so lightly that it cannot be seen. If it can be seen, there is no error.

7. Charge one error for each word wrongly divided at the end of a line.

8. Charge one error for every word that shows incorrect use of the shift key. If parts only of the proper character appear, it is an error. If, however, the complete character has been typed, there is no error.

9. Charge one error for any word in which letters are transposed.

10. Transposed *words* should be checked as though no transposition existed, but one error should be charged for the transposition.

11. Charge one error for any word written so near the top, bottom, or side of the sheet that a part of the letter is cut off.

12. Charge one error for any word that is crowded; that is, one that is written in less than its proper number of stroke-spaces.

13. Charge one error for any word that is piled. Piling is understood to mean the writing of all or any portion of the body of a character over any portion of the body of another character, or in the space between words.

14. Charge one error for any character written to the right or left of the point of the scale set for the left-hand margin. All lines, except the lines which begin paragraphs, must begin at the same point on the scale.

15. If an error is made in the last word written, whether the word is completed or not, charge one error.

16. Papers in which words are x'd or on which erasing has been done are not received or checked.

General Rule: Every word omitted, inserted, repeated, misspelled, or in any manner changed from the printed copy must be penalized by charging an error. *Only one error, however, shall be counted in any one word.*

The method of counting strokes and of determining net speed is explained on page 25.

CONTENTS

College Typing
Introduction

A few minutes spent in careful and thoughtful reading of all the instructions and explanations as they occur in the book will save you hours of work later on.

One of the most important preventives of high-frequency errors is correct position at the typewriter.

Position at the Typewriter

1. The center of the body should be opposite the letter 1.

2. Sit 8 or 10 inches back from the front frame of the machine, so that the upper arm—from shoulder to elbow—is slightly forward.

3. The body should be erect and alert; lean slightly forward from the hips.

4. The feet should be flat on the floor—not crossed or resting on the heels. One foot may be placed a few inches in front of the other.

5. The elbows should hang naturally at the sides.

Note: If the little fingers are short, it may be necessary to hold the elbows away from the sides so that the tips of the fingers may rest on the keys without arching or sagging the wrists.

Illustration 1
Correct Position at the Machine

Illustration 2
Correct Position of the Hand

6. Keep the forearm straight from elbow to hand, slanting upward at about the same angle as the keyboard. The wrists should be neither arched nor sagging.

7. The heel of the hand should be about an inch above the front frame of the typewriter.

8. The fingers should be curved sufficiently to permit them to rest on their tips, not on the balls of the fingers.

Note: The shorter the fingers, the more will be the curvature, so that the operator may reach the upper and the lower rows of keys without moving the hands. One method of determining the curvature is to rest the tips of the fingers on the guide keys, and then to bring the thumbs together on the space bar with the tips touching the b-key.

Preliminary Operations

Parts of the Typewriter. A thorough knowledge of the operative parts and their uses will greatly assist you in following the directions and will also materially shorten the time which will have to be spent on the keyboard approach.

In the following preliminary operations, the parts are taken up in the order of their use. Before proceeding with these operations, read through the instructions and become familiar with the parts mentioned. The number (in parentheses) which follows the name of a part refers to the Reference List of Operating Parts given on the inside front cover and on the front flyleaf.

Illustration 3
Picking up the Paper

Illustration 4
Inserting the Paper

Inserting the Paper

Familiarize yourself with the following operating parts:

Paper Rest (No. 5)
Cylinder (No. 1)
Paper Guide (No. 4)
Cylinder Knobs (No. 2)

To insert the paper—

1. Hold the paper with the left hand and place it between the paper rest and the cylinder, with the left edge against the paper guide.

2. At the same time grasp the right cylinder knob with the right hand—thumb well under and the first two fingers on top.

3. Twirl the knob so that the paper feeds into the machine with one movement.

Letter Writing or Carbon Copy Method. You will find it better practice to use two sheets of paper rather than one. The extra sheet serves as a cushion or *backing sheet* which helps to prevent the rubber cylinder from becoming hard or glazed. When you use two sheets (or

more, as in typing carbon copies), follow the experienced typist's method of inserting the sheets into the machine, thus:

1. Pick up the sheets with either hand—whichever is the more convenient.

2. Drop the paper loosely through the hands—between the thumbs and forefingers—and tap the edges lightly on the desk or other flat surface.

3. Insert the sheets with the *left* hand and twirl them into the machine with the right hand.

Straightening the Paper

Look up these operating parts:

Carriage (No. 3)
Line Scale (No. 17)
Paper Release Lever (No. 12)

The straightness of the paper may be tested either (a) by turning the cylinder backward until the upper edges of the sheets are in alignment with the line scale or (b) by turning the cylinder forward and putting the top and bottom edges of the sheets together.

If the paper has not been fed into the machine evenly, straighten it as shown in Illustration 5. Disengage the paper release lever, straighten the paper, and **return the release lever to position.**

Removing the Paper

To remove the paper quietly from the machine, follow this procedure:

1. Take hold of the paper release lever with the thumb and forefinger of the nearer hand.

2. Grasp the paper near the top edge with the other hand.

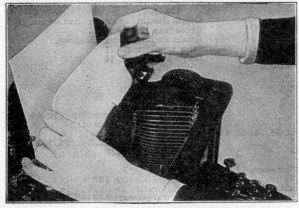

Illustration 5
Using the Paper Release to Straighten the Paper

INDEX

paper, and re-engage the release lever before removing the hand from it.

Caution: Always be sure to return the release lever to operating position. If you do not do so, the feed rolls and cylinder will not grasp the paper when it is fed into the machine; neither will the paper be held in place.

Adjusting the Paper Holders

Make sure that you understand the use of the **Paper Holders** (No. 13).

If the paper holders on your machine consist of a bail with two rolls, place the rolls about an inch and a half from each side of the paper. If there is a third roll, you may place it at the center of the sheet.

If your machine has paper clamps, adjust them in such a way that the outside edges of the rolls rest on the outside edges of the sheet.

Note: Some typewriters are equipped with both bail and clamps. You may use both, or you may leave the bail disengaged.

Moving the Carriage

Study the **Carriage Release Lever** (No. 11).

When you are typing, the carriage moves automatically from right to left with each stroke. The carriage may also be moved independently of the keys, when not typing, by depressing either of the carriage release levers. Retain hold of the cylinder knob, or the *thumb piece*, if there is one on your machine, when you depress the release lever.

Preparing for Copy

Familiarize yourself with the use of these parts:

Margin Scale (No. 10)
Type Guide (No. 14)
Margin Stops (No. 9)

In addition to a line scale and a margin scale, some typewriters are equipped with a *paper guide scale*, a *cylinder* or *platen scale*, and an *indicator scale*.

rest which is used for locating the paper guide. The cylinder or platen scale is a front scale the full width of the platen, with stroke-spaces corresponding with those of the margin scale. On some typewriters the indicator scale and the margin scale are the same; on other typewriters the indicator scale is a full-width scale directly below the cylinder or platen scale; on still other typewriters the indicator scale is on the paper holder bail, and is made available by dropping the bail forward.

Locating the Paper. If your typewriter is equipped with a paper guide scale, set the paper guide at 0. If you place the paper against the guide when you insert it, the left edge will be at 0 on the margin scale and the indicator scale.

If your machine does not have a paper guide scale, you may insert the paper with the left edge at 0 by proceeding as follows:

1. Set one margin stop at 0 on the margin scale and slide the other margin stop to the other end of the scale so that it will be out of the way.

2. Move the carriage so that the printing indicator will point to 0 on the margin scale or the indicator scale. (The printing indicator is the small projection which designates the point on the margin scale at which a character will print.)

3. Move the paper guide out of the way and insert the paper so that the left edge is directly back of the type guide.

4. Return the paper guide to position—just touching the left edge of the paper. Note carefully where the guide is now placed, and always locate it at that point when using paper of the same width.

Pica and Elite Type. Your typewriter may be equipped with either *pica* or *elite* type. Pica type is the larger of the two sizes. It measures 10 strokes to the horizontal inch (across the paper). Elite type measures 12 strokes to the horizontal inch. The difference can be observed by studying the following scale.

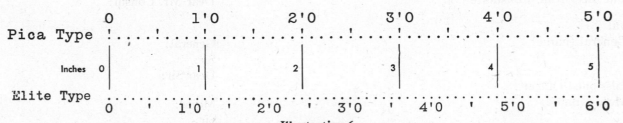

Illustration 6
Comparison of Pica and Elite Type

7

The President
The President
His Excellency, The President of the United States

Sir:
My dear Mr. President:
Your Excellency:
Mr. President:

The Vice-President
The Vice-President
The Honorable (name)
Vice-President of the United States

Sir:
My dear Mr. Vice-President:

Cabinet Officer
The Secretary of Commerce
Honorable (name)
Secretary of Commerce

Dear Sir:
Sir:
My dear Mr. Secretary:

Senator
The Honorable (name)
Senator from Minnesota

Sir:
Dear Sir:
My dear Senator:

Congressman
The Honorable (name)
The Honorable (name), M. C.

Sir:
Dear Sir:
My dear Congressman:

Chief Justice
The Honorable (name)
Chief Justice of the United States Supreme Court

Sir:
Dear Sir:
My dear Mr. Chief Justice:

Associate Justice
The Honorable (name)
Justice of the United States Supreme Court

Sir:
Dear Sir:
My dear Mr. Justice:

Governor
The Honorable (name)
His Excellency (name)
His Excellency the Governor

Sir:
Dear Sir:
Your Excellency:

Mayor
His Honor the Mayor
The Honorable (name)
Mayor of Seattle

Dear Sir:
My dear Mr. Mayor:

Judge
The Honorable (name)

Sir:
Dear Sir:
My dear Judge ——:

Consul
The Argentine Consulate

Dear Mr. Consul:

General
General (name)

General:
Sir:
Dear Sir:

Commissioned Officer
Major (name)

Major:
Sir:
Dear Sir:

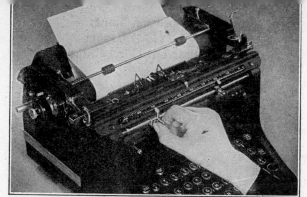

Illustration 7
Setting the Margin Stop (front)

Illustration 8
Setting the Margin Stops (rear)

Setting the Margin Stops (Centering Point Method). The margin stops are used to control the length of the writing line. They should be set in such a way that one-half of the line will be to the left and one-half to the right of the centering point.

If the side margins are to be approximately the same width, the centering point will be the center of the paper. Standard letter-size paper is 8½ inches wide; that is, 85 *pica* strokes (8½ inches x 10 strokes to the inch); or 102 *elite* strokes (8½ inches x 12 strokes to the inch). With the left edge of the paper at 0, the center will be at 42 or 43 (43 is

generally preferred) when using a machine with *pica* type; and at 51 (50 is sometimes preferred) when using a machine with *elite* type.

	Pica		Elite	
Centering Point	43	43	51	51
One-half of 5-inch line	−25	+25	−30	+30
Set Margin Stops at	18	68	21	81

The following diagrams will serve as guides in determining the margin stop locations when using the Centering Point Method.

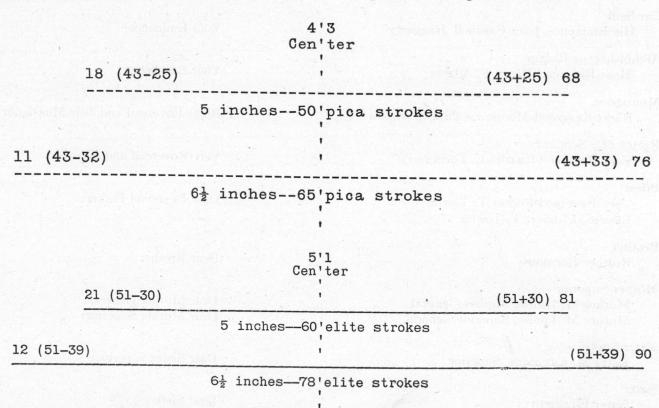

```
                          4'3
                       Cen'ter
                          '
 18 (43-25)               '                      (43+25) 68
-------------------------------------------------------------
       5 inches--50'pica strokes
                          '
 11 (43-32)               '                      (43+33) 76
-------------------------------------------------------------
      6½ inches--65'pica strokes
                          '

                          5'1
                       Cen'ter
                          '
   21 (51-30)             '                    (51+30) 81
_____
         5 inches---60'elite strokes
                          '
 12 (51-39)               '                    (51+39) 90
_____
      6½ inches---78'elite strokes
                          '
```

Professor George A. Grant	Dear Sir:
Dr. (Mr.) George A. Grant	Dear Professor Grant:
Professor of Economics	Dear Dr. (Mr.) Grant:
	My dear Dr. (Mr.) Grant:

Physician
Dr. A. L. Hampton
A. L. Hampton, M. D.

Dear Sir:
Dear Dr. Hampton:
My dear Dr. Hampton:

Note: Never write the salutation as *Dear Doctor* or *Dear Professor.*

CLERGY

Bishop (except Methodist)
Right Reverend John E. Harris
Bishop of Nebraska

Sir:
Right Reverend Sir:
Right Reverend and Dear Sir:
Right Reverend Bishop:

Methodist Bishop
Reverend Henry W. Styles
Mt. Vernon Place Church

Reverend Sir:
Reverend and Dear Sir:

Any Protestant Clergyman
Reverend Charles L. Roberts

Sir:
Dear Sir:

Rabbi
Rabbi Ezra W. Luders

Dear Sir:
Dear Rabbi Luders:

CATHOLIC

The Pope
His Holiness, Pope Pius XII

Your Holiness:

Cardinal
His Eminence, John Cardinal Haggerty

Your Eminence:

Archbishop or Bishop
Most Reverend Henry F. Adams

Your Excellency:

Monsignor
Right Reverend Monsignor Paul L. Mason

Right Reverend and dear Monsignor:

Rector of a Seminary
Very Reverend Charles C. Forbes

Very Reverend and Dear Sir:

Priest
Very Reverend Robert T. Towne
Reverend Robert T. Towne

Dear Reverend Father:

Brother
Brother Borromeo

Dear Brother:

Mother Superior
Mother M. Louise, Mother General
Mother M. Louise, Superior General

Dear Mother General:
Dear Mother Superior:

Sister Superior
Sister M. Catherine, Superior

Dear Sister Superior:

Sister
Sister Elizabeth

Dear Sister:

Familiarize yourself with the operation of these parts:

Line Space Regulator (No. 7)
Carriage Return Lever, or
Line Space Lever (No. 6)

Whether you are using a machine equipped with pica or with elite type, you will find that six lines make a vertical inch. If you are to type copy in single-spaced form and wish to leave a top margin of 1 inch, simply strike the carriage return lever six times, after you have made sure (1) that the line space lever is set for single spacing and (2) that you have adjusted the paper so that the top edge is even with the line scale.

To get the top margin, proceed thus:

1. Turn back the cylinder until the top edge of the paper is just even with the line scale.

2. Set the line space regulator for single spacing.

3. Strike the carriage return lever to space six times.

Top Edge of Sheet

XXXXXXXXXXXXXXXXXXXXXXXXX)
XXXXXXXXXXXXXXXXXXXXXXXXX)
XXXXXXXXXXXXXXXXXXXXXXXXX)
XXXXXXXXXXXXXXXXXXXXXXXXX)
XXXXXXXXXXXXXXXXXXXXXXXXX)
XXXXXXXXXXXXXXXXXXXXXXXXX)

If you wish to leave a top margin of 2 inches, strike the line space lever twelve times.

you will first set the line space lever for double spacing; next, insert the paper so that the edge is even with the line scale; finally, strike the line space lever three times for a top margin of 1 inch; six times for a top margin of 2 inches.

Top Margin Drill. Set the line space regulator for double spacing. Space down for a top margin of 1 inch; 1½ inches; 2 inches; 2½ inches; 3 inches.

Set the line space regulator for single spacing. Space down for a top margin of 3 inches; 2 inches; 1 inch; 1½ inches; 2½ inches.

The Guide Keys

The guide keys on the left, reading from left to right, are **a**, **s**, **d**, and **f**. The guide keys on the right, reading from right to left, are **;**, **l**, **k**, and **j**. See Illustration 9.

The fingers are named from the guide keys over which they are placed. Beginning with the little finger of the left hand, they are the *a-*, *s-*, *d-*, and *f-*fingers. Beginning with the little finger of the right hand, they are the *;-*, *l-*, *k-*, and *j-*fingers. The two keys in the middle of the guide row are not covered when the fingers are in position over the guide keys. See Illustration 10.

Let the fingers fall naturally over the guide keys; the finger tips should be just above, but not resting completely on, the keys.

The Stroke

A quick, easy stroke, made in correct form, plays a vital part in your typing. Each stroke is really a part of a circle or of an oval; hence. we shall call the typing stroke the "arc stroke." Think of each letter as being an **arc stroke** of

Illustration 9
Keyboard with Guide Keys Lettered

Illustration 10
**Fingers in Position over the Guide Row.
Thumbs over the Space Bar.**

APPENDIX

Reference Guide for Address and Salutation Forms

First Line of Address	*Salutation*
Individual (man)	
Mr. Henry C. Jackson	Dear Sir:
	Dear Mr. Jackson:
	My dear Sir:
	My dear Mr. Jackson:
Individual (unmarried woman)	
Miss Mary W. Milton	Dear Miss Milton:
	My dear Miss Milton:
Individual (married woman)	
Mrs. R. A. Kaylor	Dear Madam:
	My dear Madam:
	Dear Mrs. Kaylor:
	My dear Mrs. Kaylor:
Partnership (men)	
Henderson & Taylor	Gentlemen:
*Messrs. Henderson & Taylor	
Webster, Haynes & Tuttle	
*Messrs. Webster, Haynes & Tuttle	
Unmarried Women	
Misses Mary and Elizabeth Weston	Ladies:
Misses Webb and Carter	Mesdames:
	Dear Miss Webb and Miss Carter:
	My dear Miss Webb and Miss Carter:
Company	
American Machine Tool Company	Gentlemen:
Company, with Attention Phrase	
United Provision Company	Gentlemen:
(address)	
Attention Mr. K. U. Jamison	

PEOPLE IN PROFESSIONS

College President	
President Charles L. Dunn	Dear Sir:
Dr. Charles L. Dunn, President	Dear President Dunn:
	My dear President Dunn:
	Dear Dr. Dunn:
	My dear Dr. Dunn:
Dean of a College	
Dean Alfred H. Hunt	Dear Sir:
Dr. (Mr.) Alfred H. Hunt, Dean	Dear Dean Hunt:
	My dear Dean Hunt:
	Dear Dr. (Mr.) Hunt:
	My dear Dr. (Mr.) Hunt:

*The title *Messrs.* is no longer so widely used as formerly.

Illustration 11

Fingers Curved. Note the Slant of the Hand and of the Wrist.

center of the key with a quick, positive movement. This flick from the arc stroke starts the key downward, and momentum carries the type bar up to the cylinder. Your finger tip meanwhile completes the arc toward the palm of the hand or moves into position for another stroke.

Developing the Stroke

One of the most important phases of beginning typing is the development of the arc stroke. As each new key is taken up, proceed in the following manner:

1. Depress the carriage release lever and move the carriage to the left as far as it will go. The keys will lock.

2. Curve your fingers in position over the guide keys. Sit erect at the proper distance from the machine.

3. Strike quickly. Make each stroke a continuous arc from start to finish; then relax. Do not attempt to force down the locked keys. Merely flick them.

its particular finger. Do not think of the keys or their positions; think, rather, of the finger making each arc stroke and the *feel* of that stroke in the finger.

Preliminary Drill 1

Start with the *f*-finger and the *j*-finger, because they are the fingers most easily controlled. As the **f**-stroke and the **j**-stroke become more perfectly developed, try to bring the other strokes up to the same standard of evenness and speed.

In doing the following drill, observe these instructions:

1. Move the carriage to the extreme left so that the keys will lock.

2. With the keys locked, strike the f-key with the f-finger and the j-key with the j-finger.

3. Keep the other fingers in guide position while you stroke with the *f*-finger and the *j*-finger. In making the strokes, do not move your forearms or hands. Ninety per cent of the movement in stroking is made with the fingers.

4. Proceed as follows in stroking Line 1.

(a) Stroke as you count *one*; (b) pause or rest as you count *two-three*, thus:

1	2-3	1	2-3	1	2-3	1	2-3
f	*relax*	f	*relax*	f	*relax*	j	*relax*	etc.

Line 1   fffjjjfffjjjfffjjjfffjjjfffjjjfffjjjfff

Returning the Carriage

When you have written a line, the carriage must be returned quickly to continue the writing. Use the carriage return lever to throw the carriage back to start another line. This lever automatically spaces the paper up for a new line. Never push or pull the carriage across. The carriage return is a *throw of the wrist*. Instantly, after the throw has been made, return the hand to its position over the guide row. Study Illustration 12.

You will lose much time if you look up from your copy each time the carriage is returned. Cultivate the habit of throwing the carriage quickly and automatically—without watching your hands or the machine.

Illustration 12
Returning the Carriage

sions.

Yes, we shall follow the procedure you have outlined. You will agree with us, we believe, when we say that the catalog serves a useful purpose.

5. *Long Transposed Adverbial Phrases and Clauses.*

Just as soon as we hear from you again, we shall at once comply with your wishes. To arrive at a sound conclusion on any matter, it is necessary to have all the facts.

6. *Coordinate Clauses in a Compound Sentence.*

Saving will make you independent financially, and it will make you independent in your own mind. It is quite evident that an error has been made, but we do not believe that the factory is responsible for it.

7. *Non-restrictive Relative and Adverbial Clauses.*

The April issue of our house paper, which is being sent to you today, gives a full account of the new code. Shipment over the Southern Pacific will hasten deliveries, as the yards of that company are located within four blocks of our plant.

8. *Direct Quotations.*

We confirm our telegram, "Ship immediately fourteen dozen Style 572." "Genius," said Thomas Edison, "consists largely of the capacity for hard work."

Note: Do not use a comma to separate the coordinate clauses of a sentence when the conjunction is omitted. That error is called the "comma fault."

The Semicolon

The semicolon is used in these constructions:

1. Between the coordinate clauses in a compound sentence that are not joined by a conjunction.

orders will be issued in due time. The shipment was made this morning; the bill of lading is enclosed.

2. Between the coordinate clauses of a compound sentence when the second clause begins with a conjunctive adverb.

The shipment weighed only 55 pounds; consequently, we cannot allow the amount of your deduction.

The Colon

The colon is used to follow a formal introduction to a quotation or a list of items.

We have just received the following telegram from our Chicago office: "Send immediately all information relating to Illinois sales tax." The following directors were present at the meeting: Jamison, Hughes, Bard, Fulton, and Henry.

Application Exercise 20. Page 22 of the Guide is to contain a two-column tabulation giving the names of the states with the abbreviations recommended by the Post Office Department. In Exercise 3, page 126, you will find a list of state names with their abbreviations.

Application Exercise 21. Prepare a title page for the Manual. On the page you are to type the title, *Correspondence Guide*, your name, the name of your school, your town or city, state, and today's date. Plan the title page carefully.

Application Exercise 22. Type a Contents page for the Manual.

When a sheet has both a main heading and a subheading, type the main heading as the first line in the Contents and the subheading as the second line. Leaders are to be typed after the subheading.

Application Exercise 23. You are now to staple and bind the Guide. If possible, secure two sheets of heavy manila paper 8½ x 11 in size. One is to be used for the front cover, and the other for the back cover. On the cover page, type *Correspondence Guide* and your name. Punch all the sheets, including the cover pages, not less than one-half inch from the top. Two punch holes will be sufficient. Insert staples in the punch holes. You now have a valuable Guide in convenient form for reference purposes.

To cultivate a quick carriage return, proceed as follows:

1. Depress the carriage return lever and move the carriage across to 60 or more on the margin scale.

2. Place your fingers over the guide keys. Keep your eyes on these instructions for a left-hand throw.

(a) With *palm down* and fingers braced against one another, extend the left hand to the return lever about half way between the nail and the knuckle of the *f*-finger. (Hold the fingers together rather firmly, but do not make the hand tense.)

(b) Throw the carriage with a quick, forceful wrist movement, returning your hand back to the guide row before the carriage stops. Learn the proper force to put behind the wrist movement to return the carriage.

Carriage Return Drills

Repeat the following drills several times on a three-count basis.

Preparation: 1. Carry the right hand to the carriage, hooking the thumb on the thumb piece (if any) and resting the *j*-finger on the carriage release lever.

2. Depress the release lever and move the carriage across to 60 or more on the scale.

3. Return the right hand to guide position.

Drill 1: 1. Stiffen the fingers of the left hand, lifting them slightly and pointing them toward the carriage.

2. Extend the left hand, with the fingers still braced, to position against the return lever.

3. Throw the carriage, returning the left hand to its guide position while the carriage is still in motion.

Preparation: As above.

Drill 2: 1. Stiffen the fingers of the left hand, lifting them slightly and pointing them toward the carriage.

2. Extend the left hand, with fingers still braced, to position against the carriage return lever, and line-space without moving the carriage.

3. Return the left hand to its guide position.

Preliminary Drill 2

1. Insert two sheets of paper. Straighten them, if necessary.

2. Set the margin stops for a 40-stroke line (at 20 and 60).

3. Set the line space regulator for single spacing.

4. Return the carriage from the locked position to writing position.

5. Type Line 2 three times; use the same count as with Line 1, but this time space after each three-letter group, as shown below. Strike the **Space Bar** (No. 8) as you count *one*; relax as you count *two-three*.

6. Return the carriage quickly at the end of each line. Double line-space after completing the three-line group.

Line 2   fff jjj fff jjj fff jjj fff jjj fff jjj

Return the carriage quickly.

Thumb-Spacing

Spacing after words is generally done with the right thumb, although occasionally a person who is decidedly left-handed uses the left thumb. Each thumb-stroke on the Space Bar causes the carriage to space once.

The left thumb is held off the space bar and is bent in toward the *f*-finger. With the right thumb curved a very little, hit the space bar in the center with a light, quick stroke; then raise the thumb immediately.

If the carriage jumps when you thumb-space, the typewriter may be out of adjustment; usually, however, the technique of thumb-spacing is faulty. Just a flick of the bar is all that is necessary; do not follow the bar down.

Special Space Bar Drill. The following drill can be used effectively in correcting the habit of double spacing, should it occur.

j *space* j *space* j *space* j *space* j *space* j *space* j *space*

11

style, with open punctuation. The address includes an Introduction line, which is to be typed in the lower left corner. Underscore the Introduction line.

Mr. A. F. Humphreys American Oil Company Fourth and Jackson Streets Denver, Colorado Introducing Mr. Charles C. Hetherington

Application Exercise 18. The heading of page 19 is *Hyphenating Words*. Type the following material with single spacing. Underscore all italicized syllables and words. Remember that hyphenating words at the end of lines should be avoided whenever possible.

1. A word should be divided according to the syllables heard in its pronunciation and not according to its derivation. The word *represent*, for instance, is made up of the prefix *re* and *present*. It is, however, pronounced *rep re sent*. You may, therefore, correctly divide the word in either of two ways: *rep-resent* or *repre-sent*. *Presentation* is pronounced *pres en ta tion*; the first syllable is *pres*, not *pre*. Note also these syllable divisions: *pre fer, pref er ence, rec og nize, knowl edge, serv ice*.

2. Never divide a word of one syllable, such as *strength, through, wreck*. This rule applies to verbs in the past tense that end with *ed*, but which are pronounced as one syllable, thus: *planned, gained, talked, looked, charged*.

3. A two-syllable word in which either of the syllables consists of a single letter should not be divided. For that reason you may not divide these words: *about, above, again, against, abuse, away, among, bony, many*.

4. So far as possible, avoid dividing a word so that only two letters would be carried over to the second line; therefore, do not divide these words: *ever, only, horses, voices, bounces*.

5. When a consonant is doubled, the division is usually made between the two letters, thus: *fit-ted, omit-ted, spot-ted, plain-ness*. Note, however, that you may not divide such words as *referred* and *occurred* between the two *r*'s, for the reason that the final *ed* does not form a separate syllable. When a termination, such as *-ing*, which forms a separate syllable, is added to a word that ends in a double consonant, always make the division after the double consonant, thus: *fill-ing, dwell-ing, roll-ing, miss-ing*.

of a line. Carry over the entire numeral to the next line if you cannot complete it at the end of the line on which you are writing ($22,469.25, *never* $22,-469.25).

Application Exercise 19. Page 20 of the Guide is to be headed *Punctuation Marks*; page 21, *Punctuation Marks (Concluded)*. Single-space the following material, with double spacing between paragraphs. (Use a third page if necessary.)

SPACING

Space twice after the colon or after any punctuation mark—the period, question mark, exclamation point, quotation marks, or closing parenthesis mark—which closes a sentence.

Space once after the comma, semicolon, quotation marks, and closing parenthesis mark when they occur within a sentence.

Do not space before, after, or between the two hyphens which make up the formal dash (--).

Do not space before or after the hyphen (-) or the apostrophe (').

There should be no space after the opening quotation marks or the opening parenthesis mark.

USES

The Comma

The comma is used to set off expressions in the following constructions:

1. *Words in Direct Address.*

Thank you, Mr. Parker, for your courteous attention. We must believe, gentlemen, that the account has simply been overlooked.

2. *Identifying and Appositive Words and Phrases.*

Our representative, Mr. George W. Mason, will call on you on Tuesday, March 10. On June 1, 1939, the company will celebrate its fiftieth anniversary. Our factory at Trenton, N. J., has just been enlarged.

3. *Words and Phrases in a Series.* Notice that the comma is placed before the conjunction which connects the last member of the series.

Remittance may be made by check, money order, stamps, or cash.

Preliminary Drill 3

1. Lock the keys and proceed to develop the strokes for the other guide keys. Use the f-stroke as the guide for the d-, s-, and a-strokes; the j-stroke as the guide for the k-, l-, and ;-strokes.

Guide Keys

Left	Right
asdf	*jkl;*

2. Unlock the keys by returning the carriage to the writing position.

3. Now type Line 3 at least four times, spacing between the four-letter groups of the left and right guide keys. The line of typing should appear as follows:

Line 3   asdf jkl; asdf jkl; asdf jkl; asdf jkl;

4. Write Line 3 three times; double line-space after you complete the three-line group.

Preliminary Drill 4

1. Lock the carriage and develop the g-stroke and the h-stroke.

Guide Row

Left	Right
asdfg	*hjkl;*

Line 4

2. Proceed as in Drill 3. Repeat Line 4 at least three times, as follows:

asdfg hjkl; asdfg hjkl; asdfg hjkl;

asdfg hjkl; asdfg hjkl; asdfg hjkl;

asdfg hjkl; asdfg hjkl; asdfg hjkl;

12

Guide (page 15) is to be headed *Full-blocked Letter Style, with Quotation*. Type the following letter in the full-blocked style. Use mixed punctuation. Begin the date (November 24, 19—) flush with the left margin. Type the lines which form the conclusion at the left margin. Be sure to indent the quotation *on both sides*.

Judson & Clark Company West Crandall Street Erie, Pennsylvania Gentlemen: Please refer to our Order No. 105-215 for 150 gallons of freight car black semi-paste paint. Our Superintendent of Stores has written the following statement about this shipment. (P) "Analysis of this paint shows that it is four percentage points low in pigment and four percentage points high in raw linseed oil. Because of the demand for this special paint, we are accepting it. The manufacturers should be informed, however, that in the future such consignments must be condemned." (P) We also wish to call your attention to the following facts: (P) On our Order No. 107-118 delivered to us on March 15, we returned to you a quantity of freight car brown paste for replacement. (P) Order No. 206-117 for 300 gallons of freight car black, delivered to us on July 20, was rejected by us and returned to you for replacement. (P) On September 29 we wrote you about our Order No. 309-88-B, freight car black, to the effect that we were accepting the shipment, but that the paint was low in carbon and linseed oil. (P) Our relations with your company have been very satisfactory until recently, but we feel bound to call your attention to the inconvenience that results when we are compelled to reject shipments and ask for replacements. Very truly yours, ATLANTIC COAST LINE Purchasing Agent KYT/mhy (*210 words*)

Application Exercise 15. Page 16 of the Guide is to be headed *Memorandum*. With a top margin of 2 inches, center the words *Curtiss-Wright Airport*. Type the words in ALL CAPS spaced out. One double space below, write *Indianapolis, Indiana* in ALL CAPS. Date the Memorandum today. Leave a double space below the lines beginning with *From*, *To*, and *Subject*. Single-space the Memorandum and write it in the blocked style.

R. Haggerty, General Manager Subject: Additional Personnel Authority is respectfully requested to employ the following personnel: (P) Mr. G. R. Woodley as a solicitor of students for the ground school and flying school courses. We have made an arrangement with Mr. Woodley by which we shall pay him 10% commission on all sales. For the first month we have agreed to allow him a drawing account of $125. (P) Mr. H. J. Connolly as a solicitor for aerial photography. The arrangement we have made with Mr. Connolly calls for a commission of 20% on sales, with a drawing account of $20 a week for one month. (P) In both cases the solicitors will be required to stay within their drawing accounts. Their application blanks are attached. (*116 words*)

Application Exercise 16. You will now prepare pages 17 and 18 of the Correspondence Guide. Page 17 is to be headed *Envelope Address Styles*; page 18, *Envelope Address Styles (Concluded)*. On each of two sheets of paper draw two forms to represent envelopes. The forms will be 6½ inches wide by 3⅝ inches deep.

Insert one sheet into the machine. In the first envelope form which you have drawn, type the following address in the double-spaced, indented style, with open punctuation. Use four lines. In the upper left-hand corner of the form, write your own home address in the single-spaced, blocked style. Just below the form, center the caption, *Style 1*.

Mrs. Elizabeth Sawyer 615 South Street Vincennes Indiana

On the second envelope form on the sheet, type the following address in the double-spaced, blocked style, with open punctuation. Use three lines. Below the form, center the caption, *Style 2*. Type your home return address as previously instructed.

Mr. Henry C. Alexander 1187 Herndon Avenue Louisville, Kentucky

Application Exercise 17. Styles 3 and 4 are to be typed on the second sheet on which you have drawn envelope forms.

For Style 3 use the following four-line address to be written in the single-spaced, indented style, with open punctuation.

Mr. Charles W. Foster Tension Envelope Company 38 Fifty-sixth Street New York, New York

Division 1—Fundamental Skills

General Instructions. Follow these instructions throughout Division 1, unless otherwise directed. *The instructions will not be repeated.*

1. Read carefully all the *special* instructions and explanations. As often as possible, review the practice drills and operations given in the Introduction until you become thoroughly familiar with the operative parts of the typewriter.

2. Use full - size — 8½ x 11 — sheets. Two sheets are recommended when typing—one to serve as a backing sheet to protect the rubber roll (Platen); the other for the finished typing. In addition to protecting the platen, the use of two sheets develops skill in the letter writing method of inserting paper.

3. Place the Paper Guide so that the paper will be centered in the machine.

4. Set the Line Space Regulator for single spacing.

5. **Type each line three times with single spacing. Double space after each three-line group. Disregard headings.**

6. Follow the Special Instructions of each lesson for the line length and the top margin. If you have observed the foregoing instructions, your typing will be approximately centered on the paper.

7. Beginning with Lesson 2, run through each line of the Warming-up Drill several times as a preliminary drill and review. Use a separate sheet for this warming-up; then include the drill in the lesson assignment.

Explanations. The three-line repetition is an aid in locating errors. At the same time it enables one to analyze at a glance the character of the stroking.

In this Division no attempt is made to include the problem of centering the exercises. Your entire attention at this time should be given to the mastery of the letter strokes and the other basic skills in typewriting. In a later Division you will learn how to center typed matter on sheets.

Do not hurry through any lesson. Develop a smooth and even rate, free from jerkiness and hesitation. Make every effort to achieve evenness of touch, free from light and dark letters.

Begin each new line slowly. Make each stroke rapidly, sharply, and distinctly, with a rest period or interval between strokes. The one-two-three count given on page 10 is recommended—one count for the stroke and two counts for the stroke interval. Gradually decrease the time of the stroke interval until on the third line of the group the cadence is on a 4/4 time or count.

Allow one count each for the key stroke and the space bar stroke; two counts for the capital shift (one for the shift and one for the capital letter stroke); three counts for the carriage return; and five counts for the paper change.

Do not stop, pause, hesitate, or look up during the typing of the three lines of a group for the purpose of marking errors or of checking your work. Wait until you have completed the three lines; then go over your work carefully. Indicate errors (a circle drawn around the word or combination containing the error is recommended), and make a mental note of all indistinct strokes or other weak points. Try to improve these weaknesses during the writing of the next three-line group.

Remedial Practice

After typing the lesson and before removing the paper from the typewriter, read over the copy you have typed and recheck every incorrect stroke.

Be sure to circle all combinations of words in which errors have occurred. Then on another sheet, or on the back of the lesson sheet, practice all the strokes typed incorrectly in this way:

Type three times each letter incorrectly written; then type three times the letter group or word in which the error was made.

In doing remedial practice on spacing errors, type the word before and the word after the error in spacing.

13

—at the bottom of the sheets.

Dear Mr. Turner: I am glad to hear that the project for the proposed San Francisco Live Stock Show is still moving along, even though it does not show prospects for fruition as early as one might desire. Please pay my respects to Mr. Sewall the next time you see him. (P) An exposition such as you are contemplating will have a very profound effect on your city. The development of the International Live Stock Exposition made Chicago the center of the industry for a great many years; no other show has yet been developed to the point where it threatens the supremacy of the International. It has brought to Chicago every year thousands and thousands of live stock men and students of agriculture, who not only spent their money in the city but came to regard the live stock institutions which centered here in connection with the exposition as the source of information and the final authority on all things that have to do with live stock improvement. (P) The show also helped to draw to Chicago the headquarters of the National Committee on Boys' and Girls' Club Work, which has done so much in guiding and influencing the future farmers of this country. The International has helped to make the Union Stock Yards and the activities centering around them the point of greatest interest in the live stock and meat industry on this continent. It has called to this neighborhood the headquarters of a large number of pure-bred live stock associations, and has determined the location of a great many enterprises, such as farm papers, agricultural radio stations, and distributing houses for agricultural products. These institutions, we believe, would have been scattered, had not the International Live Stock Exposition been established to provide a home for them. (P) Along with the International has grown another type of institution, such as the Saddle and Sirloin Club and the Stockyard Inn, both of which are internationally famous. It has also resulted in bringing to Chicago the headquarters of such organizations as the Horse Association of America, the Society of Pure-bred Record Association, the Live Stock Loss Prevention Society, and a number of others having to live stock production and conditions. (P) I do not think that the increase in business for the industry in Chicago has been so great in proportion as one might expect, but the activities which have grown up surrounding the International Live Stock Exposition have given the city a position of prestige which it could never have attained without the existence of the exposition. (P) I do hope that your plans will work out successfully. If I can help along the good cause in any way, be sure to let me know. Sincerely yours, President HWC:PRL Mr. Charles W. Turner Merchants Exchange Building San Francisco, California (*456 words*)

Application Exercise 13. Page 14 is to be headed *Inverted Letter Style*. Type the body of the following letter in the single-spaced form, inverted style. Indent the second line and succeeding lines of each paragraph five strokes. Write the address in the blocked style. Use open punctuation. Center the date (today) on three lines. On the first line, write the name of the month; on the second, the figure representing today's date; and on the third, the year in figures. Center the second and third lines under the first. Line up the title with the complimentary close.

Mr. Walter W. Carney Secretary, Carney Products, Inc. 1876 Calvert Street Louisville, Kentucky Dear Mr. Carney A silhouette letterhead—similar to the one you are holding, but designed especially for your product—will increase the effectiveness of your Direct Mail Advertising. In today's constant battle for attention, a medium that is out-of-the-ordinary or different will help to get your message read. (P) This letterhead is only a single sample of the many ways the silhouette idea can be used. I have several interesting plans for using these letterheads, and I know from actual tests that their pulling power is three and a half times as great as that of a message written on an ordinary letterhead. (P) Will you give me a few minutes of your time to show you samples and explain the silhouette idea? You're right . . . . that's a reply card at the top of this letter; it needs no postage! Personally yours President HYTrainor—erc (*134 words*)

Special Instructions. Set the Margin Stops for a line of 40 strokes. Write each line three times with single spacing. Double-space after each three-line group. Top margin, 13 line spaces.

New Stroke Control—Guide Keys

Keep the fingers curved.

```
fff faf faf faf aaa jjj j;j j;j j;j ;;;
```

Space with the right thumb.

```
fff fdf fdf fdf ddd jjj jlj jlj jlj lll
fff fsf fsf fsf sss jjj jkj jkj jkj kkk
```

Practice Exercise

Strike the keys with the tips of the fingers.

```
fff faf faf jjj j;j j;j fdf fdf jlj jlj
fff fsf fsf jjj jkj jkj faf faf jlj jlj
```

Make the carriage return a wrist movement.

```
fds dsa jkl kl; fsf jlj ada l;j sfd jk;
ask lad fad all jad lak dad l;j sad all
```

Lesson Summary

```
as jk df l; ja ;f sk ld da js kf dj ;a
ask kjs dal ;sj kaf lad las sak kd; kas
fad all lak lad ask sad l;f ald dad sal
```

Lesson 2

Special Instructions. Set the margin stops for a line of 45 strokes. Top margin, 9 line spaces. **Do not space after the letters in Line 1 of the Warming-up Drill.** The two lines of copy will make a single line of 45 strokes without spacing, as shown in the model line.

It is suggested that you first type each line of the Warming-up Drill at least five times on a separate sheet of paper. Then write the entire lesson, including the Warming-up Drill, on a full-size sheet, according to the General Instructions given on page 13.

Warming-up Drill

Line 1
```
a s d f ; l k j s a d s f k j l k ; d a f a d
l j ; j l s d s a f ; k l j ; f d a s d ; a
```

(Model Line)
```
asdf;lkjsadsfkjlk;dafadlj;jlsdsaf;klj;fdasd;a
```

Line 2
```
af fs fa fd jj jl jk j; j; fd fd jk jk fs fd
```

Line 3
```
fad sad lad dad jad all alk lad lak ask j;j
```

stand from this statement that it will be satisfactory for us to ship you two used cleaners, and that we shall receive a credit of $10.00 to apply on the purchase price of the two machines which we are ordering from you, should we decide to keep them. We shall be glad to have you confirm this understanding. Yours very truly, STRATHMORE-COLFAX INN Manager WTO CFR P. S. May used cleaners be turned in for allowance even though they are not Premiers? (*154 words*)

Application Exercise 10. This problem, which will constitute page 10 of the Guide, is to be headed *Full-Blocked Style with Attention Line.* The following letter is, therefore, to be written in the full-blocked style, with every line, including the date, beginning at the left margin. Use open punctuation. The letter is to be dated today. The *Attention* line is to be underscored.

Berkeley Transfer Company 418 Alexander Street Berkeley, California Attention Mr. C. K. Wren, President Gentlemen When you select the company to carry your automobile insurance for next year, it will be greatly to your benefit to keep in mind the advantages offered to you by the Western Mutual. (P) Substantial increases in automobile insurance rates have recently been made. These increases, together with the discontinuance of the 10% no-accident credit, will probably mean that you will pay more for your insurance than you have been paying. (P) Western Mutual has consistently reduced the cost of insurance for its policyholders. For 524 consecutive months—nearly half a century—dividends of 20% or more of the premiums paid have been returned to policyholders. The total dividends thus paid to policyholders have saved them more than $39,000,000 on their insurance costs. (P) Let this strongest and oldest mutual company writing automobile insurance prove the value of its service to you. The enclosed booklet will explain how you can profit by availing yourself of its low rates. A few moments given to this matter now may help you to save money in your insurance costs over a period of years. Very truly yours WESTERN MUTUAL INSURANCE COMPANY Branch Production Manager CTR/jti (*178 words*)

is to be headed *Semi-blocked Style, Special Form, with Subject Line.* Center the date—today. Use open punctuation. Indent the subject line 5 strokes, just as you indent the first line of each paragraph. Block the lines which form the conclusion. Type the name of the dictator in full, with his title on the next line. For the identifying initials, type your own initials in ALL CAPS.

Hamilton-Wendell, Inc. Fort and Lincoln Streets Detroit, Michigan Gentlemen Subject: Quotation on Champion Coolers Thank you for your inquiry about the price on 300 Champion Coolers. (P) As you are thoroughly familiar with the Champion, we won't go into detail about its merits except to say that the Champion is the original cooler of this type. In order to retain the reputation which we have gained in the many years we have manufactured this cooler, we have maintained the quality in spite of price competition. (P) Because of the quantity specified in your letter, we believe you are entitled to the best possible price. We are, therefore, quoting you, on a shipment of 300 coolers, a discount of 50% from the prices shown in the enclosed folder. This quotation is made f.o.b. Binghamton. Terms: 30 days net or 2% for cash in 10 days from the date of the bill of lading. (P) Three hundred coolers would make a large carload; that is to say, the coolers would fill a car to its maximum capacity. (P) We are in a position right now to make immediate shipment on receipt of your order. Yours very truly CHAMPION COOLER COMPANY K. W. Reynolds Sales Manager (*176 words*)

Application Exercise 12. Pages 12 and 13 of the Guide will show a two-page letter with the address written at the end. The heading of page 12 will be *Two-page Letter, Semi-blocked Style, with Address at the End.*

Begin the date 15 strokes from the right margin. Type the letter in the semi-blocked style. Line up the title 4 single line spaces below the complimentary close. Begin the address 6 line spaces below the identifying marks, and write it in the blocked style, with open punctuation.

Arrange the notations at the top of the second page thus:

CWT
2
March 4, 19---

Illustration 13
The *f*-finger making the r-stroke.
The *j*-finger making the u-stroke.

Illustration 14
The *f*-finger making the inward g-stroke.
The *k*-finger making the upward i-stroke.

```
fff frf frf frf rrr jjj juj juj juj uuu fur

fff fgf fgf fgf ggg kkk kik kik kik iii jig

fur fur jig jig ruf ruf lag lag jar jar lk;
```

Practice Exercise

```
frf frf frf juj juj juj fgf fgf fgf kik kik

did lid kid rid aid fur rug dug lug jug gas

fair said rail jail full dull gull glad dusk
```

Lesson Summary

```
il is ik if id us ua ud ur rg fk rf a; l; gr

dis das dus gig gar gas gal kid rid jag jar

full fail laid raid kids girl sirs jigs lass
```

Always check for errors and write the Remedial Practice.

Lesson 3

Special Instructions. Set the margin stops for a line of 45 strokes. Top margin, 5 line spaces. Remember that there are no spaces after the letters in Line 1. Type each line of the Warming-up Drill several times before you write the entire lesson on a full-size sheet.

Warming-up Drill

Line 1   l k j u a d f g s f r f a j d ; f r k i a j s

           l d f r k i f g f j u j d f r ; k i a g ; u

Line 2   ag ar kl ui ga ra rl gl lk dr si i; du ju dg

Line 3   all ik; sad ail lid sur urs far jar gar ark

quotations on both white and red rubber of about the same softness and finish as your regular Long-Life Water Bottles. Please be sure to send us samples of the material on which you propose to base your quotations. (P) As we have prospects for large orders in the near future, we shall appreciate hearing from you promptly. Very truly yours, ALEXANDRIA DRUG COMPANY President TWF:BH (157 words)

Application Exercise 7. Page 7 is to be headed *Full-blocked Letter Style*. Type the following letter, which is a reply to the one you wrote in Exercise 6, in the full-blocked style, with open punctuation. Date the letter, March 18, 19—. Begin the date and the three lines which form the conclusion at the left margin. Write the title in the address at the end of the first line.

Mr. T. W. Frank, President Alexandria Drug Company Alexandria, Virginia Dear Mr. Frank Thank you for your letter of March 15, in which you ask us to quote prices on lots of 25,000, 50,000, and 100,000 milk bottle caps to be manufactured in accordance with the blue prints which reached us this morning. (P) As you are located near our Baltimore branch office, we are taking the liberty of referring your inquiry to the manager of that branch, Mr. R. M. Talbot. It so happens that Mr. Talbot has already arranged to be in Alexandria on Wednesday, March 21. You may expect a call from him at that time. Before we can make the quotation, we ought to have more detailed information. We feel sure that we shall get a clearer understanding of your patent from Mr. Talbot's conversation with you than we could get from an exchange of correspondence. (P) Your inquiry covers a desirable item, which is similar in process to many others that we already manufacture. If you decide to place the business with us, you will be assured of a uniform and satisfactory product. Yours very truly SANBORN MANUFACTURING COMPANY General Manager FGT/gty (172 words)

Application Exercise 8. Head page 8 of the Guide *Semi-blocked Letter Style*. Center the date of the letter, February 21, 19—. The address is to be written with open punctuation.

Strathmore-Colfax Inn 500 Irving Street Elmira, New York Gentlemen: Thank you for

ou will notice from the enclosed booklet that the PREMIER COMMERCIAL is not a household cleaner, but a specially designed, heavy-duty machine built for daily guest room cleaning. (P) Hotel executives are well pleased with the PREMIER COMMERCIAL because it gets under radiators and steam pipes, cleans along baseboards and under low-built furniture, and is fully protected with bumpers so that it will not mar furniture or woodwork. But what is most important of all is its unusual durability. (P) We should like very much to send you a PREMIER COMMERCIAL so that you can have one of your maids give it a thorough trial. Just use the enclosed addressed envelope to tell us that we may send you a PREMIER COMMERCIAL on free trial. Incidentally, it would be well to mention the voltage of the current you are using. Our standard motor operates on 110 volts AC or DC. Very truly yours, PREMIER VACUUM CLEANER COMPANY Commercial Cleaner Department RWHilton—kte Enclosure (157 words)

Application Exercise 9. The next page is to be headed *Indented Letter Style—Special Form*. Type the following letter in the single-spaced form, indented style, with 10-stroke indentations in the address and the body. Use open punctuation in the address. Center the date, February 24, 19—.

The letter contains an Attention line, which is to be centered. The complimentary close, the signature, and the title are to begin at 35 and are to be blocked. Begin the postscript two single line spaces below the identifying initials; indent the first line 10 strokes. This letter is the reply to the one you wrote in Exercise 8.

Premier Vacuum Cleaner Company 417 East 112th Street New York, New York Attention Mr. R. W. Hilton Gentlemen: We appreciate very much your letter of February 21 and the catalog which you sent us. (P) You may enter our order for two Premier Vacuum Cleaners as samples so that we may see how they will work out. If everything is satisfactory, we may be able to use several more. These are to be Standard 110 AC. (P) In your catalog we notice the following statement: "The company will make a $5 trade allowance for each full-size floor

Illustration 15
The *f*-finger making the upward t-stroke.
The *j*-finger making the inward h-stroke.

Illustration 16
The *d*-finger making the upward e-stroke.
The *l*-finger making the downward .-stroke.

```
ddd ded ded ded eee jjj jhj jhj jhj hhh had

fff ftf ftf ftf ttt lll l.l l.l l.l ... hit

her her hut hut she she hid hid has has hit
```

Practice Exercise

```
ded ded ded jhj jhj jhj ftf ftf ftf l.l l.l

she the fed led let jet set get sue kit he;

sale kale deal dear gate rate hate file just
```

Using the Shift Key

To type a capital made by the left hand, depress the right **Shift Key** (No. 15) with the little finger; for a capital made by the right hand, depress the left shift key. Study Illustrations 17 and 18. Do not allow your hands to get out of position; keep the *f*-finger and the *j*-finger over their guide row positions. Do not arch the wrists when depressing the shift keys. Hold the shift key *all the way down* until you have made the letter stroke; otherwise, the capital letter will appear cut off.

Illustration 17
The *a*-finger controlling the left shift key.

Illustration 18
The *;*-finger controlling the right shift key.

fying Initials. Plan the page carefully so that the material will be centered on the sheet.

Note: If your machine does not have the asterisk character, use the colon instead.

```
           1                              8
        THJ:MYT                      CHMcConnell/kyt

           2                              9
        KYT*TR                       RAMcReynolds--tyr

           3                             10
        RLM/mky                      CRT:jhy
                                     Enc.
           4
        LJT--cgh                         11
                                     TGE:CY
           5
        WYR                          Enclosures--2
        CHG
                                         12
           6                         ARW/lhy
        JGT
        tr                           Enclosure--Check

           7
        HGT--4
```

In all ordinary cases Styles 1 and 2 are to be preferred. In typing those styles, the shift lock may be used to type all the initials as well as the colon or the asterisk.

The Identifying Initials are included in a business letter as an aid to the sender. In a large office in which many people are engaged in correspondence, the initials serve as a quick means of identifying both the dictator and the stenographer. They are also helpful to the mail clerk in distributing the mail and to the file clerk in putting correspondence in the proper folders.

Application Exercise 5. The next page of the Correspondence Guide is to show a *double-spaced letter*. Type the following letter in the double-spaced form, indented style, with close punctuation. Begin the date (today) 15 spaces from the right margin. This sheet will be page 5 of the Guide and will be headed *Double-spaced, Indented Letter Style*.

General Electric Company, Nela Park, Cleveland, Ohio. Gentlemen: Last week Mr. Grant of your local office called and brought with him the portfolio about which you wrote us. His presentation was quite clear, and most of the material appears to be very good. We are ordering some of the sales letters and newspaper advertising mats. (P) Do you have available any sales letters addressed specifically to builders and contractors, either on lighting or simply on lamps? We serve a large number of such customers, and we find that they offer a profitable outlet. Very truly yours, **BURNS ELECTRIC COMPANY** President **KGT:NBY** (*84 words*)

Application Exercise 6. Type the following letter in the single-spaced form, indented style throughout. Begin the date, March 15, 19—, 15 strokes from the right margin. Use open punctuation in the address. Head the sheet *Single-spaced, Indented Letter Style*. Type the number of the sheet at the bottom.

Sanborn Manufacturing Company 1674 Twelfth Street Indianapolis, Indiana **Gentlemen:** Our company has used your Long-Life tires for many years. We have always found them satisfactory in every way. They have delivered excellent service. (P) We have recently been granted a patent on a milk bottle cap which, we believe, has real possibilities for volume sales. As your wide experience in the manufacture of rubber goods qualifies you to make this article, we are sending this inquiry to you. (P) Please quote us prices and approximate delivery dates on lots of 25,000, 50,000, and 100,000 of these caps, manufactured in accordance with the blueprints we

```
R;f Uaj R;f Uaj Ruf Urj Ruf Urj R;f Uaj Raj

F;a Jal R;f Hak Tjf Udh Flj Jsf Kak F;f Uah
```

Lesson Summary

```
age k;. use fat hat are his its see sir dud

Ada Ida Era Jill This Lad Is It If Ada Isla

Fred hard half hear held juts Jake kill figs
```

Lesson 4

Special Instructions. Set the margin stops for a line of 45 strokes. Top margin, 9 line spaces. Continue to write each line of the lesson three times, with single spacing. Double-space after each three-line group. The two lines of letters in Line 1 of the Warming-up Drill will make a single line of copy—no spacing after the letters. Practice the Warming-up Drill on another sheet before you begin the lesson. Be sure to do the Remedial Practice.

Warming-up Drill

Line 1
```
a d e j u h r g t h u r l . s u i d e j a ; f

g l u a s h i d e k ; f g k . u e t j d f i .
```

Line 2
```
F; Je Ka Dr Le Da Li F; Ur Gl Tu Su He Ri Kg
```

Line 3
```
Ark hat the fee Ash had ear hit Lee jut l.;
```

New Stroke Control

Illustration 19
The *d*-finger making the downward c-stroke.
The *l*-finger making the upward o-stroke.

Illustration 20
The *f*-finger making the downward v-stroke.
The *j*-finger making the downward m-stroke.

```
fff fvf fvf fvf vvv jjj jmj jmj jmj mmm met

eve eve eve vim vim vim ham ham ham gem gem

ddd dcd dcd dcd ccc lll lol lol lol ooo lot

cot cot cot jot jot jot cud cud cud cog cog
```

and Title Styles. In the full-blocked style, the complimentary close, the company name, and the title are lined up with the left writing margin of the letter.

1

Very truly yours

DETROIT AXLE COMPANY

Treasurer

2

Yours very truly,

ALPHA PRINTING COMPANY

Superintendent

3

Yours truly,

MASTER MACHINERY COMPANY

General Manager

4

Sincerely yours

BARTON & CORNELL

J. L. Cornell

5

Very truly yours,

PORTER-CHEVROLET COMPANY

R. L. Wilkinson
Sales Manager

6

Yours very truly

BALTIMORE TRANSFER COMPANY

C. K. Knudson, President

7

Very truly yours

NEW ERA COMPANY

President

8

Sincerely yours,

First Vice-President

9

Yours very truly,

Richmond Oil Company

C. R. Springer
Sales Manager

10

Yours very truly,

WORTHINGTON MACHINERY COMPANY

President

am do go so to uc us ma me ic of ov or vi v.

ace act ago got ave ava arm are him hum for

came card care love loss lost meet miss joke

Lesson Summary

same save case cash free gram goes does silk

Space once after the semicolon. Call at the old Hill farm; ask to see Marie.

Lesson 5

Special Instructions. Use a line of 50 strokes. Top margin, 7 line spaces. Be sure to do the Remedial Practice each day.

Warming-up Drill

Line 1
a d c s ; l c j f v l s r j m d e o g t j i d m o

d c k . a m a c u i e k t r o l g e j m . d r l v

Line 2
ie ct mi dv lo so to gu ou cc ok ov ti oc gt ia el

Line 3
Tom too our out car cat Tim jot ear eat mat met to

New Stroke Control

Illustration 21
The *s*-finger making the upward w-stroke.
The *j*-finger making the downward n-stroke.

Illustration 22
The *f*-finger making the downward b-stroke.
The *j*-finger making the upward y-stroke.

sss sws sws sws www jjj jyj jyj jyj yyy how why

Jew few saw caw vow low gay day rum hum vat kit

fff fbf fbf fbf bbb jjj jnj jnj jnj nnn ban bad

and hay boy buy job vow sow fun can rim leg oak

18

1

Mr. George W. Matthews,
   Scienceville, Ohio.

2

Mrs. Elizabeth C. Coulter

   Oakford, Georgia

3

Breton Flooring Company
   1786-1790 Timmins Street
      Cedar Rapids, Iowa

4

Charles W. Hawkins, Esq.,

   Guarantee Trust Building,

      Reading, Pennsylvania.

5

Miss Anna H. Worthington
1876 K Street, N. W.
Washington, D. C.

6

Messrs. Lawton & Billings

      418 Raymond Avenue

         Lima, Ohio

7

Mr. W. C. Redway, President
   Hunt Radio Service Company
      Fifth and Main Streets
         Afton, Iowa

8

Mr. Charles E. Bangor, Jr.
Manager, Bangor Tool Company
Saginaw, Michigan

9

Mr. James W. Woolson
   Care of Hotel Trimble
      Lockport, New York

10

Mr. R. A. Rutt, Secretary
Fielding Furniture Company
1987 Wilmington Road
Dover, Delaware

11

Dr. Raymond T. Fenway
Dean, School of Education
University of Wisconsin
Madison, Wisconsin

12

National Social Service Bureau
2256 Michigan Boulevard
Chicago, Illinois

Attention Miss Agnes L. Sherman

13

Trexler Importing Company
   1189 Market Street
      Xenia, Ohio

Attention Mr. C. W. Meyers

14

Lawton Provision Company

   716 Tenth Street

      Kansas City, Kansas

Attention of Charles C. Kinyon

Note: The *Attention* line may also be centered with reference to the length of the writing line in the body of the letter.

```
bl br yl wn ga cy ny sw do ef hb bj kf dm r. vy ‚tu

May any man yes yet you jab big bit try now own

book both done down find fine walk warm year sign

June July fact deck half very wait want back baby
```

Lesson Summary

Space once after
the abbreviations
Dr., J., and *V.*

```
able away boys blue city kind even long nice whom

Dr. J. V. John made his call very late that day.
```

Lesson 6

Special Instructions. Use a line of 50 strokes. Top margin, 7 line spaces. Be sure to do the Remedial Practice.

Warming-up Drill

Line 1
```
j m l o f a s d e u h g b n y c . s w ; i r k f v

h n g b o w . d t i a j e y c u v m t r k e g l n
```

Line 2
```
he ma ly eg un ow mb je oa bi ck tc nd ws f. yt rv
```

Line 3
```
caw cad van was hen kin bag bat boy run fog job
```

New Stroke Control

q   **p**   **x**   **,** *(comma)*

Illustration 23
The *a*-finger making the upward q-stroke.
The *;*-finger making the upward p-stroke.

Illustration 24
The *s*-finger making the downward x-stroke.
The *k*-finger making the downward comma-stroke.

```
aaa aqa aqa aqa qqq kkk k,k k,k k,k ,,, quq q,q

sss sxs sxs sxs xxx ;;; ;p; ;p; ;p; ppp six sap

open page paid part quit quid quad quay next text
```
19

Your work in this Division will consist of the preparation of a Correspondence Guide. Each problem is to occupy one page unless otherwise noted. If possible, make carbon copies of all your work. Keep the originals in a folder. At the conclusion of your work in this Division you will make a title page and a Table of Contents for the Guide; then bind it with a manuscript cover.

This Division, therefore, provides a review of various phases of typewriting. Your work will determine whether you can center material attractively; whether you know how to set up letters in various styles; and whether you have mastered the principles of tabulation. Pay careful attention to the subject-matter. It gives specific instruction on English and punctuation—details which are the secretary's responsibility.

Application Exercise 1. The first page of the Guide is to be headed *Date Styles*. Leave a margin of at least 2 inches above the heading. Here is the copy you are to type. Use the current year date instead of the year given. You are to use your own judgment in centering and arranging your work. Be sure to type the footnote. At the bottom of the sheet—in the center about half an inch from the lower edge— type 1, the page number.

```
            1                                       8
February 14, 1942                            July Thirty-first
                                             Nineteen Forty-two


            2
21 December, 1942*
                                                    9
                                             October
                                             Thirty-first
            3                                Nineteen Forty-two
November 12
19        42

            4                                      10
March 12                                     September
    1942                                     Fifteenth
                                             Nineteen
                                             Forty-two


            5
September 15
    1 9 4 2
                                                   11
                                             April
                                             Twenty-fourth
            6                                Nineteen
October Fourteenth                           Forty-two
19                    42

            7                                      12
     May                                     November
  Fourteenth                                 25
Nineteen Forty-two                           1942
```

*This form is often found on letters originating in foreign countries.

```
ix sp pm og mn xc an xp nq qu bu fo hd ek ep tl ps

No. not new six box pay yes que qui aqu pa, up,

keep kept face view lieu hope home edge jars quid

gash quit deft jump waxy even ever fort pack back
```

Lesson Summary

```
If you of you by you we had he had to pay to the

about black draft given happy jewel month quite

The pluck of a big, queer Texan moved Will Jason.
```

Make one space only after the comma.

Optional Letter Review

```
a b c d e f g h i j k l m n o p q r s t u v w x y z

z y x w v u t s r q p o n m l k j i h g f e d c b a

ab cd ef gh ij kl mn op qr st uv wx yx wv ut sr qp

on ml kj ih gf ed cb ac be ce df eg fh gi hj ik jl
```

Lesson 7

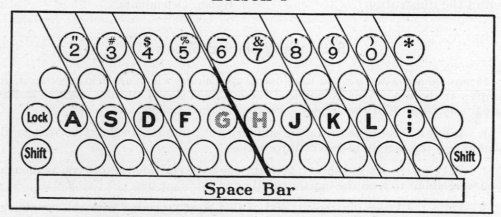

This chart shows the standard control of the Figure Row. The illustrations in Lessons 7, 8, and 9, pages 21, 22, and 23, show the standard method of fingering the figures. The drills in those lessons are based on that standard method.

Note: Drills for the optional method of fingering the figures are given on page 24.

Warming-up Drill

Use a line of 55 strokes. Top margin, 9 line spaces.

Line 1
```
j y h a q f s w l o e ; t p , g b n m r v k i j u d . s
x ; p d c o i t r e l w a q n v , c f h k i y v m n x c
```
Line 2
```
jo bt um xa wo dy xi ob sq pf cs hu ex ik tg nl pr ev
```
Line 3
```
the thy air aim his tax lax jam but rut ask put eve wit
```

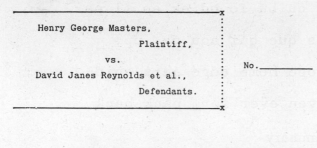

CITY AND COUNTY OF NEW YORK

```
Henry George Masters,

                Plaintiff,

        vs.                          No. _____

David Janes Reynolds et al.,

                Defendants.
```

```
     IN THE SUPERIOR COURT OF THE STATE OF
     CALIFORNIA, IN AND FOR THE CITY AND
            COUNTY OF SAN FRANCISCO

F. H. Benzinger, a Corporation,

                Plaintiff,

        vs.                          No. _____

Nevada Mining Company, a Corporation

                Defendant.
```

Illustration 84
Other Ways of Arranging Boxes

Note that in the first illustration the caption is centered over the box. The lines are made by the use of the underscore. How will you adjust the carriage to strike the small x in the position shown in the illustration?

tered between the rulings on the sheet. The top line is omitted.

Application Exercise 31. Arrange the following data in the form of the first illustration.

Supreme Court City and County of New York Alfred Chase Mason et ux., Plaintiffs, vs. United Traction Company, a Corporation, Defendant.

Surrogate's Court County of New York Mary W. Kilburn, Plaintiff, vs. Carl Quincy and Walter H. Downey as Executors of the Estate of Charles Wilson Morrison, deceased, Defendants.

Application Exercise 32. Arrange the following in the form of the second illustration.

In the Superior Court of the City and County of San Francisco, State of California Mary Weston Duncan, Plaintiff, vs. Northwestern Drug Company, a Corporation, Defendant.

In the Circuit Court of the United States, Ninth Circuit, Northern District of California Jamison Manufacturing Company, a Corporation, Plaintiff, vs. Henry Grayson Kernan and Albert Wiggin Hylan, Defendants.

Reinserting Stapled Sheets

It may be necessary for you to reinsert typed sheets which are held together with staples at the top. You cannot feed these stapled sheets into the machine in the usual way because of the staples. Proceed in this manner:

1. Insert a sheet of paper in the ordinary way; turn it into the typewriter until you have a top margin of two or three inches.

2. Take up the stapled sheets; keep the one to be corrected before you as though you were about to read the matter typed on it.

3. Drop the lower (unstapled) end of that sheet, together with the remaining sheets, between the inserted paper and the *front* of the platen.

4. Turn the single sheet *back*, or out of, the typewriter. As you turn back that sheet, the stapled sheets will feed into the typewriter in the proper typing order.

Illustration 25
The *d*-finger making the upward 3-stroke.
The *k*-finger making the upward 8-stroke.

Illustration 26
The *a*-finger making the downward z-stroke.
The *;*-finger making the upward hyphen-stroke.

aaa aza aza aza zzz kkk ki8 k8k k8k k8k 888 azf zer 8ik

ddd de3 d3d d3d d3d 333 ;;; ;p- ;-; ;-; ;-; --- d3d ;-;

Joel zeal zero aqua lack wear next sign ship hair etc.

Practice Exercise
Make two spaces after a period ending a sentence.

ve 38 83 kp be ws ut go zy nx h, cl nk do f. nj ru aq

Jump king bawl chop dent five quit raze sent quiz pity

I am. He will be. You can find the road, I am sure.

Lesson Summary

to you to see to our to him to put in the in his in all

quay quid quit ribs zinc queer open quite backs quacks

Ask for a very quiet place; it must be away from noise.

Lesson 8

Special Instructions. Use a line of 60 strokes. Top margin, **7** line spaces.

Warming-up Drill

Line 1 k i c m b s h y g e n a z u x d ; e - f l q u p v k 8 j s x

      e w j r n t z m k 8 s ; 3 d - t r g v o b w t n b - s y z i

Line 2 ta pi ed 38 or ju kn az ph sb vy cl a- gm eq ax 83 ol za mn

Line 3 are not and not did not and the but the you are you can ark

testimony in three ways: (1) With the Q's and A's two strokes to the right of the double ruled line; (2) with the Q's and A's two strokes to the left of the double rule; and (3) with the answers "run in." Interpolations by the court or by an attorney should be indented 10 strokes from the writing margin.

To put you on your mettle, the copy is given in solid form with a diagonal at the end of each question and its answer.

HOWARD ALLEN EDWARDS, plaintiff being first duly sworn, testified as follows:

DIRECT EXAMINATION

BY MR. TILTON: Q What is your name? A Howard A. Edwards./ Q Also known as Ned Edwards? A Yes, sir./ MR. KENNEDY: Now, if the court please, I do not know whether this is the right time to speak or not, but it is my understanding that all the testimony that was given in the other case is now incorporated in this case and is before the court./ THE COURT: That is my understanding./ MR. TILTON: Yes, certainly. I don't even know why he was sworn again./ THE COURT: Because it is a different law suit./ MR. KENNEDY: That is agreeable to me. By stipulation I understand that all the testimony in the chancery case is now before the court in the law case./ MR. TILTON: That is correct. And we are entitled to offer enough testimony to prove this case./ THE COURT: That is right./ (Documents were marked Exhibits 12, 13, 14, and 15.)/ Q I hand you Exhibits 12, 13, 14, and 15 and ask you whether these are assignments of land contracts and quit-claim deeds that you executed to the Harrington Corporation and W. R. Winggate. A They are./ Q And those are the assignments and quit-claim deeds on lots 935 and 936 of Hastings Boulevard Villas subdivision No. 3? A They are./ Q Now, you have testified that you found out about ten days before this suit was started that the lots were not in Jefferson Park? A I have./ Q Did you instruct your counsel to draft the quit-claim deeds and other necessary papers to put the Harrington Corporation and W. R. Winggate in the same position that they were when you purchased the lots? A I did./ Q And did you instruct your attorney and agent to make a tender of Exhibits 12, 13, 14, and 15 to the Harrington Corporation

the deeds, are they?/ A Yes, sir./ Q And believe you testified that all your dealings were with the Harrington Corporation? A Yes, sir./ Q Have you ever seen W. R. Winggate or Charles Winggate before this law suit? A No, sir, not to my knowledge./ Q Have you ever had any dealings with them? A No, sir./ Q I show you Exhibits 2 and 4, the land contracts, and ask you whether you made all the payments of principal and interest that are endorsed thereon. A I did./ Q Does that amount to approximately $1370? A I believe it does, yes, sir./ MR. TILTON: I offer Exhibit 16 at this time./ MR. KENNEDY: No objection./ Q I show you Exhibit 16 and ask you whether you know what that is. A It is a returned receipt for a registered or insured article./ Q Whom was it signed by? A Harrington Corporation per Katherine McCullough./ Q What is the date on it? A October 14, 1934./ MR. TILTON: Any objections to this Exhibit 16? I offer Exhibit 16./ Q Now, Mr. Edwards, are you ready, willing, and able to deliver the deeds and assignments on these pieces of property? A Yes, I am./ Q That is all from this witness.

Application Exercise 30. Arrange the following data in the form of a title page of an Abstract of Record. Box the names of the appellee and of the appellant. Refer to Illustration 78, page 190.

STATE OF MICHIGAN/ APPELLATE COURT, FIRST DISTRICT/ October Term, A. D. 19--/ CHARLES A. LITTLETON, Appellee,/ vs./ MILTON & WINTERS, Appellant/ No. 33885/ Honorable D. G. Kennedy, Presiding Judge/ ABSTRACT OF RECORD/ELLSWORTH, KENYON & RICHARDS/ Attorneys for Appellant

The form in which court documents are typed varies in different jurisdictions. Should you be employed in a law office, your first duty will be to inform yourself of the details of the forms that are in vogue in the jurisdiction in which the office is located.

Study again the "box" form shown in Illustration 78, page 190. On the next page are shown two other ways of boxing the names of the plaintiff and the defendant.

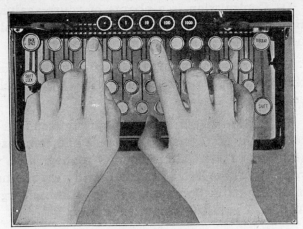

Illustration 27
The *f*-finger making the upward 4-stroke.
The *j*-finger making the upward 7-stroke.

Illustration 28
The *s*-finger making the upward 2-stroke.
The *l*-finger making the upward 9-stroke.

The small 1 is used for the figure 1.

fff fr4 f4f f4f f4f 444 jjj ju7 j7j j7j j7j 777 474 834 378

sss sw2 s2s s2s s2s 222 lll lo9 l9l l9l l9l 999 242 l9l lll

de3d ju7j fr4f ki8k sw2s lo9l 3489 2347 4789 aqua zeal play

Practice Exercise

June care word five high bank many plan quit zone axes 3388

Jane nigh vain exit item obey bone rusk chop zero left twig

Rajah rapid quote azure awful exalt giant saved cough monks

I did as he asked. He saw the paper. She came home later.

Lesson Summary

and are end was who are who was for him for the you can see

4477 8822 join zeal 911, both cars 3399 apex 1191 fuzz pair

The way to be the most happy is to make other people happy.

Lesson 9

Warming-up Drill

Special Instructions. Use a line of 65 strokes. Top margin, 3 line spaces.

Line 1

f r v d e c s w x a q z j u m k i , l o . ; p z f t b j y n s q j

7 9 3 1 9 2 8 2 7 3 8 4 9 1 3 9 2 8 1 4 7 4 1 3 7 2 8 1 2 3 4 7 8

Line 2

12 34 78 99 19 pa cw 21 ob s. gn ke dn lv tr xh lm fy xc eb jo ay

Line 3

why not yes was you who may and our are for the can has see him

A They would send us money by cable.

Q You did not have any general deposit for them?

A No.

Q Did you have any power of attorney or other authority to act for them?

A That is what I am trying to find here. Because we were not able to ship, they instructed us to resell some of the goods.

A second method of transcribing testimony is to "run in" the answers; that is, the answers are continued on the line on which the question is finished. Each question and answer then makes a paragraph. The letter Q (for question) is typed two strokes to the right of the double ruled line. Study Illustration 83.

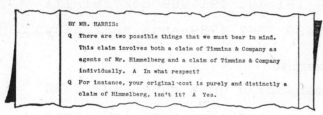

Illustration 83
Testimony with A's run in

Application Exercise 28. Type the following testimony with the answers run in.

BY MR. HARRIS: **Q** There are two possible things that we must bear in mind. This claim involves both a claim of Timmins & Company as agents of Mr. Himmelberg and a claim of Timmins & Company individually. **A** In what respect?

Q For instance, your original cost is purely and distinctly a claim of Himmelberg, isn't it? **A** Yes.

Q Interest likewise is a claim of Himmelberg's? **A** Yes.

Q Storage is a claim of Timmins & Company against Himmelberg? **A** Yes.

Q You paid that with Himmelberg's money? **A** Yes.

berg's money? **A** Yes, sir.

Q Commission is a charge of yours against Himmelberg? **A** That is paid with Himmelberg's money; that has already been paid.

Q I know, but you reimbursed yourself for that commission. **A** I made out a regular bill to him, yes, sir.

Q Wait until I finish. You reimbursed yourself for the storage and insurance and commission out of Mr. Himmelberg's money, didn't you? So those items in their origin were claims of Timmins & Company against Himmelberg. **A** Yes, I paid the amount for him.

Q You were primarily responsible? **A** Yes.

Q Whose is the overhead expense—Himmelberg's or yours? **A** Himmelberg's.

Q How did you arrive at that? **A** Merely his statement to me to charge that amount for overhead in my account.

Q For whom is the profit intended? **A** Himmelberg. We have no interest in the matter at all.

Q You have no idea how that overhead is made up? **A** I suppose it is cable expense and things of that kind. I have no idea what he had in mind. I am merely following his instructions.

Q Did you have any contract with Mr. Himmelberg as to the commission you would receive? **A** Any written contract?

Q Yes. **A** No different from what we have had all along. We get one per cent.

Q Was the storage all carried on one warehouse? **A** No, there were different warehouses.

Q How was the interest calculated? **A** Six per cent.

Q On what? **A** On the time payments which were made up to the first of August.

Q That is to say, the interest on your cost up to the date of requisition? **A** Yes. And another thing—I think that interest is charged only on the cost of the material. It is not charged on the storage, insurance, or commission. You will notice that it is charged right on the original price of the material.

Illustration 29
The *f*-finger making the upward 5-stroke.
The *;*-finger making the upward 0-stroke.

Illustration 30
The *j*-finger making the long upward and inward
6-stroke.

jjj jyj jy6 j6j j6j j6j 666 ;;; ;p; ;p0 ;0; ;0; ;0; 000 j;0 ;0;

fff frf fr5 f5f f5f f5f 555 ;;; ;p; ;p0 ;0; ;0- ;-; ;-; --- 0-;

up-town one-half one-third two-thirds first-class three-fourths

Practice Exercise

Make no spaces before or after the formal dash; that is, the dash made with two hyphens.

We come to which of your on this in that we take as they if this

Friday church become Aztecs packer axioms avails quaint judges

34 89 76 56 90 23 19 you see to speak in reply no doubt we have

Two strokes of the hyphen make the dash. A crash--then silence.

Note that there are no spaces before or after the formal dash.

Lesson Summary

with that with your with this from this that this very glad this

12 34 56 78 90 10 12 13 14 15 16 17 18 19 28 37 41 95 62 20 10 27

The talent of success is doing well without any thought of fame.

I must never let my attention waver for an instant while I type.

pare the title page of the transcript of the case you have been following. Use a sheet of ruled legal paper. On the upper part of the sheet type the caption, *State of Michigan*, etc., and the box with the names of the plaintiff and of the defendants, just as in preceding exercises. Then leave two double spaces and arrange the following material on the remainder of the page.

Before Hon. John W. Raymond, Circuit Judge
December 5, 19—

APPEARANCES:
Lorenzo A. Hughson, Esquire,
For Plaintiff.

William W. O'Neill, Esquire,
For Defendant Redway.

INDEX

There are two other methods of arranging testimony which are sometimes followed. In the first method, the Q's and A's are typed two strokes to the *left* of the double rule. The questions and answers themselves, with the name of the attorney or THE COURT, then begin two strokes to the right of the double rule. Study Illustration 82.

Illustration 82
Testimony (Special Form)

Application Exercise 27. Type the following testimony in the form of Illustration 82.

BY COLONEL KINGSTON

Q What is your claim in this matter, Mr. Geary?

A a claim.

Q Whom do you represent?

A G. van Hendricks of Holland.

BY COLONEL HAGGERTY

Q Just a minute. The award from which you protest was made to you as agents, was it not? There was a claim—an original claim—made in this matter, and an award was made. All of the original correspondence, claims, and data as to quantities, etc., indicated that you were the owners of the material that was requisitioned. At least I think you filed the claim as agent, and the award was made to you.

A Yes, but in the requisition papers I think it is stated that the goods belonged to van Hendricks of Holland. They were stored and insured in our name, but that was a matter of convenience in shipping.

Q When the property was taken, it was on storage; I suppose your name was furnished at that time. Do you now state the owner is van Hendricks? In your letter of October 3 to us you state the real owner was Matthieu van Hendricks.

A Matthieu van Hendricks doing business under the name of G. van Hendricks of Waalwick, Holland. G. van Hendricks is a firm name. The firm was established in—

Q Well, then, Mr. Geary, the award which you protested, though made out to you, should in fact have been made out to G. van Hendricks.

A Yes, or to us.

Q Or to you as agents?

BY COLONEL KINGSTON

Q How long have you been doing business for the van Hendricks firm?

A About five years—that is, any large business. We did a very small business with the firm before that.

Q What is the character of the business that you have done with them?

A Merely buying leather and tanning material.

Do not practice the following drills if you are using the standard method of fingering as given in Lessons 7, 8, 9, 10, 11, and 29.

In this optional method the 2, 3, and 4 keys are controlled by the *a*, *s*, and *d*-fingers, respectively; the 5 and 6 keys are controlled by the *f*-finger. On the right hand, the 7, 8, and 9 keys are controlled by the *j*, *k*, and *l*-fingers, respectively; the 0 and hyphen keys are controlled by the *;*-finger.

Lesson 7

```
aaa aza aza aza zzz kkk ki8 k8k k8k k8k 888 azf zer 8ik

sss sw3 s3s s3s s3s 333 ;;; ;p- ;-; ;-; ;-; --- s3s ;-;
```

Lesson 8

```
ddd de4 d4d d4d d4d 444 jjj ju7 j7j j7j j7j 777 474 834 378

aaa aq2 a2a a2a a2a 222 lll lo9 l9l l9l l9l 999 242 l9l lll

sw3s ju7j de4d ki8k aq2a lo9l 3489 2347 4789 aqua zeal play
```

Lesson 9

```
fff ftf ft6 f6f f6f f6f 666 ;;; ;p; ;p0 ;0; ;0; ;0; 000 j;0 ;0;

fff frf fr5 f5f f5f f5f 555 ;;; ;p; ;p0 ;0; ;0- ;-; ;-; --- 0-;
```

Lesson 10

```
sss sw3 sw# s#s s#s s#s #33 kkk ki8 ki' k'k k'k k'k '88 #38 83#

ddd de4 de$ d$d d$d d$d $44 jjj ju7 ju& j&j j&j j&j &77 $43 4's
```

Lesson 11

```
aaa aq2 aq" a"a a"a a"a "22 lll lo9 lo( l(l l(l l(l ((( aq"

fff fr5 fr% f%f f%f f%f %55 ;;; ;p0 ;p) ;); ;); ;); ))) ;p)
```

Lesson 29

```
fff ft6 f6_ f_f f_f f_f ___ ;;; ;/; ;/; ;/; /// j/-

;;; ;p- ;p* ;*; ;*; ;*; *** ;;; ;/? ;?; ;?; ;?; ???
```

24

testimony all went in, and then you put Mr. Redway on the stand as part of your principal case—as part of your defense. Now, I am sitting here as a jury, as far as this case is concerned. If a jury were here, they would be instructed on what constitutes the relationship of principal and agent; they would be instructed on how they would find that relationship; and they would be told that they have a right to draw all reasonable inferences from the testimony in determining the question as to whether or not the relationship existed.

You put Mr. Redway on the stand yesterday as part of your defense, and he was asked this question: "What was the agreement between you and Hinton as to the Martin deal?" His answer was, after some hesitation, "I don't remember." That was his answer. The court was not exactly satisfied with that answer, because it did not seem reasonable; so I asked him some questions. Then Mr. Redway informed the court that he did not pay Hinton a penny; and that, to the best of his recollection, Grimm gave him four lots, subject to the $300 basic price which Grimm was evidently to have on these lots. He went into a long explanation to the court as to how, to the best of his recollection, this commission was paid.

It is apparent to me, gentlemen, that Mr. Hinton and Mr. Redway were working together in the consummation of this deal. Whether they were both principals or whether Hinton was Redway's agent is not of a great deal of importance, after all, in deciding this particular issue. If they were both principals, they were partners in a joint enterprise engaged in trading this farm for these lots, and either one or both of them are liable for fraud, if a fraud exists. I have already found that, as far as I am concerned, Mr. Hinton is guilty of fraud in several respects, which resulted to this plaintiff's damage. I cannot come to any other conclusion.

I am going to hold that Mr. Hinton was, during this transaction, the agent of Mr. Redway. Any other conclusion would do violence to reason and common sense, if this record is examined.

sion, I would find against Mr. Redway, and that is exactly what I am going to do. I shall order a judgment entered against Mr. Redway and in favor of Mr. Martin for the amount in question with interest.

Application Exercise 24. After the testimony and the opinion are transcribed, the official court stenographer prepares the following affidavit, which forms the last page of the transcript. Type the copy on ruled legal paper.

State of Michigan)
) ss.
County of Wayne)

I hereby certify that as the official court stenographer I reported in shorthand the proceedings had and the testimony taken in the case of George Lambert Martin, plaintiff, vs. Frank W. Grimm and Henry Walters Redway, defendants, tried before Judge John W. Raymond on November 4, 19—, and November 5, 19—, and that the foregoing transcript is a true and correct transcript of my notes taken in said case.

—————————————————————
Official Court Stenographer

Application Exercise 25. The clerk of the court disposes of the case by making the following record for the court journal. Type the copy on a sheet of ruled legal paper. Prepare the caption, *State of Michigan*, etc., and box the names of the plaintiff and of the defendants just as you did in the preceding exercises. Write the number of the case—167,543. Leave two double line spaces; then continue with the following copy. Indent paragraphs 10 strokes.

The issues joined in this cause having heretofore been tried by the court without a jury, and the court, after mature deliberation, having rendered a decision in favor of the plaintiff against the defendants; and having assessed the plaintiff's damages over and above his costs and charges by him about this suit in his behalf expended at the sum of $5400; therefore, it is ordered and adjudged that plaintiff recover against the defendants his damages as aforesaid in the sum of $5400; together with his costs and charges to be taxed, and have execution therefor.

—————————————————Circuit Judge

Division 2—Developing Speed and Accuracy

This Division consists of twenty-five lessons devoted to the development of those skills and techniques which are essential to the business phases of typing.

Lessons 10 and 11 include a Warming-up Drill, a New Stroke Control (the shift characters on the figure keys and on the semicolon key), and a Practice Exercise.

Each lesson from 12 to 28 inclusive is made up of four parts: (1) Warming-up Exercise, (2) Acceleration Drill, (3) Concentration Development, and (4) Timed Writing.

The paragraphs which make up the Concentration Development material give the high points in the history of the automobile and the airplane. These paragraphs require careful reading and will develop your copy-getting ability as well as your typing skill. You cannot type accurately unless you read accurately.

The Timed Writings are all graded according to difficulty. Never start typing the Timed Writing any faster than you typed the Concentration Development. Your speed will gradually increase, and that natural rate of increase will mean more accurate typing.

Lessons 29 to 34 take up certain new strokes and also bring in special characters. In addition, each lesson contains a Warming-up Exercise, an Acceleration Drill, and a Timed Writing. Special instructions and explanations for the writing and use of the special characters are given in each lesson.

Remedial Practice. After completing a lesson and before proceeding with the next one, go over your typing carefully to find all the errors you made in the lesson. Analyze each error to see whether you can determine its cause. The object of that analysis is to aid you in avoiding similar errors in the future. Check up your position at the machine. Are you sitting to the right of, and away from, the keyboard? Are your wrists straight—neither arched nor sagging? Are your fingernails too long to permit you to strike the keys with the finger tips? Do you keep your mind on your typing?

For corrective practice on each error, do remedial drill work according to the following procedure:

1. With firm, quick strokes, type three times the letter stroke made incorrectly.

2. Type three times the word in which the error was made. Write at an even pace.

3. Type the word just before the one in which the error was made; then type the word written incorrectly; finally, type the word immediately following.

4. Write these three words as a group two more times, gradually increasing your speed. Do not, however, force your speed at any time.

Example: Assume that b was struck for v in the word have, and that the word before have was we and the word after, not. Your practice would then be as follows:

vvv have have have we have not we have not we have not

If you transpose strokes, as tkae for take, write three times the word in which the error was made—*slowly*. To get vivid stroke impressions, close your eyes as you type. Next, write the three-word series —the word itself, the word before, and the word following—at a medium rate. Gradually increase the rate, repeating the series of three words until you are sure of the strokes. Transpositions, such as tkae for take, are caused by reading ahead and by uneven typing.

Correct your spacing errors by writing several times the series consisting of the word before and the word after the omitted space. If your carriage jumps several spaces, your thumb is not "getting away" fast enough from the space bar. Practice the Special Space Bar Drill on page 11 of the Introduction.

Timed Writing. These assignments will accustom you to writing under a time limit. Two methods of timing may be followed. You may either start and stop at the signal given by the teacher, or you may time yourself. In timing yourself, record or make a mental note of the time when you begin to type, type through the entire Timed Writing, and then again record the time. The difference between the starting and stopping time is the amount of time taken to type the article.

Finding Your Typing Rate

For convenience in determining typing speed, 5 strokes are counted as one word. For many years International Typewriting Contests were held. The following paragraphs are adapted from the rules for those contests.

The figures printed at the end of each line of the copy given in the Timed Writing indicate the total stroke count up to that point. The count includes 1 stroke for the end of each line if the last word in that line is completed (not hyphenated). In other words, the strokes are counted as though the entire test were written in one continuous line.

that is right or the other is right, my recollection is that Mr. Redway was there.

Q   And at the other trial your recollection was that you had never seen him until the trial of the case?

A   Well, that may be there, but I think I was wrong.

Application Exercise 21.   After the cross examination has been concluded, the attorney for the plaintiff begins his Re-direct Examination. Type the following copy.

RE-DIRECT EXAMINATION

BY MR. HUGHSON:

Q   Just a moment, please.   In this suit against Mr. Grimm, $3600 was required. Is that right?

A   Yes, sir.

Q   Did you have any part of the $3600 at that time?

A   Yes, sir, I had $1200 of it.

Q   Had you made any arrangements with anybody else—any member of your family, your son, or anybody else—for the balance?

A   Yes. My son was going to give me the balance if they would have taken it, but they would not take it.

Q   Mr. Grimm refused to take the money?

A   Yes, sir.

Q   So that is the reason you did not go through with raising it?

A   Yes, sir.

Application Exercise 22.   The attorney for the defendant is now given an opportunity to re-cross examine the witness on matters brought out on the re-direct examination.   Type this copy.

RE-CROSS EXAMINATION

BY MR. O'NEILL:

Q   Just one question, Mr. Martin. Now Mr. Grimm refused to take that $3600 after he had already repossessed himself of these lots. Isn't that true?

A   What is that? Come around here. I cannot hear you.

of those lots, hadn't he, when he refused to take that money?

A   No, I don't think he had. No, he had not.

Q   He had not taken them back?

A   The lots had gone up then. Mr. Grimm was holding on to the lots for his own good.

Q   Was this during the time of one of your extensions that you came to him with $3600?

A   Yes, sir.

Q   And he would not take it?

A   He would not take it, no. The lots were disposed of, he said.

Q   That is all.

MR. HUGHSON: Suspend now, your honor?

THE COURT: Yes, I shall suspend. Now I anticipate that at two o'clock you are going to try to put in Hinton's testimony, aren't you?

MR. HUGHSON: Yes.

THE COURT: Then that is your case?

MR. HUGHSON: That will be.

THE COURT: That will be your case, won't it?

MR. HUGHSON: Yes.

THE COURT: Well, see whether you can find some law to let Hinton's testimony in, will you?

MR. HUGHSON: Yes.

THE COURT: I am dubious about that.

(Noon recess)

Application Exercise 23.   The case which we are following was tried without a jury. A part of the opinion of the Court, which is in the nature of a verdict, is given here. Type the copy. Leave two stroke-spaces inside the ruled lines. Indent paragraphs 10 strokes.

THE COURT: You made your motion at the end of the plaintiff's case yesterday, and I indicated at length on the record what I thought about this entire situation. I further indicated that if an agency was established between Hinton and Redway, I would hold Redway liable.

ters, when paragraphing, and when returning the carriage are not counted. If it is necessary to strike a second key to complete a character, as in the exclamation point, the extra stroke *is* counted.

Two strokes are counted for every dash printed in the copy, for every exclamation point, and for the two spaces which should be left after the colon, the interrogation mark, the exclamation point, and the period (when used at the end of a sentence).

To find your gross and net typing rates:

(1) Find in the book the last line you have typed; note the number of strokes printed at the end of that line. Add to that number any additional strokes which you typed on the last (uncompleted) line in your copy.

The total of the two numbers is the *gross strokes* typed.

divide the total found in (1) by 5. The result is the *gross words* typed.

(3) From the gross words deduct 10 words for each error. The result is the *net words* typed.

(4) To get your net rate per minute, divide the number of *net words* by the number of minutes you wrote.

Example: 5-minute writing with 2 errors.

(1) Stroke count given in the book at the
end of the last line completely typed.. 502
Add—Strokes in uncompleted last line
of typed copy...................... 12
Gross strokes................... 514

(2) 514 ÷ 5 =   102.8 Gross words

(3) 2 (errors) x 10 =   20 Words deducted
82.8 Net words

(4) 82.8 ÷ 5 (minutes) = 16.5, net words per minute, or rate of typing.

Record Keeping

Half the joy in learning to typewrite comes from keeping a record of your progress. For this reason, you will use two charts in your work from now on—a "Speed and Accuracy Chart" and an "Error Classification Chart."

Speed and Accuracy Chart. Look at the chart, Illustration 31. The figures across the sheet are the numbers which appear in parentheses after the Timed Writing headings throughout the book. Those at the left edge represent net words per minute.

Let us assume that in Timed Writing No. 1 (page 31) your rate of writing is 9 net words a minute. That score is represented by the dot placed in the center of the square opposite 9 in the column under 1. Let us also assume that you made 3 errors. Place a dot 3 spaces below, or in the center of the square opposite 6. The two dots are then joined by a *light* straight line as shown on the chart. That straight line is the "error line." The shorter you keep the error lines on your chart, the better typist you are.

In Timed Writing 2, we'll say your net writing rate is 13 words; you again made 3 errors. Those facts are recorded on the chart. A dot is placed in the square opposite 13 in the column under 2. Another dot is put in the square opposite 10 (13 − 3 = 10). You will then join the dot in the 9 square to the dot in the 13 square by a *heavy* line. Join the dots in the 6 square and the 10 square with a broken line, as shown on the chart.

For Timed Writing 3 the chart shows 13 net words —no errors; therefore, a *star* is placed in the square

opposite 13 and under 3. Try to get as many stars as possible.

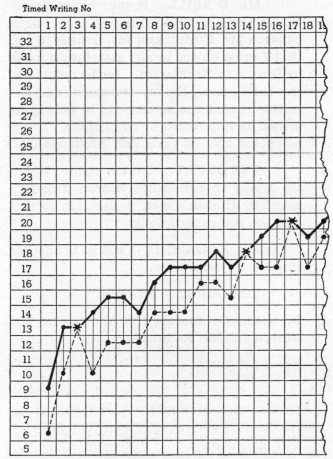

Illustration 31
Graph Showing Net Speed and Errors

26

Q Did you know a man by the name of Hinton?

A Yes, sir.

Q In February, 1930, did you have any transactions through Mr. Hinton?

A Yes, sir, I did.

Q State whether or not in 1930 you agreed to purchase some lots as shown by this contract, Exhibit 1?

A Yes, those are the lots in the Greenwood subdivision.

Q And this is the contract you entered into?

A Yes, sir.

Q How did you first learn of these lots?

A Mr. Hinton came to me.

Q What did he say?

A He said—I had this farm—

MR. O'NEILL: If your honor please, unless there is a showing of a connection between Mr. Hinton and Mr. Redway, I feel that I must object to any statements made by Hinton to Mr. Martin. In the first place, the chief reason for my statement and objection is that the agency can in no way be proved by statements or admissions. It can be proved only by facts and circumstances.

THE COURT: That is right. If you are trying to constitute Hinton Redway's agent by Hinton's own declaration to this witness, you cannot do it.

MR. HUGHSON: I will go to another stage of it, your honor.

THE COURT: All right.

Q On the first of March, 1930, did you see Mr. Hinton and Mr. Redway?

A Yes, I saw them.

Application Exercise 20. After the direct examination is concluded, the witness is cross-examined by the attorney for the other side. Type the following excerpts from the cross examination of the witness whose direct examination you typed in Exercise 19.

BY MR. O'NEILL:

Q Just to run over your testimony a little, Mr. Martin. You say—

A Come up just a little bit closer, please.

MR. HUGHSON: He is a little hard of hearing.

Q You say when this deal was consummated by which you became the vendee in this land contract that there were present at that time three people. Is that right?

A What?

Q That there were present at that time three men—Mr. Redway, Mr. Grimm, and Mr. Hinton.

A At what time now?

Q The time when you closed the deal.

A Yes, that is my best recollection; there were three there at that time.

Q You say that at that time Mr. Redway said to you, "I am paying $450 a lot to Mr. Grimm?"

A I would not say it was Mr. Redway, but it was said there.

Q It was said, but now you can't say whether Mr. Redway said it?

A No, I would not say whether he said it or not. It was said.

THE COURT: What was said?

A That Mr. Redway was paying $450 on each lot—had paid it.

Q You are certain Mr. Redway was there?

A Yes, I am very certain he was there. Now I might—

Q I will read you a question and answer given by you in the last trial of this case.

A All right, sir.

Q "Q Now when did you meet Mr. Redway?

"A When did I?

"Q Yes.

"A The first time I saw Mr. Redway was at the other trial."

Is that a correct statement of what you said?

tration 32. This chart is used to classify the errors made in your writing. Opposite Timed Writing **1** you will find *i* written under *E*. That notation shows that the error consisted of writing *i* instead of *e*. The other errors made in Timed Writing 1 are

The four wide columns at the right of the chart are included to record errors not otherwise provided for. Under "Mechanical" you might note "Wrong paragraph indentation" or "Left margin uneven"; under "Others," you would record letters omitted.

TIMED WRITING	A	B	C	D	E	F	G	H	I	J	K	L	M	N	O	P	Q	R	S	T	U	V	W	X	Y	Z	'	.	?	;	—	FIGURES	SPACING	Mechanical	OTHERS	TOTAL
1					*i*						*d*						*f*																			3
2																		*g*		*s*													✓			3
3	*Perfect*																																			0
4				*d*	*d*																												✓			4
5													*o*							*b*			*l*											*m omitted*	4
6	*s*													*i*				*r*																		3
7	*&v*																																	*Left Margin*		3
8													*w*																							1
9					*r*							'	*b*																							3
10																	*f*																	*¶ indentation*		2
11															*o*																					1
12						*g*																														1
13	*Perfect*																																			0
14																																				
15																																				
16																																				
17																																				
18																																				
19																																				
20																																				
21																																				
22																																				
23																																				
24																																				
25																																				
26																																				
27																																				
28																																				

Illustration 32

Error Classification Chart (Record Sheet)

To the Teacher: Students may be instructed to prepare their own charts on graph paper. Printed forms are contained in the accompanying Workbook of Laboratory Materials.

Lesson 10

Special Instructions. Use a line of 60 strokes. Top margin, 1 inch. *Note:* Hereafter the top margin, when given, will be designated in inches. There are 6 lines, or line spaces, to the inch. A top margin of 1 inch is equivalent, therefore, to 6 lines of single-spaced typing. Type each line of this lesson three times with single spacing; double-space after each three-line group. Use the Margin Release Lever if necessary.

Figure Row Shift Characters. When typing the shift characters in this lesson and in Lesson 11, remember that you are to use the same fingering for them that you used for the corresponding figures. The shift characters of the figures, reading from left to right, are:

"	#	$	%	_	&	'	(	)
2	3	4	5	6	7	8	9	0

The Colon (:). The colon is the shift of the semicolon. The **Question Mark** (?) on some machines is the shift of the comma; on other machines it is the shift of the diagonal (/).

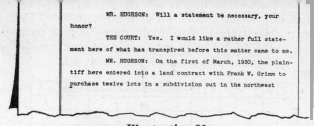

Illustration 80
Opening Statement

MR. HUGHSON: Will a statement be necessary, your honor?

THE COURT: Yes. I should like a rather full statement here of what has transpired before this matter came to me.

MR. HUGHSON: On the first of March, 1930, the plaintiff here entered into a land contract with Frank W. Grimm to purchase twelve lots in a subdivision out in the northwest section. The negotiations were opened some time in the month of February with a Mr. Hinton, who was a real estate salesman.

THE COURT: Mr. who?

MR. HUGHSON: Mr. Hinton approached Mr. Martin, the plaintiff, as to whether or not he would be interested in trading a farm that he owned in Green County for some lots in Wayne County. Mr. Hinton informed Mr. Martin that a Mr. Grimm owned these lots and was buying them from Henry Redway at $750 each and had paid $450 on the lots and owed a balance of $300.

THE COURT: Hinton informed Martin, the plaintiff, that Redway was buying these lots on contract from Grimm?

MR. HUGHSON: Yes.

THE COURT: All right. Whose agent was Hinton?

MR. HUGHSON: Mr. Redway's.

MR. O'NEILL: And I say he was not.

MR. HUGHSON: That is in dispute.

MR. O'NEILL: Yes.

MR. HUGHSON: Well, all right, to go ahead. As I say, we were approached by Mr. Hinton, who offered these lots to Mr. Martin. On the first of March, then, the parties all got together, that is, Martin, Hinton, and Redway at Hinton's office, and Mr. Martin made a deed to his farm to Redway.

called to testify, he is first sworn. Type the following copy in which a witness is introduced and examined. Write the name of the witness in ALL CAPS spaced out, as shown in Illustration 81. The heading, DIRECT EXAMINATION, is centered between the rulings on the sheet. The letters A (Answer) and Q (Question) are typed two strokes to the right of the double ruling. There are two stroke-spaces between Q or A and the testimony. Notice where the name of the examining attorney, Mr. Hughson, is typed. When interpolations occur, the name of the attorney or the words THE COURT are indented 10 strokes. Overrun lines always begin under the first line of the testimony—not under Q or A.

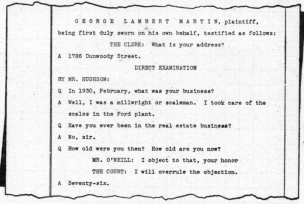

Illustration 81
Testimony

GEORGE LAMBERT MARTIN, plaintiff, being first duly sworn on his own behalf, testified as follows:

THE CLERK: What is your address?
A 1786 Dunwoody Street.

DIRECT EXAMINATION

BY MR. HUGHSON:

Q In 1930, February, what was your business?

A Well, I was a millwright or scaleman. I took care of the scales in the Ford plant.

Q Have you ever been in the real estate business?

A No, sir.

Q How old were you then? How old are you now?

MR. O'NEILL: I object to that, your honor.

THE COURT: I will overrule the objection.

your year work than said love hope just busy much five quit
value usual story items enjoy dance dozen apply music extra
There is nothing at all in life except what we put into life.

The Shift Characters # $ & ' :

Spacing Rules. There is no space between the #-sign and the adjacent figure: #45 68#. Except in a tabulation, there is no space between the $-sign and the adjacent figure: $45.00.

The &-sign (ampersand) is both preceded and followed by a space when used in partnership or company names: James & Wheeler Henry Bryce & Sons.

No space precedes or follows the apostrophe (') when used in contractions or in the possessive case of a noun: couldn't men's suits.

The colon is followed by two spaces.

New Stroke Control

ddd de3 de# d#d d#d d#d #33 kkk ki8 ki' k'k k'k k'k '88 #38 83#

fff fr4 fr$ f$f f$f f$f $44 jjj ju7 ju& j&j j&j j&j &77 $43 4's

Preceding a figure, the #-sign stands for the abbreviation No.

Following a figure, this same sign is used to indicate pounds.

Item #473 weighs 128# and must now be insured for at least $15.

The small l is used for the figure one: 1, 12, 13, 18, 19, 61.

McMillan & Sons' invoices #4378 and #4379 amounted to $1520.00.

Important: If you are using the optional method of fingering, turn back to page 24 for the drills.

Practice Exercise

The only limitations set on a man are those within himself.
Manhood, not scholarship, is the first aim of all education.
Every war is a national calamity, whether victorious or not.

Paragraph Writing

Indenting for Paragraphs. Except in writing letters in the blocked style, the opening sentence of every paragraph is indented from five to fifteen strokes—generally five strokes. These paragraph indentations are made by using the **Tabular Key.**

Operating the Tabular Key. Observe the position of the tabular key or keys, or the tabular bar, on your machine. Study the illustrations on page 29 and the illustrations on the back cover and the back flyleaf of this book. You will note that the multiple-key tabulator and the tabular bar are located in the center above the figure row. With the multiple-key tabulator, the decimal key is used for paragraph indentations. When the tabulator consists of a single key, the key is operated by the little finger. **Use a push stroke. Be sure to hold down the tabular key until the carriage comes to a complete stop.** Keep your hands in correct position.

gaged in the buying and selling of real estate for themselves and for others in and about **Wayne** and **Green** Counties and elsewhere and were well informed as to values of farms and subdivision properties.

3. At about said time defendant Grimm owned a certain subdivision in Wayne County, the lots in which (as plaintiff has recently learned) were of a market value of approximately $300.00 each on subdivision terms, which defendants, by virtue of their arrangement, were offering for sale to the public at said price, defendants then well knowing said lots to have no greater value, and which premises are described as follows:

Greenwood Boulevard Heights, part of the northeast quarter of the northeast quarter of Section 17, Town 2 South, Range 14 East, Lincoln Township, Wayne County, Michigan, as recorded in Liber 34 of Plats, page 67.

4. That shortly prior to March 25, 1930, plaintiff informed defendant Redway that he desired to dispose of his farm for property in Detroit, whereupon defendants conspired together and with their servants, agents, and others to obtain from plaintiff his farm without giving any consideration therefor and offered plaintiff lots 59 to 70, both inclusive, of said subdivision at $9,000.00 and to take his equity in said farm at $5,400.00 as a down payment, the balance to be payable July 1, 1931.

5. As a part of their unlawful scheme defendants falsely and fraudulently represented to plaintiff that said lots were of the fair market value of $750.00 each, though well knowing the contrary and that the fair market value of said lots did not exceed $300.00 each and well knowing plaintiff was inexperienced and unfamiliar with such values and particularly ignorant of the value of the lots aforementioned; and likewise defendants well knew and were informed that plaintiff was relying upon their honesty to deal fairly with him, whereupon it became and was defendants' duty to take no unfair advantage of plaintiff and to impart to him all the facts as to values and to refrain from perpetrating any fraudulent deal.

ants' unlawful acts and their false and fraudulent conduct, has lost said farm to his damage in the sum of $10,000.00, to recover which this suit is brought.

Attorney for Plaintiff

Business Address:
615-621 Majestic Building,
Detroit, Michigan.

Dated: Detroit, Michigan,
October 6, 19—.

The next step is for the defendants' attorney to plead. In this case he pleads the General Issue. On the filing of the Plea, the issue is joined and the case is ready for trial.

Application Exercise 17. For the Plea, type the same caption with the names of the plaintiff and of the defendants which you used in the preceding documents. Insert the number of the case—167,543. The body of the Plea follows:

PLEA OF THE GENERAL ISSUE

And now come said defendants by William W. O'Neill, their attorney, and demand a trial of the matters set forth in plaintiff's declaration.

To the above-named plaintiff: You will please take notice that under the plea of the General Issue above pleaded the defendants will give in evidence and insist in their defense that the cause of action alleged in said declaration arose more than six years before said suit was instituted and is therefore barred under the Statute of Limitations of the State of Michigan.

Attorney for Defendants

Dated: October 16, 19—

Application Exercise 18. You will now type excerpts from the testimony given at the trial of this case, so that you may become familiar with the form in which reporters' transcripts are prepared. First, you will type a part of the opening statement of the attorney for the plaintiff. The material is to be typed within the rulings on a legal-size sheet. Leave at least two blank stroke-spaces at the beginning and at the end of the lines. Indent the name of the speaker 10 strokes and write it in ALL CAPS. Study Illustration 80, page 194.

Illustration 33	Illustration 34	Illustration 35
Operating the Tabular Key	Operating the Tabular Key	Operating the Tabulator Bar

Tabular Key Drill. Before proceeding with the paragraph writing, practice the following drill:

1. With the margin stop set at **10**, set four tabular stops at intervals of fifteen strokes: **25, 40, 55,** and **70.**

2. Tabulate across the sheet on a two-count; thus, (1) Tab, (2) Release; (1) Tab, (2) Release; etc.

3. Return the tabular key finger to guide position on completing the release.

On another sheet of paper type the following paragraph. Reset the margin stops for a line of 50 strokes. Reset the first tabular stop for a 5-stroke indentation. Set the line space regulator for double spacing. If you have time, write the paragraph twice. Be sure to hold down the tabular key until the carriage comes to a full stop; then release the tabular key finger and return it to guide position.

	*Strokes**
Hold down the tabular key until the carriage stops. I do not know how long I sat there on that	43
rock. It was too hot to move. I was also high	91
over the creek and could get down only along the	140
slick face of the rock.	163

(37 Words; Stroke intensity, 4.41)

* The figures give the total stroke count at the end of each line. To find the number of standard stroke words, divide the number of strokes by 5. Thus, 163 ÷ 5 = 32.6, or 33 standard stroke words.

Lesson 11

Use a line of 60 strokes. Top margin, 1 inch. Single-space. Type each line three times, with double spacing after each three-line group. Use the Margin Release Lever if necessary.

Warming-up Drill

Special Words   many mean cold even zero quay post bank fast this jump girl

relax house women today won't usual quite seven books extra

Joe sent the extra check for $181.74 to O'Farrell & Johnson.

Figures and Characters   38 74 14 31 56 190# $118.42 #491 John Daly & Sons, Portland.

The Shift Characters " % ( )

Spacing Rules. There is no space between the opening quotation marks and the quoted matter following. The spacing after closing quotation marks is governed by the rules for the other punctuation marks used with them—one space when the quotation marks follow the comma; two spaces when the quotation marks follow the period, the question mark or the exclamation mark at the end of a sentence. If no other mark is used with the closing quotation marks, they are followed by one space only. "Hurry," he called to them.

There is no space between the per cent sign (%) and the figure preceding. One space follows the per cent sign: 45% increase. There is no space between either parenthesis mark and the matter enclosed. Space once before the opening parenthesis mark and once after the closing parenthesis mark.

29

Mason W. Quigley. Please get in touch with me and let me know whether they can come to my office at 2 p.m., Friday, September 18. I should also like to have you present at that time. Very truly yours, *(86 words)*

Application Exercise 14. Prepare an endorsement for the paper you wrote in Exercise 12, page 190. Use the following data. Space out properly.

No.————————————————

```
        STATE OF MICHIGAN
     In the Circuit Court
   For the County of Wayne
```
———————————————————

```
George Lambert Martin,
              Plaintiff,

   vs.

Frank W. Grimm and
Henry Walters Redway,
              Defendants.
```
———————————————————

```
   PRAECIPE FOR SUMMONS
```
———————————————————

```
   Lorenzo A. Hughson
   Attorney for Plaintiff.
```
———————————————————

```
615-621 Majestic Building
   Detroit, Michigan
```

After the Praecipe has been filed, the county clerk makes out the Summons. The Summons is ordinarily a printed sheet which is filled in. The original, with one copy for each defendant in the case, is given to the sheriff of the county, who serves the Summons on the defendants. The Summons also includes a printed affidavit which is filled in. Since you have had practice in typing on ruled or dotted lines, the Summons is omitted from the papers which you are preparing in this case.

has been served, the attorney retained by the defendants prepares an "Appearance of Defendants." You are to type the document. The caption, *State of Michigan*, etc., and the matter in the box are to be precisely the same as shown in Illustration 78, page 190. The clerk has assigned the number 167,543 to the case. Type that number after the abbreviation *No.* The copy for the rest of the paper follows.

APPEARANCE OF DEFENDANTS
The appearance of the above defendants is hereby entered in the above entitled cause.

————————————————————
Attorney for Defendants

To Lorenzo A. Hughson,
   Attorney for Plaintiff.

Please take notice that I have this day entered my appearance as attorney for the defendants in the above entitled cause.

————————————————————
Attorney for Defendants

Dated September 24, 19—.

Business Address:
   1765 Second National Bank Building,
   Detroit, Michigan.

Application Exercise 16. The attorney for the plaintiff now prepares a Declaration, which gives the substance of the matter in controversy. The Declaration in this case was quite long; hence, you are asked to type only the part given below. The caption and the box are made up of the same data that you typed in Exercise 12. Insert the number of the case—167,543. Double-space, with 10-stroke paragraph indentations.

DECLARATION
Now comes the above-named plaintiff by Lorenzo A. Hughson, his attorney, and complains of the within defendants in a plea of trespass on the case and says:

Count 1
1. On, to wit, March 25, 1930, plaintiff was the owner in fee of a certain 80-acre farm situated on Silver Lake, Green County, Michigan, of the reasonable value of $10,000.00 and subject to a mortgage of $4,000.00.

```
sss sw2 sw" s"s s"s s"s "22 111 lo9 lo( 1(1 1(1 1(1 ((( sw"
fff fr5 fr% f%f f%f f%f %55 ;;; ;p0 ;p) ;); ;); ;); ))) ;p)
```

The period and the comma are typed inside the quotation marks.

When used in numbers, no space follows the comma.

The semicolon and colon are typed outside the quotation marks.

Mr. John's invoice #509 (I enclose a copy) is for $43,510.90.

Your money will not earn any more than 7% this coming quarter.

Important: If you are using the optional method of fingering, turn back to page 24 for the drills.

Practice Exercise

```
We shall be very glad to have you call if you have the time.
I shall also send the postal cards to you as I did last year.
Clear thinking and real concentration are quite necessary now.
Only the wise use of effort and time will bring you success.
```

Paragraph Writing

Use a second sheet of paper for the paragraph writing. Double-space. Set the margin stops for a line of 65 strokes and the tabular stop for a 5-stroke indentation. Make three copies of this paragraph if time permits.

	Strokes
The fact that a man knows what is right does not mean that	59
he will do what is right. Often you will see men who have had	122
good training and whose minds are active do things which they	184
know are harmful to themselves or to others.	228

(46 Words; Stroke intensity, 4.96)

Lesson 12

Throughout Lessons 12 to 28 inclusive, use a 70-stroke line and a 2-inch top margin, unless otherwise directed.

Put the Warming-up Exercise, the Acceleration Drill, and the Concentration Development on one sheet and the Timed Writing on a second sheet.

Type each line of the Warming-up Exercise and the Acceleration Drill twice, single-spaced, with double spacing after each two-line group.

Double-space the Concentration Development and the Timed Writing. Indent all paragraphs; set the tabular stop for a 5-stroke indentation.

Sometimes it is necessary to extend a line of typing a few strokes into the right margin. If the typewriter is in proper adjustment, from four to seven strokes can be typed after the bell rings and before the carriage locks. Additional strokes may be typed beyond the right margin point without moving the margin stop by simply depressing the **Margin Release Key** (No. 16).

In order to familiarize you with the use of the Margin Release Key, some of the lines in the Warming-up Exercises and in the Acceleration Drills are longer than 70 strokes. Set the margin stops for a 70-stroke line, however, and use the Margin Release Key to write the longer lines.

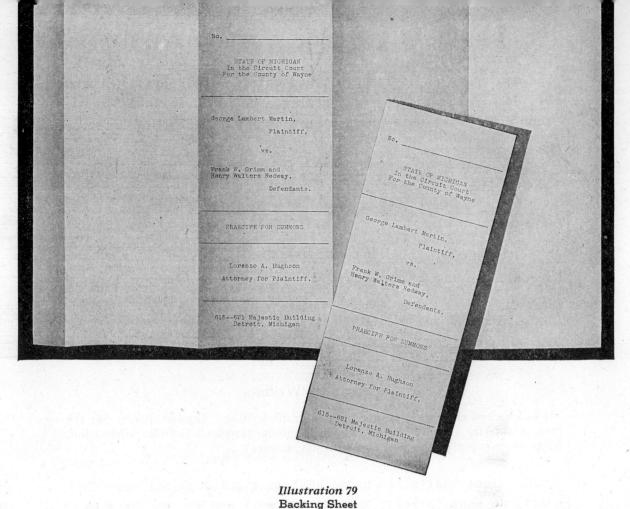

Illustration 79
Backing Sheet
Endorsed and Folded

Endorsements. Every paper that is filed with the court and every copy that is served on the opposite side must be bound in a backing sheet and endorsed. Such backing sheets are made of heavy paper cut to 9″ wide by 15″ long, often blue in color. On the backing sheet is written certain information identifying the contents of the paper which is bound in it. That writing is called the *endorsement*. To prepare an endorsement, proceed in this way:

1. Fold down the upper edge of the backing sheet one inch and crease evenly.

2. Bring up the lower edge even with the crease you have just made. Fold the sheet. Crease this second fold neatly and evenly.

3. Now fold over the crease made in Step 2 and bring it up even with the crease made in Step 1. Crease this third fold.

Unfold this last crease and feed the backing sheet into the machine in such a way that the crease made in Step 1 will be at the left of the cylinder and facing you. The endorsement is to be typed on the right-hand section of the folded sheet as you now have it in the machine. Study Illustration 79.

Application Exercise 13. Type the following letter in the double-spaced style. The letter was written on September 16, 19—, by the attorney, Lorenzo A. Hughson, to his client, Mr. George Lambert Martin. Mr. Martin's address is 417 North Avenue, Detroit, Michigan. Use your own initials as those of the stenographer. Type the attorney's name four line spaces below the complimentary close.

Dear Sir: Summons will shortly be issued in your case against Frank W. Grimm and Henry Walters Redway. As soon as the date of the trial has been set, I shall notify you. (P) I should like to have another talk with two of

191

am an as at be by do go he if in is ma me my no oi on oh or pa so to
act add age ago all and any are arm ask bad bed beg. big bit box boy
able also away baby back bank been best bill blue book both boys busy
call came card care cars case each city club cold come copy cost date
days deal dear does done door down each else etc. even ever eyes face

Acceleration Drill 1

Sentence Writing. Each line in this drill contains 72 strokes. Set the margin
stops for a 70-stroke line, and use the Margin Release Key to release the margin.

It is your duty to aid the man if he will promise to do as you tell him.
The letter ought to bring replies. It has an appeal to a certain class.
Let me hear from you as quickly as possible so that I may make the call.
We can assure you that this course will be a great help to you later on.
On February 23, 24, and 25 we shall place on sale 6,987 men's silk ties.

Concentration Development 1

The possibility of power-driven vehicles was visualized as early
as the fifteenth century by that versatile genius, Leonardo da Vinci.
In 1680 Newton proposed a steam carriage, which he expected to propel
by a jet of steam. The first successful road vehicle, however, was not
developed until 1769, when Joseph Cugnot, a captain in the French
army, built and operated a quaint steam carriage.

(65 Words)

Timed Writing 1

Write for 2 or 5 minutes, as your instructor directs. If you finish before time is
called, start again from the beginning.

	Strokes
Once in a while you meet a person who tells you that he has a	62
right to do what he wants to do without any regard to what others may	132
think or say. Such a person is very likely to be left to go his own	201
way; he will have few or no friends. If you want to live a rich and	270
full life, you need to think of others as well as of yourself.	332

(75 Words; Stroke intensity, 4.43)

Lesson 13
Warming-up Exercise 2
Common Words

us up we to so pa or am as be go by he ma no my if he an in to on oh
but buy can car cut day did due eat end eye far fat fee few fit for
fact fair fall farm fear feel feet felt file fill find fine fire five
form four free from full game gave girl give glad goes gone good hair
about above after again agent agree allow alone along among apply

31

taken without waiving any rights reserved to the Commonwealth Casualty Company by virtue of the aforesaid policy, and that the Commonwealth Casualty Company hereby disclaims any and all liability under the aforesaid policy. Very truly yours, HAWKINS, MEYER & HINTON HYH:CGT *(208 words)*

Application Exercise 10. A *proxy* is a legal paper which conveys authority to an agent to perform a specific act for the principal. Type this proxy with a line for the signature. Arrange the affidavit below the proxy as shown in Illustration 77, page 188.

PROXY

KNOW ALL MEN BY THESE PRESENTS: That I, Charles Thurber Wiggin, do hereby constitute and appoint Henry Atkinson my true and lawful attorney, for me and in my name, place, and stead, to vote as my proxy at the annual meeting of the shareholders of the Tredway Art Metal Company, a corporation duly organized under the laws of the State of Delaware, all the 350 shares of the capital stock of said corporation now standing on its books in my name, as fully and amply as I could or might do were I personally present, with full power of substitution and revocation. (P) WITNESS my hand at Muskegon, Michigan, this   day of   , A. D. One Thousand Nine Hundred and   . _____
State of Michigan County of Muskegon ss. On   , 19   , before me personally appeared Charles Thurber Wiggin, to me known to be the same person described in and who executed the foregoing instrument and acknowledged that he executed the same as his free act and deed. (P) IN TESTIMONY WHEREOF, I have hereunto set my hand and official seal.

_____Notary Public County of Muskegon, State of Michigan. My commission expires January 30, 1940.

Application Exercise 11. Form 45 in the Workbook is a Lease that has been completed in longhand. The next sheet—Form 46—is a blank Lease. Fill in Form 46 from the longhand insertions in Form 45.

First, you will write the documents that are prepared prior to the suit; then you will type extracts from the testimony given at the trial; finally, you will type the Opinion of the Court and the final judgment.

Application Exercise 12. The first paper prepared when a suit is undertaken is the *Praecipe for Summons*. Study Illustration 78.

Type the document on a sheet of ruled legal paper. The number of the case is filled in by the county clerk. He also stamps the date of filing on the back of the paper. Study the arrangement of the "box" in which the names of the parties are typed. The plaintiff, of course, is the party who brings the suit; the defendant is the person against whom the suit is brought. This paper was prepared by the attorney for the plaintiff. Type from the copy at the bottom of this column.

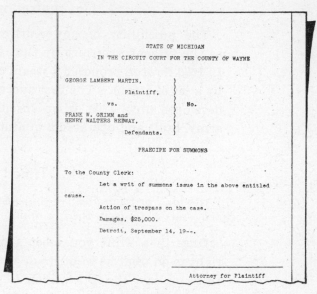

Illustration 78
Praecipe for Summons

STATE OF MICHIGAN IN THE CIRCUIT COURT FOR THE COUNTY OF WAYNE GEORGE LAMBERT MARTIN, Plaintiff, vs. FRANK W. GRIMM and HENRY WALTERS REDWAY, Defendants. No. PRAECIPE FOR SUMMONS To the County Clerk: Let a writ of summons issue in the above entitled cause. (P) Action of trespass on the case. (P) Damages, $25,000. Detroit, September 14, 19—.

_____**Attorney for Plaintiff**

It is not necessary for you to return to us now the receipted invoice.
Call at the new store address for all goods returned today for credit.
As soon as a reply is received, I shall send you the complete results.
Magazine and newspaper advertising rates must depend upon circulation.
Collect $426.86 from Schmalz, Exeter & Co. due on their April account.

Concentration Development 2

In 1802, Richard Trevithick patented a steam vehicle and actually suc-
ceeded in operating it. It was equipped with all the essential mecha-
nisms present in refined form on modern vehicles--handle bar, change
speed gearing, and differential drive. In succeeding years, principally
between 1810 and 1830, Anderson, James, Gurney, Hancock, and Maceroni
all built road carriages in England.

(57 Words)

Timed Writing 2

Do not type the author's name at the end of a paragraph unless you are instructed
to do so.

	Strokes
Knowledge cannot be stolen from you; it cannot be bought or sold.	67
You may be poor, and the sheriff may come into your house and sell	134
your furniture at auction, or drive away your cow or take your lamb,	203
and leave you homeless and penniless; but he cannot lay the hand of	271
the law upon the jewelry of your mind.	309

—Elihu Burritt
(60 Words; Stroke intensity, 5.15)

Lesson 14

Warming-up Exercise 3

Common Words

fun fur get got had has hat her him his hot how its job kid law let
half hand hard have head hear held help here high hold home hope hour
idea into item July June just keep kept kind knew know lady land last
late left less life like line list live long look loss lost lots love
April asked awful basis begin being bills black blank board books

Acceleration Drill 3

Phrase and Sentence Writing

this which is may be with you which are very much in regard to that
we shall be pleased, for some time, I should be glad, I should like it
two or three, in the last year, if we may, we shall be very glad, I am
The foes of the tariff fought to free all farm fruits from the tariff.
Their notices state that new discounts of 20% to 50% are being made.

second part, the receipt whereof is hereby acknowledged, does by these presents grant and convey unto the said party of the second part, and to his heirs and assigns forever, the following described real estate situated in the County of Montgomery, State of Pennsylvania, to wit: (P) All that certain lot or parcel of land known as lot number 25 in the Jackson Farm Plan of lots in Madison Township, Montgomery County, State of Pennsylvania; said plan being recorded in Plan Book, Volume 27, page 143, and further bounded and described as follows, to wit: (P) Beginning at a point on the southerly line of Lambert Avenue in the dividing line between lots numbered 14 and 15, distant 37.56 feet north, 25 degrees 41 minutes west from the northwest corner of Lambert Avenue 40 feet to a point in the line of lot numbered 13; thence southwestwardly along the line of lot numbered 13 in said plan 120 feet to a point in the southerly line of Fulton Alley; thence south 25 degrees 41 minutes east 40 feet to a point in the dividing line between lots numbered 14 and 15 aforesaid; and thence northeastwardly along the dividing line between lots numbered 14 and 15 a distance of 210 feet to the point on the southerly side of Lambert Avenue aforesaid, the place of beginning, as more fully described in the deed from Henry West Walton et ux. to Walter Hamden Davidson, dated September 16, 1930, and recorded in Montgomery County in Deed Book, Volume 768, page 542. (P) Together with all and singular the tenements, hereditaments, and appurtenances thereunto belonging, or in anywise appertaining, and the rents, issues, and profits thereof. (P) TO HAVE AND TO HOLD, all and singular, the above-mentioned and described premises, together with the appurtenances, unto the said party of the second part and to his heirs and assigns forever. And the said party of the first part and his heirs, the said premises, in the quiet and peaceable possession of the said party of the second part, his heirs and assigns, against the said party of the first part and his heirs, and against all and every person and persons whomsoever lawfully claiming or to claim the same, shall and will WARRANT and by these presents forever DEFEND. (P) IN WITNESS WHEREOF, the said party of the first part has hereunto set

(P) State of Pennsylvania County of Montgomery ss. On this   day of   , 19—, before me, Charles C. Yarnall, a Notary Public in and for the said County of Montgomery, State of Pennsylvania, personally appeared Alfred Roe Bentley, known to me to be the person whose name is subscribed to the foregoing instrument, and acknowledged to me that he executed the same. (P) In witness whereof, I have hereunto set my hand and affixed my official seal the day and year in this certificate above written._____
Notary Public   County of Montgomery, State of Pennsylvania

Application Exercise 8. Many legal papers are in the nature of forms which are filled in by the typist. In the Workbook you will find Form 43, which is a Power of Attorney. It has been filled in. The next sheet is Form 44, which is a blank Power of Attorney form. You are to type the fill-ins on Form 44. The "copy" which you are to fill in is that given in longhand on Form 43.

Application Exercise 9. Type the following letter in the single-spaced style with mixed punctuation. Write the subject on two lines. *Et al.* is Latin for *and others*.

Mr. William Bolton 765 Ashland Boulevard Camden, New Jersey Dear Sir: Re Leslie Beckwith, Administrator, vs. William Bolton et al. A few days ago a copy of a summons pertaining to the above entitled cause was mailed to the Commonwealth Casualty Company. On checking up the matter in the court records, we find, according to the return made on the back of the original summons, that you were served with a copy about a month ago. (P) The first knowledge we had of any law suit pending against you was when we received this summons through the mail. As you contend that you were not personally served with a copy of the summons in this case, we shall file your special and limited appearance for the sole and only purpose of vacating a default entered against you and thus quashing the return of the summons in this case. (P) We hereby notify you that we are taking this action under a reservation of rights in your policy No. 257,764, which you have with

Thereafter, the attention of other zealous and inventive minds was directed to the possibilities of the internal combustion engine. The general form of the present-day reciprocating gas engine was worked out by the Frenchman, Lenoir, in 1860. To his quite basically sound idea successive contributions were made by Siemens, Hugon, Otto, and Brayton.

(54 Words)

Timed Writing 3

	Strokes
How shall I live? How shall I make the most of my life and put	64
it to the best use? How shall I become a man and do a man's work?	132
This, and not politics or trade or war or pleasure, is the question.	202
The primary consideration is not how shall one get a living, but how	271
shall he live; for if he lives rightly, whatever is needful he shall	339
easily find.	351

—John Lancaster Spalding

(72 Words; Stroke intensity, 4.88)

Note: For control of the Question Mark, see the bottom of page 27.

Lesson 15

Warming-up Exercise 4

Common Words

lot low man may May men met Mr. new No. not now off old one our out made mail make many mean meet mind mine miss Miss more most Mrs. much must name near need news next nice note once only open over page paid bring can't carry cases cause check child claim class clear close accept action advice advise afraid almost always amount answer anyone

Acceleration Drill 4

Phrase and Sentence Writing

work out will be then the are devoting the time we were I was will be will not permit will not this pleasure may this be the last member in per minute you will also to typing first hand any great success in it It was not too late for them to fill the order which we sent in today. On December 12 car #3780923, S. P., was shipped on your order #668B12.

Concentration Development 4

By 1855 the internal combustion engine had been quite effectively developed as a general principle. The earliest pioneers to experiment in the development of a practical automobile were Daimler, Benz, Mayback, Krebs, Panhard, Levassor, Serpollef, De Dion, Bouton, Gibbon, and Roots. Of these, Benz, with his tricycle of 1885, must be credited with the first successful road vehicle with an internal combustion engine.

(62 Words)

desks, chairs, filing cabinets, and office furniture and fixtures now located in his offices at Rooms 368, 370, and 372 of the Professional Building at the corner of Broadway and Tenth Street in the City of Seattle, above mentioned, a list and description of the said furniture and equipment being appended hereto as ''Appendix B,'' all of which are estimated and valued by the parties hereto at the sum of Five Thousand Dollars ($5,000.00); these contributions to constitute the capital stock and equipment of the firm to be used and employed in common between them for the support, promotion, and conduct of the said law business in the City of Seattle, to and for their mutual benefit and profit. (P) III. At all times during the continuance of their partnership they and each of them will give their time and attention to said business and profession, and will exert themselves for their joint interest, benefit, and profit, and will employ their skill and knowledge of the law in the trial of causes and the care of all such legal business as may be entrusted to them by their clients. (P) IV. That they shall and will at all times during the said partnership bear, pay, and discharge equally between them all rents, charges, and expenses that may be required for the maintenance of offices and the conduct of said business, and that all gains, profits, fees, retainers, and compensations of any and every sort that shall come from or arise out of their said business, either directly or indirectly, shall be divided and shared equally between them on the first day of March, June, September, and December of each year during the continuance of this partnership. (P) V. That accurate and complete books of account of said business shall be kept by double entry of all money transactions of said firm, to which each partner shall at all times have access. At the expiration of the agreed term or sooner termination of the partnership, the said partners, each to the other, shall and will make a true, just, and final accounting of all things relating to their said business, and in all things truly adjust the same. (P) IN WITNESS WHEREOF, the above-named parties have hereto set their hands and seals the day and year first above written.

for the document from the following data. If you are using ruled legal sheets, center the lines of the title with reference to the right and left rulings on the sheet. Use today's date instead of the one shown here.

ARTICLES OF CO-PARTNERSHIP
between
EDWARD JENKINS HUTTON
Seattle, Washington
and
JAMES WALTON HARRINGTON
Spokane, Washington
March 1, 19—

Application Exercise 7. Type this Warranty Deed. Follow the capitalization exactly. In the blanks in the first paragraph and in the affidavit, fill in the current date. The expression *et ux.* means *and wife* (Latin *et uxor*).

Study Illustration 77. It shows the last three lines of the Deed together with the Affidavit. The abbreviation *ss.*, which appears in the affidavit, means *namely* (Latin *scilicet*).

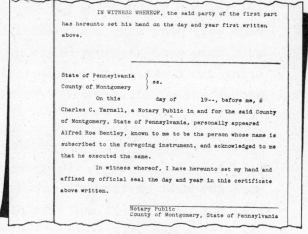

Illustration 77
Affidavit

WARRANTY DEED
THIS INDENTURE, made this   day of   , One Thousand Nine Hundred and   ; (P) **BETWEEN** Alfred Roe Bentley of the city of Norristown, County of Montgomery, State of Pennsylvania, party of the first part, and James Calhoun Perry of the same place, party of the second part. (P) **WITNESSETH:** That the party of the first part, for and in consideration of the sum of Sixteen Thousand Seven Hundred and Forty Dollars ($16,740.00)

One day, so runs the old fable, all the beasts met in an open 62
field.   A ring was made, and a monkey came out to dance.   So well did 132
he dance that he won the praise of all.   A camel, moved by envy, began 203
to dance too.   He made such a silly show of himself that the other 270
beasts drove him out of the ring. 304

Do not let envy tempt you to do things for which you are not 365
fitted.   Be yourself. 386

(82 Words; Stroke intensity, 4.71)

Lesson 16
Warming-up Exercise 5
Common Words

own pay red run saw say see set she sir six ten the too try two use
part past plan play poor post rain rate read real rest road room said
comes could cover dance dated delay doing don't doubt dozen draft
dress early eight enjoy error every extra favor files first floor
anyway appear around asking assure attend August become before better

Acceleration Drill 5
Phrase and Sentence Writing

their to the amounts of their invoices will you be will be in still in
and I I know same problem then on the subject there will be results at
from your letter you wrote you said about it from our you are you can
If you will be good enough to specify a certain hour, I shall be here.
July 15, 1911, fell on Saturday; November 17, 1904, fell on Thursday.

Concentration Development 5

In America such geniuses as Duryea, Olds, Haynes, Winton, Ford,
King, Maxwell, Apperson, Riker, Clarks, Stanley, White, and Franklin
developed steam, electric, and internal combustion engine vehicles.
Duryea built the first American automobile that ran. Ford's first
machine, built just about the same time, was the first forerunner of
the Model "T."

(52 Words)

Timed Writing 5

A good way to relieve the monotony of any job is to think up 61
ways of improving it. 83

It is said that for horses the hardest road out of London is the 148
most level one.   There are no hills to climb and descend, and the 214
tired horse has no chance to rest one set of muscles while another 281
works.   Monotony produces fatigue; and because this particular road 349
is one dead, monotonous level, more horses die on it than on any other 420
road out of the city. 441

—P. W. Goldbury
(86 Words; Stroke intensity, 5.13)

34

tation resulting from strikes, severe storms, or other causes beyond the control of the party of the first part; or in case of a stoppage of his mines caused by a strike among his miners or other employees, the said party of the first part shall be released from all obligation to furnish coal to the said party of the second part during such suspension. (P) It is further agreed that the said party of the first part will, if required, use his best endeavors to purchase some other corresponding grade of coal and furnish the same to the said party of the second part, at the lowest market price at which it can be obtained by the said party of the first part; or the said party of the second part, at his option, may secure his supply of coal elsewhere during such suspension. (P) WITNESS our hands and seals the day and year first above written.

Application Exercise 4. Legal letters are frequently technical in character; hence, you will need to exercise special care in the writing. Before you turn in any work, always read and check the typing.

Write the following letter in the single-spaced style, with 10-stroke paragraph indentations. Type the letter with close punctuation. Write the address on four lines. The subject line is to be typed below the salutation and indented ten strokes. Use Form 42.

Hon. W. A. Lowell, Auditor General, Capitol Building, Dover, Delaware. Dear Sir: In re Capital Stock Tax of Roland Oil Company Enclosed you will find a petition for a reassessment of capital stock tax determined against the above-named company for the year 19 *. The company admits that a tax in the sum of $1,456.62 is due, and we enclose a certified check for that amount. (P) If you will refer to the company's capital stock report, you will readily see where the error lies. The report sets forth, on page 1, that the non-manufacturing assets for 19—* are $856,743.00, of which $221,435.76 is represented by property held in Delaware. The officers of the company included in this calculation all the real estate and tangible personal property held in Delaware, as well as the cash on deposit in Delaware banks, and excluded the cash and current assets and bills receivable connected with its business in other states.

* Last year.

on the part of the officers of the company. (P) We assume that, in accordance with your general practice, in the event of an adverse decision by you on our petition, you will grant us sixty days from the date of your decision within which to appeal. Yours truly, **HAWKINS, MEYER & HINTON GLM:MRT** (*198 words*)

Application Exercise 5. Type this agreement. Use ruled legal paper, if possible; 10-stroke paragraph indentations. Type two lines for the signatures, with (SEAL) at the end of each line. Two double spaces below the second signature line type *Witnessed by*, beginning at the left writing margin. Space down two more double line spaces and type a line beginning at the left writing margin and extending about half way across the sheet.

ARTICLES OF CO-PARTNERSHIP

THIS AGREEMENT, Made this   day of   , One Thousand Nine Hundred and   , between Edward Jenkins Hutton of the City of Seattle, County of King, State of Washington, and James Walton Harrington of the City of Spokane, County of Spokane, State of Washington, WITNESSETH AS FOLLOWS: (P) I. That the said parties above named have agreed to become partners in the law business, and by these presents do agree to be partners together under and by the firm name of Hutton & Harrington, at and in the City of Seattle, County of King, State of Washington, in the business and profession of attorneys and counselors at law. The said partnership is to BEGIN on the first day of   * , One Thousand Nine Hundred and   , and to continue for a period of seven years, to the first day of   †   , One Thousand Nine Hundred and   †   , unless sooner dissolved by mutual consent or terminated by the death or disability of one of the parties thereto. (P) II. To this end and purpose the said Edward Jenkins Hutton has contributed the sum of Five Thousand Dollars ($5,000.00) in cash, and the said James Walton Harrington has contributed all his certain law library, containing about one thousand (1,000) volumes, the titles and descriptions of which are hereto appended as ''Appendix A''; together with the said library

* Next month.
† Seven years hence.

Warming-up Exercise 6

Common Words

war was way who why win yes yet you tan tax lag hub sob hit job top
sale same save says seem seen sell send sent ship show sick side sign
folks found fully funny girls given gives going goods grade great
guess hands happy heard heart hours house inst. isn't issue items
bought called cannot chance change church coming common copies charge

Acceleration Drill 6

Phrase and Sentence Writing

can it be can be very much from you with our letter your letter is in
if you will come as soon as you will be they have this letter now the
a time when you can come today is the time it will not be for a time.
Your charge account is now open and ready to use at your convenience.
Note #432 for $567.89 from Jones, Fall & Frye is to bear 6% interest.

Concentration Development 6

It is said that Mr. Ford made his first cylinder from the exhaust pipe
of an old steam engine. The front and rear wheels of the queer-looking
machine were taken from bicycles, and the body was of current carriage
construction. Although there were 300 automobiles built in the United
States between 1886 and 1898, there was no automobile industry in the
sense that we know it today.

(68 Words)

Timed Writing 6

Most people are content to spend their lives carrying out the	62
purposes of others. They work only for the pay. They care more for	131
the pay than for the purpose. Give them the pay and you can have the	201
purpose, for all they care. And in this way millions of unhappy lives	272
are spent.	283
If you lack a purpose, why not look the matter squarely in the	346
face? Why not have a purpose of your own? You can still serve	410
another's purpose--can serve it even better; you can still have the	478
pay and yet be working out your own purpose.	522

(101 Words; Stroke intensity, 5.17)

Word Division.   In dividing a word at the end of a line, the hyphen must always
be placed at the end of a *complete* syllable.   Syllabication—not derivation—is the
standard to be followed in word division.

One-syllable words may never be divided.   This guiding rule applies to past tense
verb forms which are pronounced as one syllable; as, *trained*, *dredged*, *wrecked*,
stamped.   If the word cannot be completely typed at the end of the line, the entire
word must be carried over to the next line.

A two-syllable word in which either syllable consists of a single letter may never
be divided; as, *about*, *around*, *again*, *bony*, *many*.

son Landor, the testator, in the presence of each of us, and was at the same time declared by him to be his LAST WILL AND TESTAMENT; and we are at his request signing our names hereunto in his presence as attesting witnesses.

_____(SEAL)

_____(SEAL)

Application Exercise 2. You will now type a letter which gives the opinion of an attorney based on his examination of an abstract of title. Use double spacing, but single-space and indent (5 stroke-spaces on either side) the descriptive paragraph—"Beginning for the same," through "page 531."

Mercantile National Bank   Houston, Texas   Gentlemen: In re Abstract of Title 123 Fulton Avenue Brenham, Texas Having made a careful examination of the records of Washington County as to the record title of the following described premises situated in Worth Township, County of Washington, State of Texas, bounded and described as follows, to wit: (P) Beginning for the same on the southwest side of Fulton Avenue at the distance of 130 feet southeasterly from its intersection with the southwest side of Marblehead Street and running thence southeasterly, binding on the southwest side of Fulton Avenue 130 feet to the northwest side of an alley 15 feet wide there laid out; thence southwesterly parallel with Jackson Street and binding on the northwest side of said 15-foot alley, with the use thereof in common with others, 136 feet 8 inches more or less to the northeast side of another alley 15 feet wide there laid out; thence northwesterly parallel with Fulton Avenue and binding on the northeast side of said last mentioned 15-foot alley, with the use thereof in common with others, 130 feet; thence northeasterly parallel with Marblehead Street 136 feet 8 inches more or less to the place of beginning, together with the right and privilege of the open space 20 feet wide between the lot hereinbefore described and the lot adjoining to the northwest, as more fully described in the deed from George Lambert Johnson et ux. to Henry Davison dated February 8, 1932, and recorded in Washington County Deed Book, Volume 324, page 531. (P) I HEREBY CERTIFY that the said records show a good and indefeasible title

following, to wit: (P) Subject to the building line and all building and other restrictions set forth in the explanation endorsed on plan of record. (P) This statement is made to include the date of   , 19   .

Application Exercise 3. Written contracts are frequently referred to as Articles of Agreement. Write the following paper. Type lines for two signatures at the end. The word SEAL in parentheses is to be written at the end of each line.

ARTICLES OF AGREEMENT

THESE ARTICLES OF AGREEMENT made this   day of   , One Thousand Nine Hundred and   , between Carl Estes Hemingway of the City of Erie, County of Erie, State of Pennsylvania, party of the first part, and William James Farmsworth of the City of Cleveland, County of Cuyahoga, State of Ohio, party of the second part: (P) WITNESSETH that the parties to this agreement, in consideration of payments to be made as hereinafter stated, stipulate and agree as follows: (P) The said party of the first part agrees, subject to the reservations hereinafter named, to sell to the said party of the second part five thousand (5,000) tons of coal, in such quantities as the said party of the second part may require for use in his factory situated in Cleveland, Ohio, from the date hereof until the first day of January, A. D. 19 *, at the rate of Five Dollars and Twenty-five Cents ($5.25) a ton, said coal to be delivered by the party of the first part to the said factory of the party of the second part. (P) The said party of the second part agrees to buy of the party of the first part all the coal he may need for use in said factory from the date hereof until the first day of January, A. D. 19 *, and to pay the said party of the first part the rates above mentioned for all coal used under these Articles of Agreement, said moneys to be due and payable on the fifteenth day of each month, for all coal delivered during the immediately preceding calendar month. (P) It is further mutually agreed that the said party of the first part shall not be held responsible for failure to deliver coal to the said party of the

* Next year.

Warming-up Exercise 7

Word Building. In a number of lessons from this point on, this part of your work will consist of word building exercises. These drills are designed to help you to write by letter groupings rather than by single strokes. These words are correctly divided and will aid you in making word divisions at the end of typed lines. Use the Margin Release Lever to complete any line which has more than 70 strokes.

```
ad ad ad just just just ment ment ment adjustment adjustment adjustment
frac frac frac tion tion tion fraction fraction fraction ob ob ob serve
serve serve observe observe observe pas pas sen sen sen ger ger ger pas-
senger passenger passenger ward ward ward robe robe robe wardrobe ward-
robe wardrobe taxi taxi taxi cabs cabs cabs taxicabs taxicabs taxicabs
```

Acceleration Drill 7
Phrase and Sentence Writing

```
that I that I that I will that he more than a letter the letter with him as
would have you have they have who have have you would be which would
which will be they will be he will this will who will she will it will
Strive every period to make some real gain in your speed and accuracy.
James Wellton & Co. offer 20% to 25% discount during July and August.
```

Concentration Development 7

The first references in literature to flying are to mythological attempts on the part of one Daedalus, a Greek architect, who sought to flee from the island of Crete, where he and his son Icarus were to be served as dainties on the Minotaur's bill of fare. Daedalus built for himself and his son a set of wax wings, "took off" from the scene of his imprisonment, and journeyed through the air for home.

(74 Words)

Timed Writing 7

If you were to ask a busy man how he gets so much done, he would tell you that when he starts a job he finishes it; then goes on to the next one.

Some people start well enough; they are all aglow and they pitch in with a vim. But the trouble is that they do not keep on; every little thing that comes along takes their minds off their work. They tire of the job at hand; then they begin another one, only to tire of it also. Unless you form the habit of going through with a piece of work, you won't get far.

(107 Words; Stroke intensity, 4.78)

65
133
146
211
278
348
418
487
511

Word Division. It is a good rule not to divide a word in such a way that only two letters are carried over to the next line. The hyphen-stroke, which would be required if the word were divided, takes up one of the two stroke-spaces needed to type the two letters. Do not, therefore, divide such words as *frozen, happy, hardly.* Do not carry over to the next line the *ly* ending in such adverbs as *formerly* and *morally.* These words may, however, be divided thus: *for-merly, mor-ally.*

LAST WILL AND TESTAMENT

The last will and testament of Mervin Jackson Landor
of the City of Springfield, County of Sangamon, State of
Illinois, made and published this   day of   ,
in the Year of our Lord, One Thousand Nine Hundred and   .

In the name of God, Amen: I, Mervin Jackson Landor
of the City of Springfield, County of Sangamon, State of
Illinois, of the age of 47 years and being of sound and disposing mind and memory, do hereby make, publish, and declare
this my last will and testament in manner following, that is
to say:

FIRST: I direct that all my just debts and funeral
expenses be paid as soon after my decease as conveniently may
be done.

SECOND: To my daughter, Mary Wilson Landor, I give
and bequeath the sum of Five Thousand Dollars ($5,000.00).

THIRD: To my brother, Charles Jackson Landor, I
give and devise my apartment property known as No. 301 Tenth
Street in the City of Springfield, County of Sangamon, State of
Illinois, to have and to hold, and to his heirs and assigns
forever.

FOURTH: To the Trustees of Washington College in the
City of Springfield, County of Sangamon, State of Illinois, I
give and devise the sum of Five Thousand Dollars ($5,000.00) to
be added to the general endowment fund of said College.

the rest, residue, and remainder of my
estate I give, devise, and bequeath to my
Kingston Landor, for and during the term of
after her death, to my daughter, Mary Wilson
and assigns forever.

I hereby nominate and appoint Charles
attorney-at-law of the City of Springfield,
State of Illinois, to be the executor of
and testament, hereby revoking all former
tary instruments made.

SS WHEREOF I have hereunto subscribed my name
and set my seal this   day of   in the year of
our Lord, One Thousand Nine Hundred and

_____(SEAL)

The above instrument, consisting of two sheets, was
now here subscribed by Mervin Jackson Landor, the testator, in
the presence of each of us, and was at the same time declared
by him to be his LAST WILL AND TESTAMENT; and we are at his
request signing our names hereunto in his presence as attesting
witnesses.

_____(SEAL)

_____(SEAL)

2

Illustration 76
Will with Attestation

185

Warming-up Exercise 8
Word Building

super super super in in in tend tend tend ent ent superintendent
superintendent superintendent reason reason reason able able able
reasonable reasonable reasonable mag mag mag net net magnet magnet
magnet kind kind kind ness ness ness kindness kindness kindness
dif dif dif fer fer fer ent ent ent different different different

Acceleration Drill 8
Word and Sentence Writing

arts part sort lark park sign sins when whip whom what base fact fail
lost race here hate pair coal none wash wide rush rule role rail pain
It is not necessary to return the postal card if you are going to buy.
What is the meaning of the maxim, "Nothing succeeds like success"?
Act immediately if you wish to take advantage of the free offer made.

Concentration Development 8

Leonardo da Vinci sketched three of the possible seven varieties of
aircraft--the ornithopter, the parachute, and the helicopter. Even
though he did not go further, this fact alone justly stamps him as the
"grandfather" of aviation. There are unconfirmed references in literature to several gliding flights by an expert Frenchman by the name of
DeBacqueville and an Italian by the name of Dante, contemporaries of
da Vinci.

(67 Words)

Timed Writing 8

As you do your work day after day, keep in mind the fact that 62
your teacher has been over the road before you. He or she knows the 131
hard spots and how to get over or around them. It may be that some- 199
times, in your zeal to get ahead, you may think you are being held 266
back. That is not the case at all. What you no doubt need is more 334
practice on some detail which you have not yet mastered. You may not 404
be able to see, as you go along, the reason for each step that is 470
taken; but rest assured that there is a reason. 517

(108 Words; Stroke intensity, 4.79)

Lesson 20
Warming-up Exercise 9
Word Building

what what what ever ever ever whatever whatever whatever some some
some one one one someone someone someone tele tele tele scope scope
scope telescope telescope telescope zeal zeal zeal ous ous ous zealous zealous zealous fir fir fir ing ing ing firing firing firing
em em em pha pha pha size size size emphasize emphasize emphasize

Division 5 — Law Office Typing

In this Division you will learn how to prepare legal papers and court documents. Because of the high standard of accuracy which such work demands, the training you will get here will be extremely valuable to you, no matter what sort of typing you may be called on to do.

Note: A comprehensive course in all phases of law typewriting is provided in the text, *Legal Typing Practice*, published by The H. M. Rowe Company.

A large part of the work of a law office consists of the preparation of such papers as agreements, deeds, mortgages, abstracts of titles, and wills. The papers are generally typed on ruled legal sheets, which are 8½" wide by 13" long. The ruling at the left of the sheet consists of a double line from top to bottom printed 1½" from the left edge. The ruling at the right is a single line printed ½" from the right edge. All the typing must be done within the rules. Set the margin stops so that there will be two stroke-spaces at the beginning and at the end of the typed lines. Headings must be centered with reference to the space between the rulings.

Use ruled legal sheets for the law office work you will do in this Division. If such sheets are not available, use ordinary paper ruled with red ink. In actual work, carbon copies of legal papers are always made.

Type the title of each document 2" or 3" from the top of the sheet. Leave a margin at the bottom of 1½". Triple-space below the heading, and double-space all your work in this Division, unless otherwise directed. Indent all paragraphs 10 stroke-spaces. If a piece of work calls for more than one page, number each page. Type the figure about one-half inch from the bottom of the sheet.

Application Exercise 1. Type the following will on a ruled legal sheet. Insert the current date in the blanks. Do not use figures; write out the date in words.

When you have written the last line of the will, double-space and type a line about 3 inches long—for the signature, followed by the word (SEAL). Then space two more double spaces and type the Attestation, which is the sentence beginning, "The above instrument." Below the Attestation type two signature lines. Study Illustration 76, page 185.

LAST WILL AND TESTAMENT

The last will and testament of Mervin Jackson Landor of the City of Springfield, County of Sangamon, State of Illinois, made and published this   day of   , in the Year of our Lord, One Thousand Nine Hundred and   . (P) In the name of God, Amen: I, Mervin Jackson Landor of the City of Springfield, County of Sangamon, State of Illinois, of the age of 47 years and being of sound and disposing mind and memory, do hereby make, publish, and declare this my last will and testament in manner following, that is to say: (P) **FIRST:** I direct that all my just debts and funeral expenses be paid as soon after my decease as conveniently may be done. (P) **SECOND:** To my daughter, Mary Wilson Landor, I give and bequeath the sum of Five Thousand Dollars ($5,000.00). (P) **THIRD:** To my brother, Charles Jackson Landor, I give and devise my apartment property known as No. 301 Tenth Street in the City of Springfield, County of Sangamon, State of Illinois, to have and to hold, and to his heirs and assigns forever. (P) **FOURTH:** To the Trustees of Washington College in the City of Springfield, County of Sangamon, State of Illinois, I give and devise the sum of Five Thousand Dollars ($5,000.00) to be added to the general endowment fund of said College. (P) **FIFTH:** All the rest, residue, and remainder of my personal and real estate I give, devise, and bequeath to my beloved wife, Anna Kingston Landor, for and during the term of her natural life; after her death, to my daughter, Mary Wilson Landor, her heirs and assigns forever. (P) **LASTLY:** I hereby nominate and appoint Charles Swinburne Elliott, attorney-at-law of the City of Springfield, County of Sangamon, State of Illinois, to be the executor of this my last will and testament, hereby revoking all former wills and testamentary instruments made. (P) **IN WITNESS WHEREOF I** have hereunto subscribed my name and set my seal this   day of   in the year of our Lord, One Thousand Nine Hundred and

_____(SEAL)

Word and Sentence Writing

dated sated place found makes relay ready doubt price wrote write
yours guess world state steak stake plans notes peace piece clear
Please accept our thanks for the cash payment you sent for the order.
We ask you to give this matter your immediate attention if possible.
Checks #240, 351, 462, 573, 684, 761, and 843 have not reached us yet.

Concentration Development 9

The first successful authentic aerial voyage did not come until 1783,
when Lenormand, a zealous Italian expert, jumped from a tower in a
parachute quite similar in its design to da Vinci's, and descended safely
to earth.

The balloon, the flotation of which is independent of propulsion, took
the honor of first ascending with a human passenger.

(56 Words)

Timed Writing 9

A miser once hid all his money in an earth bank near the foot of	65
an azalea bush. Each evening he went to enjoy a glimpse of his tiny	134
hidden mine. A mean man, who had seen the miser at his queer evening	204
pastime, came one night and carried off the money. The next night the	275
miser, finding his money gone, moaned and groaned, filling the night	344
with his lamentations. One of his neighbors told him that he must see	415
the matter aright. The miser had really lost nothing. "Come each	482
evening," he said, "and fancy your money at the foot of the azalea	549
bush. Wealth unused might as well not exist."	595

(112 Words; Stroke intensity, 5.31)

Lesson 21

Warming-up Exercise 10

Word Building

cap cap cap tain tain tain captain captain captain fog fog fog horn
horn horn foghorn foghorn foghorn un un un der der der lie lie lie
underlie underlie underlie jug jug jug gler gler gler juggler juggler
juggler main main main tain tain tain maintain maintain maintain
ref ref ref er er er ence ence ence reference reference reference

Acceleration Drill 10

Word and Sentence Writing. Keep your typing even and continuous when
writing all words, especially the left-hand and right-hand words.

size sold some soon sort stay stop such suit sure take talk tell than
attar hilly aster lymph abate hippo agate knoll addax nullo areas
after holly bares nippy asset linum babes mummy bards Polly bases
Honesty in advertising must be a requirement in this era of business.
This 3-in-1 insurance policy is for $2500.   The premium is $147.36.

Filling in the addresses and salutations on reproduced letters requires care, skill, and patience. The best results are obtained when the color of the ribbon on the typewriter matches exactly the color of the ink used on the stencil copies.

Follow this procedure: First, insert the sheet into the machine and adjust the paper so that the alignment is accurate. Select an **l** or an **i** and move the paper to the right or to the left until it is properly aligned. Next, set the stop for the left margin. Finally, use the cylinder knobs to raise the paper to the first line of the duplicated material; then space up the required number of lines for the address and salutation. For a three-line address, space up six lines—three for the address, one for the space between the address and the salutation, one for the salutation, and one for the space between the salutation and the first line of the letter.

Begin writing the address on the line to which you have spaced up.

Application Exercise 45. From the following addresses, fill in four copies of the letter you reproduced in Exercise 43. (If you have not cut a stencil, fill in the four copies—one original and three carbons—which you typed.) The salutation in each case will be *Dear Miss—* or *Dear Mrs.—*, followed by the name given in the address.

1. **Miss Mary W. Warner 567 West 79th Street New York, New York**

2. **Mrs. Elizabeth W. Judson Monmouth Apartments Montpelier, Vermont**

3. **Miss Anna C. Sherman 1987 Princeton Avenue Trenton, New Jersey**

4. **Miss Helen W. Weldon The Jefferson South and French Streets Albany, New York** *(four lines)*

Reference List of
NUMERALS

ARABIC				ROMAN*
Cardinals		Ordinals		
One	1	First	1st	I
Two	2	Second	2d	II
Three	3	Third	3d	III
Four	4	Fourth	4th	IV
Five	5	Fifth	5th	V
Six	6	Sixth	6th	VI
Seven	7	Seventh	7th	VII
Eight	8	Eighth	8th	VIII
Nine	9	Ninth	9th	IX
Ten	10	Tenth	10th	X
Eleven	11	Eleventh	11th	XI
Twenty	20	Twentieth	20th	XX
Twenty-one	21	Twenty-first	21st	XXI
Thirty	30	Thirtieth	30th	XXX
Forty	40	Fortieth	40th	XL
Forty-four	44	Forty-fourth	44th	XLIV
Fifty	50	Fiftieth	50th	L
Fifty-five	55	Fifty-fifth	55th	LV
Sixty	60	Sixtieth	60th	LX
Sixty-six	66	Sixty-sixth	66th	LXVI
Seventy	70	Seventieth	70th	LXX
Seventy-seven	77	Seventy-seventh	77th	LXXVII
Eighty	80	Eightieth	80th	LXXX
Eighty-eight	88	Eighty-eighth	88th	LXXXVIII
Ninety	90	Nintieth	90th	XC
Ninety-nine	99	Ninety-ninth	99th	XCIX
One Hundred	100	One Hundredth	100th	C
Two Hundred	200	Two Hundredth	200th	CC
Three Hundred	300	Three Hundredth	300th	CCC
Four Hundred	400	Four Hundredth	400th	CD
Five Hundred	500	Five Hundredth	500th	D
Six Hundred	600	Six Hundredth	600th	DC
Seven Hundred	700	Seven Hundredth	700th	DCC
Eight Hundred	800	Eight Hundredth	800th	DCCC
Nine Hundred	900	Nine Hundredth	900th	CM
One Thousand	1000	One Thousandth	1000th	M

* Roman numerals may be written by indenting from the right or from the left, depending on their relative position. They are generally tabulated in the same order as Arabic numbers; that is, with units under units, tens under tens, etc.

Just what had been predicted by Sir Roger Bacon, Black, Gavallo, and others was realized when the Mongolfier brothers successfully piloted their paper-covered bag, filled with hot air, before the awed royalty and intelligentsia of Paris.

It was not, however, until 1784, when the Roberts brothers elongated the gas bag, applied their rudders and silken oars, and made short, slow, but controlled progress through the air, that the first human flight can be said to have been made.

(79 Words)

Timed Writing 10

This copy contains all the letters of the alphabet and stresses particularly the a, s, d, and k strokes. If you complete the copy before time is called, start again at the beginning.

A man drove his donkey to the seaside to purchase a load of salt.	67
On the road back home the donkey unexpectedly stumbled and fell as he	137
crossed a brisk stream. It was some time before he was able to regain	208
his feet. By that time the salt had just about washed away. The lazy	279
donkey was quite delighted because his burden was gone. A few days	347
later, with a basket of sponges lashed to his back, the donkey had	414
occasion to pass over the same brisk stream. Shrewdly remembering his	485
pleasing experience with the salt, he stumbled--this time on purpose.	556
To his intense surprise his load, instead of disappearing, was many	624
times heavier than before.	650

(117 Words; Stroke intensity, 5.56)

Lesson 22
Warming-up Exercise 11

Frequent Letter Combinations. The words in the first four lines of this Exercise and of the Warming-up Exercise in Lesson 23 contain the three hundred most frequent letter combinations. The words in the last line are from the Thousand Commonest Words. Line of 60 strokes.

```
Lewis tired comb many select liter than Fageol onerous cook
Roslyn write wiggle rolled third staid rascal pretense kiln
James ajar jeopardy riled Sally reverse telephone sing stay
Hague silent lead sent inert merely heretic medium telegram
known large later learn least leave light lines local makes
```

Acceleration Drill 11
Sentence Writing

Use a line of 70 strokes.

```
Thank you for your prompt answer to our recent letter on discounts.
We regret very much that your June and July payments were not sent.
It may not be just the best thing for you to do the work at this time.
It is always most difficult for most of us to avoid talking too much.
58# indicates 58 pounds; #49 indicates number 49.  62#, 137#, #1, #13.
```

An important phase of typing is the preparation of stencils from which duplicate copies are to be produced. Before typing the stencil, type the copy on a sheet of paper placed over the backing sheet from a stencil. Keep all typing within the border lines on the backing sheet.

When you have made an exact copy of the material to be stenciled, place the top edge of the typed paper even with the top line and the corner marks of the stencil sheet. In that way you can determine how far down on the stencil sheet the first line should be typed. The numbers, or line spaces, at the sides of the backing sheet will help you to arrive at this starting point. When you insert the stencil sheet, line-space down to the number on which the first line is to be written.

If your stencil is provided with a "cushion sheet," lift the stencil carefully from the backing and insert this cushion sheet between the stencil and the backing sheet.

Now take this pack of backing, stencil, and cushion sheets and place it, top first, in the typewriter with the *backing* next to the typewriter platen. Hold the stencil sheet and the backing sheet firmly together while you turn up the stencil to the point of writing which you have previously determined.

Adjust the machine for stencil cutting (or remove the ribbon if necessary). Be sure that the type of your machine is clean. It is always well to brush the type thoroughly before you start writing. See that the stencil is in the machine straight. Check again the starting point and begin typing.

Whenever you roll back the platen to make a correction on the stencil, hold the loose ends of the stencil and the backing sheet firmly together. Unless you do so, the stencil will wrinkle.

Type with a firm, even touch. The capitals require a harder stroke than that used on small letters.

If you make an error, rub the place where the error was made gently with the back of your finger nail or some other hard, smooth object. Then place a very small quantity of the correction fluid on a piece of paper. Dip the brush into this small quantity of fluid and apply it lightly over the error. Let the fluid set for a few seconds and then type the correction *lightly*.

Do not type beyond the lines around the backing sheet. All copy written outside of those lines will fail to print.

When the stencil cutting has been finished, remove the cushion sheet and attach the stencil to the cylinder of the reproducing machine.

The stenciled reproduction on the paper can be raised, lowered, or moved to the right or left by certain mechanical adjustments. Your teacher will show you how to operate the duplicating machine, how to ink the drum or cylinder, and how to change the ink pad if necessary.

Application Exercise 43. Type the following letter in the semi-blocked style, with mixed punctuation. Use today's date. Four single line spaces below the complimentary close, write the title, **Secretary.**

Miss Flora C. Hepburn 1567 Adams Street Dover, Delaware Dear Miss Hepburn: At the last meeting of the Executive Committee of our class, it was decided to raise a fund of $1,000 as our contribution toward the equipment of the new library at Witherspoon College. The fund will be devoted to the purchase of books on history and sociology. We are having made an attractive book plate showing the college seal and the phrase, "Gift of the Class of 1935." (P) As a loyal classmate, I am sure you will want to have a part in making up this fund. With this letter you will find a subscription blank and a stamped and addressed envelope. I hope you will fill in the blank for as large an amount as possible and mail it to me promptly. It is not necessary to send the money immediately. (P) I want to make my report about two weeks before commencement, which will be held this year on June 15. Sincerely yours, *(152 words)*

Identifying Marks: Your teacher's initials and your own, both in ALL CAPS and separated by the colon. Below the initials, type **Enclosures—2.**

Application Exercise 44. On the copy you have typed, cross out the address and the salutation. Prepare a stencil for the remainder of the letter. Determine accurately how far down on the stencil sheet to begin the first line. Run off a number of copies. (If stencil sheets are not available, type the letter with three carbons, omitting the address and the salutation.)

It is quite generally conceded that Cayley and Henson, English engineers, established the general form of the airplane. Henson built a model which is today housed in an English museum. Penaud was the first man to understand the stabilizing action of the airplane tail. Stringfellow built a triplane model of his own. Langley made extensive model flights.

(57 Words)

Timed Writing 11

The people who get things done are the ones who win our respect.	66
They know how to work. They have tasted of the inner joy that comes	135
from a good job well done.	162
God meant for all of us to get real joy out of the things our	224
hands or minds have found to do. So far from being a curse, work is	293
really one of the chief sources of joy in our lives. Indeed, the	359
happy man is the one who has found work which he likes to do.	421
A way to get joy out of any sort of work is to stick by it until	486
you have learned to do it well. You must hold yourself at the task set	558
before you with all the will power you have.	602

(131 Words; Stroke intensity, 4.60)

Lesson 23

Warming-up Exercise 12

Frequent Letter Combinations. Use a line of 65 strokes.

Manley thistle system throne around Leyden uric leading quail
Howard theory routed Coleman stamen insect malice Bayard josh
Steuart demand burl pogy forgery putter youth jutted reunions
Zander packer ominous pansy Rubicon teethes light tram mantles
maybe means might miles money month music never night notes offer

Acceleration Drill 12
Word Building and Sentence Writing

Use a line of 70 strokes.

young younger youngest youngster youngest younger youngsters younger
excite excited exciter excites exciting excitedly excitement excited
Act now, for this free offer may be withdrawn at any time this month.
The rest of the work will be up to us. We can surely make good at it.
Here is our check for the first quarter's rent less commission to us.

Concentration Development 12

The major portion of the glider experimentation was performed by Lilienthal, Chenot, and the Wright brothers, all of whom realized the necessity of studying the characteristics of an airplane without power plant before attempting mechanical flight. About fifty years ago, at Kitty Hawk, North Carolina, Orville Wright made the first successful flight of a mechanically driven, heavier-than-air machine carrying a man.

(63 Words)

Afternoon

12:30 p.m., Kiwanis Club

Evening

6:30 p.m., Dinner, Hillen Country Club

Thursday
Forenoon

10 a.m., Mr. C. L. Sylvester (Halsey & Grant)

Afternoon

3:30 p.m., Buyers' Conference

Friday
Forenoon

10:30 a.m., Mr. Henry W. Jacobs (City Planning Commission)

Afternoon

12:30 p.m., Lunch with Mr. W. L. Jackson

Evening

8 p.m., Credit Association Meeting, Hopkins Hotel

Afternoon

1 p.m., Lunch with Mr. W. P. Salmon, Hopkins Hotel

Application Exercise 41. The two forms marked Form 41 in the Workbook are "Call Slips." Fill out the slips from the following data.

1. At 2:30 p. m. Mr. George F. Elton of the Simmons Manufacturing Company called in person. He wanted to make an appointment for tomorrow with the General Manager to discuss a new line of beds, as well as the new discount rates which go into effect on the first of next month. He can be reached by telephone at his hotel—MAin 7200.

2. At 3:00 o'clock Mr. George L. Walker, President of the Chamber of Commerce, telephoned to tell the General Manager about a brief special meeting of the Public Relations Committee in the Chamber of Commerce offices at five o'clock tomorrow afternoon.

On the first line of the call slip fill in the name of your teacher. Type your initials after "Taken by."

Application Exercise 42. Prepare the following itinerary. Double-space your work, but single-space the names of the stations and railroads which appear in parentheses. Make a carbon.

ITINERARY
for
Mr. and Mrs. James W. Hamilton

Saturday, September	2	Leave Baltimore (Pa. Station)	4:58 p.m.,	E. T.
Sunday, ''	3	Arrive Chicago (Union Station)	8:25 a.m.,	C. T.
Monday, ''	4	In Chicago		
Tuesday, ''	5	'' ''		
Wednesday, ''	6	'' ''		
Thursday, ''	7	Leave Chicago (C & N W)	10:30 a.m.,	C. T.
'' ''	7	Arrive Omaha	11:00 p.m.,	C. T.
Friday, ''	8	Leave Omaha (Union Pacific)	10:20 a.m.,	C. T.
'' ''	8	Arrive Cheyenne	8:55 p.m.,	M. T.
Saturday, ''	9	Leave Cheyenne (Union Pacific)	12:01 p.m.,	M. T.
Sunday, ''	10	Arrive Ogden	12:05 a.m.,	M. T.
'' ''	10	Leave Ogden (Southern Pacific)	9:00 a.m.,	P. T.
Monday, ''	11	Arrive San Francisco	10:50 p.m.,	P. T.

Note: The abbreviations E. T., C. T., M. T., and P. T. mean, respectively, *Eastern Time, Central Time, Mountain Time,* and *Pacific Time.*

Long words get into the minds of men; short words get into their 65
hearts. When we wish to talk of the things that lie at the roots of 134
life--of birth and death, youth and age, joy and pain--we use the 200
short words that have come down to us through the stream of time. 267
They are the words that touch and move us. 310

The only way we have to set out our ideas is by our words. If 373
we wish to make those ideas clear, we shall do well to learn the 438
right use of the short words in our tongue. 482

Long words may be all right when we want men to know; but when 545
we want them to act, short words are the ones to use. Keep in mind 613
the fact that we act when we feel, not when we know. 665

(143 Words; Stroke intensity, 4.65)

Lesson 24

Warming-up Exercise 13

Common Words, Hyphenated Words, Difficult Sequences. The first line
of this drill is made up of common words; the second line consists of hyphenated
words; the third, fourth, and fifth lines are made up of sequences, each of which consists of a word ending with a certain letter, the space stroke, and a second word beginning with the same letter. Line of 65 strokes.

```
county couple course credit decide desire didn't direct divide
mother-in-law sister-in-law air-speed-meter up-to-date one-half
Damp places should dry yearly.  It traveled due east this season.
Oil leases seem most timely, new wells supplying greater returns.
Pleasant times seemed daily yours sightseeing great cities.
```

Acceleration Drill 13
Word and Sentence Writing

Use a 70-stroke line.

```
died sake fail rove move dove crop drop deep gets fast more mile mole
pass slow load grow grew knew slew true sued coat bear cake film firm
You have not used your charge account with us for many weeks.  Why?
Examine the book carefully.  Remit to us in ten days if you keep it.
The Star of Zealand, a sailing ship, was built at Bath, Maine, in 1901.
```

Concentration Development 13

In 1907 the Signal Corps, after a study of the Wright machine, laid
down specifications for bids on a military observation machine. The
specifications called for a useful load of 350 lbs. and a duration of one
hour at an average speed of 40 miles an hour. The maximum cruising
radius was to be 125 miles. The Wright brothers secured the contract
for $25,000.

(64 Words)

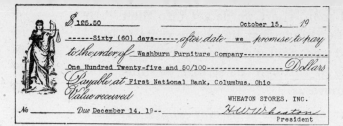

$ 125.50   October 15, 19—
------Sixty (60) days------ *after date* we *promise to pay*
to the order of Washburn Furniture Company------------
One Hundred Twenty-five and 50/100----------------- *Dollars*
Payable at First National Bank, Columbus, Ohio
Value received
                     WHEATON STORES, INC.
No _____ *Due* December 14, 19--   *H. W. Wheaton*
                            President

Illustration 74
Promissory Note

The typing problem involved in filling in other business instruments, such as receipts, promissory notes, and drafts, is precisely the same as that involved in filling in checks. You will need to use the ratchet release and turn the cylinder by hand.

Study the Promissory Note shown in Illustration 74.

Application Exercise 37. From the following data prepare promissory notes. Fill in the word *we* before *promise*. The notes are both to be made payable at Second National Bank, Columbus, Ohio. Use the blank promissory notes marked Form 37.

Date	Time	Payee	Amount	Due Date
July 24, 19—	60 days	Payson Tool Co.	$675.67	September 22, 19—
January 4, 19—	3 months	Gillett & Byers	57.87	April 4, 19—

Business men often draw drafts on debtors. Such drafts are filled in and then frequently turned over to the creditor's bank. That bank sends the draft to a bank in the town or city in which the debtor lives, with instructions to present it to the debtor for payment. Study the draft shown in Illustration 75.

Notice that the debtor, A. W. Swanson, is directed to pay the amount, $145.87, to the Mercantile Trust Company. Mr. Swanson is the *drawee* of the draft; the Mercantile Trust Company is the *payee*. The

drawer of the draft, whose signature of course is not typed, is the person who signs it.

$ 145.87   *Baltimore, Md.*   January 14, 19—
------------------At ten (10) days' sight---------------- *Pay to*
the order of Mercantile Trust Company----------------
One Hundred Forty-five and 87/100------------------ *Dollars*
Value received and charge the same to account of
To A. W. Swanson _____
No _____   *A. F. Adams*

Illustration 75
Draft

Application Exercise 38. Fill in drafts from the following data. Use the blank drafts marked Form 38.

Date	Time	Drawee	Payee	Amount
March 15, 19—	At sight	W. L. Carey	Union Trust Company	$ 78.97
September 5, 19—	At ten days' sight	Burton Motor Co.	First National Bank	212.50

Application Blank

Application Exercise 39. When applying for a position, the typist is usually asked to fill in an application blank. You will find an application blank—Form 39—in the accompanying Workbook. Detach the blank and fill it in. Give the facts about yourself.

Appointment Schedules

Application Exercise 40. The secretary keeps a calendar of her employer's engagements. From the following data, fill in the engagement slip, Form 40.

Monday

Forenoon
11 a.m., Conference of Department Heads

Afternoon
2 p.m., Mr. F. C. Romer (Acme Lace Company)

Tuesday

Forenoon
11:05 a.m., Leave for San Francisco

Evening
8 p.m., Speech—Traffic Club, Hopkins Hotel

I do not know that a man who loves books can quite explain the hold they have on him. When he gets with his books, he feels at home. He knows that in books he can find the best that has been thought and said in all ages. When his friends grow cold or when cares press down on him, he can always go to his books, for they never change.

It is with books as with men: A very few play a great part; all the rest are lost in the crowd. The books that help you most are the ones that make you think the most. Books which do not make you think may be all right when you wish to pass an idle hour, but books which call for thinking on your part are the ones that will add to your mental growth.

135
205
276
338

403
473
543
612
678
692

(146 Words; Stroke intensity, 4.74)

Lesson 25

Word Division.   Divide between double consonants, thus: *bet-ter, mat-ter, neces-sary* (or *nec-essary*).   If, however, you wish to divide a derivative formed from a root word that ends with a double consonant, the division must be made *after* the double letter, thus: *dress-ing, spell-ing.*

In derivatives which are formed by doubling the last consonant in the root word, the division must be made between the double consonant, thus: *refer-ring* (or *re-ferring*), *admit-ting* (or *ad-mitting*).

Warming-up Exercise 14

Common Words

that them then they this till time told took town trip true turn upon
often order other ought paper parts party piece place plans plant
point power price quite quote reach ready refer reply right sales
fellow filled finish follow forgot Friday friend future giving ground
handle happen hardly having health hoping indeed inform kindly latter

Acceleration Drill 14

Word Building and Special Stroke Combinations

dream dreams dreamer dreamed dreamers dreaming dreamily dream dreams
Verge. Nestled close beneath. He wore spats. Save him. I did not.
Men gathered. By this time the bell rang. Get him. Make them easy.
The figure 500 in a telegram should always be written "five hundred."
The Union Trust & Savings Bank, Capital and Surplus, $3,800,000.

Concentration Development 14

America's entrance into the World War brought into existence two distinctly American products--the Curtiss J. N. 4 D training plane, known affectionately to the expert war-time pilots as "Jennie," and the Liberty Motor, which was used in a number of record flights after the war--notably the first world flight.

(52 Words)

data prepare checks which are to be signed by A. W. Quigley, Secretary of the Scott-Franklin Motor Car Company. Date all the checks today. Use the four blank checks marked Form 35.

(1) **No. 1761; to Hawkins Adjustment Co.;** $56.76.

(2) **No. 1762; to Henry W. Silver; $200.**

(3) **No. 1763; to Franklin Motor Company;** $3,278.20.

(4) **No. 1765; to W. C. Sylvester; $5.50.**

Application Exercise 36. Study the Voucher Check shown in Illustration 73; then prepare four voucher checks from the following data. Use the blank voucher checks marked Form 36. Remove the two sheets on which those forms are printed; then separate the vouchers at the perforations. Amounts are frequently perforated into checks by means of a device, such as the Protectograph. In your work, however, you will type the amounts. Date all the checks today.

Illustration 73
Voucher Check

Voucher checks of this character are often prepared in triplicate. The original is sent to the payee; the duplicate is attached to the invoice, or invoices, paid and filed by the voucher number; the triplicate is filed alphabetically according to the name of the payee.

Voucher No.	Payee	Amount	Check No.	Invoice Date	Invoice Amount	Dept.	Frt. & Exp.	Discount Rate	Discount Amount	Pay Last Amount in this Column
9456	Acme Lace & Embroidery Works	2181.80	478	19— *— 20	515.24	FG		2%	10.30	504.94
				— 22	146.88	FG		2%	2.94	648.88
				— 25	1236.50	FG		2%	24.73	1860.65
				— 29	327.70	FG		2%	6.55	2181.80
9457	Baker & Emmart Company	790.15	479	— 15	196.72	RC	1.85		—	194.87
				— 19	96.45	RC	1.26			290.06
				— 21	510.30	RC		2%	10.21	790.15
9458	Union Printing Company	300.62	480	— 15	85.10	DA		2%	1.70	83.40
				— 24	110.70	DA		2%	2.21	191.89
				— 24	18.50	DA		2%	.37	210.02
				— 25	92.45	DA		2%	1.85	300.62
9459	Clara F. McHenry	1.22	481							

9459 Clara F. McHenry   1.22   481   Type across the columns on this voucher the following notation: **Return allowance, Invoice No. 6378.** Insert the amount, **$1.22,** in the last column on the voucher.

* Use the figure which represents the last month.

Figure and Character Review Drill.   Use a 70-stroke line.

$14 $95 $78.36 $920.76 $1,743.85 $16,845.20 $35,768.29 $116,783.24
#45 #178–B #275C 1,876# 3,567# 4' 6" 28' 9" 168' 10" 6 x 9 8½ x 11
27% 148% 854 yards @ $1.39 a yard; 164 feet @ 10¢ a foot; 10' x 15'

Tell me what you do in your off time, and I can tell you what 62
sort of person you are. The way in which a man spends his leisure is 132
a good index to his character and his habits of thinking. 190

One of the great aims of the school is to teach us how to make 253
proper use of leisure time. It is so easy to fritter away the free 321
hours which, if rightly spent, will enable us to live rich and full 389
lives. The man who really lives, in the best sense of the word, tries 460
all the time to broaden his interests in a wholesome way. He sets 527
apart a time for reading good books, so that he may learn to commune 596
with the great masters of prose and poetry; he develops a sport or a 665
hobby--something to which he can turn his mind and his thoughts in his 736
off time. 745

(154 Words; Stroke intensity, 4.84)

Lesson 26

Word Division. An amount in figures should not be divided at the end of a line. Carry over all the figures to the next line if you cannot type them all at the end of the line, thus: 786,543 (not 786,-543).

A compound word which is spelled with a hyphen may be divided only at the place where the hyphen comes in the word, thus: *three-quarters* (not *three-quar-ters*).

Avoid dividing the last word on a page. Carry the entire word to the next page.

Warming-up Exercise 15
Common Words

used very view wait walk want warm week well went were what when whom
seems sense serve seven shall sheet short shown since sleep small
sorry speak spend spent stand start state still stock store story
letter little living locate longer looked lovely mailed making manner
market matter moment Monday months mother myself nature nearly notice

Acceleration Drill 15
Word Building and Special Stroke Combinations

Use a 65-stroke line.

Independence. On above. In plains. Early. The days gone by.
Rough floor. The travelers. I am. We had. Westport, Oregon.
Great buoyancy. Richard continued. An hour passed. Time in.
trade trader traded trades trading tradings trading traditional
4 2 42 4 3 43 1 6 16 5 7 57 8 9 89 9 4 94 7 2 72 9 5 95 5 0 50

Concentration Development 15

Directly after the war, the air mail service, created by the Post Office
Department, not only made a remarkable record for safety and reliability, but continued to build up steadily in number of lines and quantity
of mail carried. More important still was the excellent record of con-
sistent and relatively safe operation.

(52 Words)

Klotzman, Mrs. Fannie W.	516 Culver Street	Citrus	
Edmunds, Mrs. Clara H.	Medical Arts Building	Sacramento	MArket 1876
Porter, Charles R.	456 Ludlow Street	Fairoaks	
Forbes, Henry W.	516 North 21st Street	Sacramento	BElmont 6543-J
Barker, Stanley	418 East 10th Street	Sacramento	WAlnut 2176
Carter, Edwin F.	415 University Avenue	Sacramento	UNiversity 1540-J

Labels

Sometimes the typist is asked to prepare labels to be pasted on bottles and cartons of various sizes. Such labels are often gummed on the back. Study Illustration 71.

Labels to be pasted on shipments are generally typed. If such labels have horizontal rulings, the writing line should be carefully adjusted.

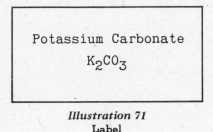

Illustration 71
Label

Application Exercise 33. On a half sheet of paper, rule in pencil three rectangles 1½″ deep by 3″ wide. From the following data, prepare labels for bottles in the form shown in Illustration 71. When you have written in the information, remove the sheet and cut out the labels.

(a) **Potassium Carbonate K_2CO_3**

(b) **Potassium Dichromate $K_2O_2O_7$**

(c) **Formaldehyde Solution H. CHO   Use as a preservative and disinfectant.**

(d) On paper cut to postal card size, type a label for a parcel post package. Use your own name and address. Supply a return address.

Checks

The filling in of checks on the typewriter is simply a matter of writing on ruled lines. Use the ratchet release lever whenever you write on odd-spaced lines. Study Illustration 72. Notice how the amount is written. The words indicating the dollars are spelled out, and the cents are represented by figures separated by the diagonal, thus: 48/100. If the check is to be written for an even amount in dollars—that is, an amount that does not include cents—type "and 00/100." Type the name of the payee close to the printed matter. Use closed hyphens to fill out the lines on which the name of the payee and the amount are written. The signature of a check, of course, should never be typewritten. The amount written out should begin at the extreme left, and the amount in figures should be typed close to the dollar sign.

In business offices, the amounts on checks are often inserted by means of a machine which produces perforated figures. The typist then fills in only the date, the number of the check, and the name of the payee. Keep the typing above the line as it would appear above an underscore.

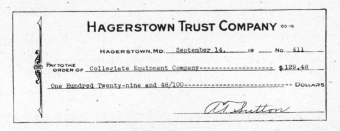

Illustration 72

Check

Application Exercise 34. Fill in four checks from the following data. Use the four blank checks marked Form 34.

	Date	Number	Payee	Amount
1.	Today	421	Mason Stationery Co.	$21.48
2.	Tomorrow	432	O'Sullivan & Bros.	67.76
3.	Next Tuesday	467	Frank W. Hirschman	25.00
4.	Saturday of next week	488	Charles W. Higginson	10.50

When you know the goal at which you are aiming, you will need to   65
practice the act which you wish to form into a habit. The only kind   134
of practice that is worth anything is the kind that is done with all   203
your mind and thought fixed on what you are doing. You must put your 273
heart into your work and do it with fire and vim.   323

Here is a vital point: Do not allow any exceptions to occur   384
while you are forming a habit. Let us say that a person wishes to   451
break up the bad habit of swearing and form in its place the good   517
habit of using clean speech. If that person allows just one lapse to 587
occur, he can easily break down the result of days of care and thought. 659

You may think that one lapse does not count. Well, you may not   723
count it and a kind Heaven may not count it, but all the time it is   791
being counted against you in your nerve cells where habits are stored 861
up.   864

(176 Words; Stroke intensity, 4.91)

Lesson 27
Warming-up Exercise 16
Common Words

wife will wire wish with word work year your haze raze quit pose axle
study style sweet taken teach terms thank their there these thing
think third those three times tired today total touch trade train
number oblige office orders others papers passed people period person
account address advance advised against allowed already another anxious

Acceleration Drill 16
Word Building and Sentences

Line of 65 strokes.   Use the Margin Release Lever if necessary.

face faced faces facer facing faction factions factional faced
quench quenched quencher quenches quenching quencher quenchable
The worst sorrows in life are not in its trials, but in its fears.
Control your tongue; then you will be able to control yourself.
Your orders #82 and #91, dated March 30 and 31, amounted to $345.21.

Concentration Development 16

Mr. W. R. Stout of Detroit had for many years been doing research
and experimental work which he hoped would lead to the development
of a transport airplane really suitable for quantity production. His
premise was that the monoplane was the ideal type for this purpose.
The development and production of the Ford Transport plane and the
operation of the Stout Air Services are too well known to need description.

(70 Words)

Reply Cards. Illustration 69 shows a form of reply card that is often enclosed with letters about a meeting. The person who receives the card is expected to fill in and return the card. If he plans to be present, he simply runs his pen through *shall not;* if he cannot be present, he crosses out *shall*.

Application Exercise 30. Type the message shown in Illustration 69. On the other side write this address: **Mr. George R. Roberts, Secretary Rotary Club Bellevue-Stratford Hotel Philadelphia, Pennsylvania**

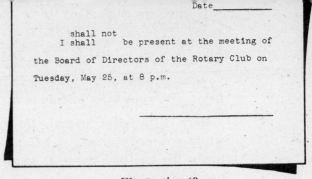

```
                                    Date_____

              shall not
          I shall       be present at the meeting of

          the Board of Directors of the Rotary Club on

          Tuesday, May 25, at 8 p.m.


                                    _____
```

Illustration 69
Reply Postal Card

Index Cards

The typist frequently has occasion to type material on cards of various sizes. Records of one kind and another are kept on index cards. Such cards are usually 5 inches wide by 3 inches deep—to fit into standard card index file drawers.

```
 Yarmouth
 Ellis Furniture Company



 10,000--20,000
```

Illustration 70
Index Card

Application Exercise 31. From the following data, prepare a set of 5 x 3 cards giving the names of companies in certain towns in Massachusetts. Each card is to show also the financial worth or rating of the company. Study Illustration 70.

Ellis Furniture Co.	Yarmouth	10,000—20,000
G. B. Everett	Spencer	3,000— 5,000
Snedden Bros.	Woburn	30,000—40,000
Martin Company	Uxbridge	40,000—50,000
Harry W. Whipple	Andover	15,000—20,000
Turner & Collyer	Medford	10,000—15,000
Shoemaker Store	Salem	40,000—50,000
White Brothers	Abington	5,000—10,000
Wolfe & Stearns	Medford	20,000—25,000
Peter R. Reilley	Newton	5,000—10,000
J. W. Walker	Middlesex	10,000—20,000
W. C. McLeod	Lawrence	10,000—15,000
Eyler Supply Co.	Lynn	20,000—25,000
Garvey & Ray	Medway	10,000—15,000

Application Exercise 32. Make out cards from the following data. Type a separate card for each name. When a telephone number is included, type the information on four lines. Double-space. Center the lines horizontally and vertically. When you have typed the cards, arrange them alphabetically according to the surnames of the individuals.

Name	Street Address	City	Telephone
Curtis, Mrs. Mary W.	Unwin Apartments	Sacramento	PLaza 1433
Sanders, Miss Margaret F.	1876 Portland Street	Sacramento	HOpkins 6547
Gaskin, Miss Flora H.	1923 Lawnview Street	Sacramento	
Abbott, Mrs. Josephine A.	2789 Market Street	Sacramento	MArket 7865-J
Mackenzie, Mrs. Martha J.	417 Holden Road	Sacramento	BRighton 6576
Hargreaves, Mrs. Edith C.	417 Floral Avenue	Sacramento	HOpkins 6754
Ascher, John C.	1176 Montague Avenue	Sacramento	
Dobler, Harry F.	416 Main Street	Davis	
Birdsong, Miss Jennie C.	418 Altamont Street	Sacramento	MAdison 1706

If you are a student in a college, seize upon the good that is there. You get good by giving it. You gain by giving. Give sympathy and cheerful loyalty to the institution. Stand by your teachers; they are doing the best they can. If the place is faulty, make it a better place by an example of cheerfully doing your work every day the best you can.

If you work for a man, in heaven's name work for him. If he pays you wages that supply your bread and butter, work for him, speak well of him, stand by him, and stand by the institution he represents.

I think if I worked for a man, I would work for him. I would not work for him a part of the time and then the rest of the time work against him. I would give undivided service or none.

Do this, or if for any reason you should prefer not, then take your choice of these: Get out--or get in line. You must do one or the other--now make your choice.

—*Elbert Hubbard*

(183 Words; Stroke intensity, 4.95)

Lesson 28
Warming-up Exercise 17
Common Words

tried truly trust under until using usual value visit waste water
placed places please policy pretty prices prompt proper public rather
arrange arrived article balance because believe brother brought calling
careful carried catalog certain charged charges college company correct
yourself whatever vacation trusting tomorrow together Thursday thousand

Acceleration Drill 17
Word Building and Sentences

Line of 65 strokes. Use the Margin Release Lever if necessary.
move moves mover moved moving movable movement moving movement
revoke revokes revoked revoker revoking revoked revoker revoke
hurry hurried hurrying hurries jail jails jailer jailed jailer
Investments of $150, $300, $500, $1000 would now yield 3% to 5%.
It has been said that truth is truth, to the end of the reckoning.

Concentration Development 17

The development of public confidence in the airplane was hastened principally by the memorable flight of Colonel Lindbergh from New York to Paris in 1927. This tremendous accomplishment made clear to us all that the airplane, and particularly its engine, had reached the point where we might depend on it for everyday flying.

(53 Words)

ing, use the cylinder knob instead of the line space lever.

Study the arrangement of these messages written on Government postal cards. Care and judgment are required in centering the message. The long way of the card, measured in strokes, makes a writing line of 55 strokes (pica type). If you leave a margin of 5 strokes on each side, your type line will be 45 strokes. On that basis you can determine about how far down on the card to begin the salutation. If the message is short, you can leave 4 or even 6 line spaces between the heading and the salutation; if the message is fairly long, leave only 2 line spaces.

```
                           Rochester, New York
                           January 14, 19--

Dear Sir:

The January meeting of the Board of Trade will
be held in Room 406, Board of Trade Building,
at 8 p.m., January 24.

Final action will be taken on the referendum,
which was recently sent to the members of the
Board, on the proposed merger with the Chamber
of Commerce.

                 Secretary, Board of Trade
```

Illustration 67
Postal Card Style 1

Application Exercise 24. On a sheet of paper cut to postal card size, write the message given in Illustration 67. On the other side type this address in the double-spaced, blocked style, with open punctuation:

Mr. Charles W. Forbes 214 Webster Street Rochester, New York

Application Exercise 25. Type also the following postal card. Use today's date. Center the heading, "Dividend Notice."

The Board of Directors of the Binghamton Wholesale Corporation has declared the regular quarterly dividend of 1½% as of March 31, 19—, payable to stockholders of record on March 1, 19—. (P) Checks will be mailed on April 4. No receipt is necessary. Binghamton Wholesale Corporation

On the other side type this address: **Mr. C. F. Ford Fidelity Building Buffalo, New York**

Application Exercise 26. Type the message shown in Illustration 68. Use today's date. On the other side, write this address: **Mr. C. R. Mason 748 Jackson Street Fulton, Ohio**

```
                      Cincinnati, Ohio
                      June 4, 19--

Dear Sir:

    Thank you for your
order for 10 gallons of
Lucas Flat White Paint
No. 6 placed with our
representative, Mr. John
Walton, on May 25. The
order is being shipped
today.

    Our new price list
of Ready Mixed Paints is
being sent to you today.

    Many thanks for your
courtesy to Mr. Walton.


    LUCAS PAINT COMPANY
```

Illustration 68
Postal Card Style 2

Application Exercise 27. Type the following message in the same form.

The Siphon Company Davenport, Iowa July 15, 19— Dear Madam: It is a pleasure to send you today, in accordance with your request, a catalog describing the new Siphon Refrigerator. (P) Our refrigerators are sold in your city by the H. J. Hampton Company, 617 South Street. At that store you can personally inspect our various models. THE SIPHON COMPANY

On the other side type this address: **Mrs. C. R. Eggleston 422 Ward Street Cedar Rapids, Iowa**

Application Exercise 28. Type this message in the form of Illustration 67. Use today's date.

Gentlemen: Shipment of your order No. 6531 was made last evening. We are temporarily out of stock on item 2876-A. These rockers, however, are in process of manufacture. We expect to be able to make shipment in about two weeks. ARMSTRONG FURNITURE COMPANY

Type this address for the card: **Meyer & Wilson South and Front Streets Sandusky, Ohio**

Application Exercise 29. Type the following message in the form of Illustration 68. Use this date: July 20, 19—.

Dear Sir: Our August Sale of Men's Summer Suits will start on August 5. We are giving a three-day pre-showing, starting with August 2. Visit the store during those three days, and you will have the pick of the lot—at extraordinarily low prices. MENDEL'S—THE MEN'S STORE.

Supply an address and type it on the other side of the card.

From time to time you set yourself to the task of forming new habits or of breaking yourself of bad habits into which you may have fallen. To save time and to aid you to reach your goal, you ought to know the best way to go about the job. 131

First of all, you must have clearly in your mind all the details of the new habit you wish to form. If, for instance, you wish to form habits that will make you a good pole vaulter, you need to study correct form in all the aspects of that sport. 489

Next, you will want to make sure that you have clearly in your mind the goal at which you are aiming. If you wish to learn to write a better hand, you need to learn correct posture at the desk; but you also need to have in your mind a picture of how well-written letters look. 767

Of course, you always want your typewritten notes and letters to look neat and attractive. For that reason you will need to study the well-written and properly arranged typewritten notes and letters which appear in this book. 998

(195 Words; Stroke intensity, 5.09)

Lesson 29

In this lesson and the remaining lessons of Division 2, put the drills on one sheet; then type the Timed Writing on a separate sheet. Use a line of 70 strokes and a paragraph indentation of 5 strokes; double-space the Timed Writings.

Unless you are otherwise instructed, type each line of the drills twice with single spacing; double-space after each two-line group.

Warming-up Exercise 18

Common Words. Use a line of 70 strokes. Top margin, 1½ inches.

weeks where which while white whole woman women won't words world
really reason recent record regard regret remain report result return
sample saying school season second secure seemed should signed sister

New Stroke Control

The Underscore (_). The underscore, which is the shift of the 6-key, is used for emphasis. When isolated words are to be underscored, write through the word, return the carriage to the beginning of the word, and type the underscore. When there is a series of words in a line to be underscored, type through the entire line; then depress the **Shift Lock**, and make the necessary underscores. *Do not underscore between words or under punctuation marks.*

The Diagonal (/). The diagonal is used in writing "made" fractions not on the keyboard. It is also used in writing identifying marks and a few contractions, thus: 3/5 ED/ce B/L.

The Asterisk (*). When included on the keyboard, this symbol is the shift of the hyphen stroke. It is used to indicate footnotes.

Illustration 36
The ;-finger making the downward /-stroke.

Illustration 65
Telegram Style 1

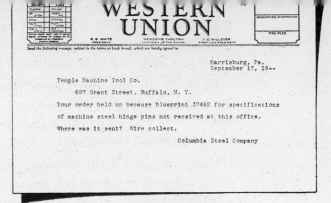

Illustration 66
Telegram Style 2

Application Exercise 22. Type the following messages in the form of Style 1. Use the Postal telegraph blanks marked Form 32. Indicate by a checkmark or by a typed x the class of service desired.

Telegram

Address of Sender: **Rochester, Minn.** *Date:* **October 13, 19—** *Address of Telegram:* **Sylvester H. Lamar, 876 Montrose St., Peoria, Ill.** *Signature:* **Alfred Martin**

Arriving train due station 10:47 Tuesday morning, October 14. *(10 words)*

Day Letter

Address of Sender: **Pittsburgh, Pa.** *Date:* **February 14, 19—** *Address of Day Letter:* **Consolidated Electric Company, Fidelity Building, Baltimore, Md.** *Signature:* **Pittsburgh Steel Company**

Slugs will run from 36 to 44 carbon. The lengths will be from 16 to 40 inches. Net price for immediate shipment is $40 a gross ton f.o.b. Pittsburgh. The work can be completed in one week from the time order is received. Wire your order at our expense. *(50 words)*

Application Exercise 23. Write the following messages in the form of Style 2. Use the Western Union blanks marked Form 33.

Telegram

Address of Sender: **Fresno, Calif.** *Date:* **February 15, 19—** *Address of Telegram:* **Kingston Paper Company, 672 Market St., San Francisco, Calif.** *Signature:* **King Printing Company**

Our order No. 78 has not arrived. Trace at once. *(10 words)*

Night Letter

Address of Sender: **Freeport, Ill.** *Date:* **October 15, 19—** *Address of Night Letter:* **Brighton Athletic Supply Co., 614 Winter St., Minneapolis, Minn.** *Signature:* **The Rapid Review**

Advertisement for November issue inadvertently omitted from your letter October 13. Paper goes to press October 19. If not already sent, mail copy special delivery. *(25 words)*

Postal Cards

Cards are often used in sending notices and announcements of various kinds. A Government postal card is 5½ inches wide by 3¼ inches deep.

The writer's address and the date, which form the heading, may be centered at the top of the card or placed so as to end at the right writing margin. To save space, the address of the person to whom the card is sent is usually omitted, and the message begins with the salutation.

In inserting a card into the machine, place the card holders in position and make the necessary

```
jjj jy6 jy_ j_j j_j j_j ___ ;;; ;/; ;/; ;/; /// j/_

;;; ;p- ;p* ;*; ;*; ;*; *** ;;; ;/? ;?; ;?; ;?; ???

one-half well-read 8-story ;-; far-reaching ;/; j_j
```

Type this <u>three</u> times.   This year* shows improvement.

Important: If you are using the optional method of fingering, turn back to page 24 for the drills.

Special Characters

The Dash (――).   The formal dash is made by two strokes of the hyphen (–).   Do not space before, after, or between the two hyphen strokes (――).   A single hyphen with a space before and after it (the informal or open dash) is sometimes used.

Note these examples.   In the first sentence the formal dash is used; in the second, the informal dash.

This is the point--let it be emphasized--learn to labor and to wait.

All three offices - Chicago, New York, and Boston - show increases.

Made Fractions (5/6).   To write fractions not on the machine, type the numerator, the diagonal, and finally the denominator; as, 2/3, 4/5, 9/10.   Ordinarily, made fractions, such as 2/3, and the fraction characters $\frac{1}{2}$ and $\frac{1}{4}$ should not be used together.   In writing business papers of which several carbon copies are desired, the made fractions are more satisfactory than the characters.

Mixed Numbers (4–5/6, 5 5/8).   When a whole number and a fraction are written together, a hyphen may or may not be used after the whole number.

Typing Special Characters

Use a line of 60 strokes.

We knew that great danger lay ahead--that was to be expected.

The colon (:) is the shift of the semicolon (;) key.   ;: ;: ;:

Use the "/" in writing these fractions: 1/6, 4/9, 3/7, 5/8.

The symbol (*) - the asterisk - is used to indicate footnotes.

Writing on Ruled Lines.   The underscore may be used to make horizontal lines or rulings (across the sheet).   Make a 70-stroke line with the underscore.   Use the Shift Lock.   Type several words above this underscore.   Note the relative position of the base of the letters and of the underscore.

Type two more 70-stroke lines with the underscore; use double spacing.   Remove the paper from the machine and then reinsert it.   Disengage the **Variable Line Spacer*** and turn the paper up or down, as required, until the typing is in writing position.   Reengage the Variable Line Spacer and type on these underscore lines the first two sentences of Acceleration Drill 18.

* Refer to the illustration of your machine on the back cover or on the back flyleaf of the book.

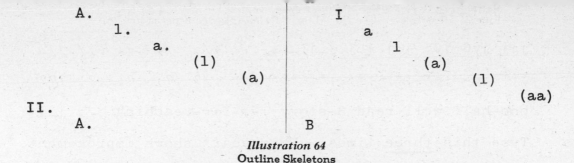

```
A.                              I
  1.                              a
    a.                              1
      (1)                             (a)
        (a)                             (1)
                                          (aa)
  II.
    A.                            B
```

Illustration 64
Outline Skeletons

Application Exercise 21. Single-space the following outline; triple-space below the main heading and double-space after each of the principal divisions. Set tabular stops for indentations of 5 strokes. Type the outline twice, first with the Roman numerals justified on the left and then with the Roman numerals justified on the right. Omit periods after the numbers in the second outline.

THE FINANCING OF PUBLIC EDUCATION

I. Introduction
  A. Maintaining services for the public
  B. Society and community interests

II. Public education a common interest
  A. The right of children to an education
  B. Cost of public education compared with cost of private education

III. The basic reason for taxation
  A. Taxes in ancient times
  B. Taxes in modern times
    1. The police department
    2. The public health department
    3. The fire department
    4. The public schools

IV. The sources of taxation
  A. Real property taxes
    1. Real property overburdened
    2. Inequalities in property taxation
      a. Function of Tax Courts
      b. Tax strikes
  B. Income tax laws
    1. Federal
    2. State
      a. Centralization of authority
      b. Equitable distribution
  C. The sales tax
    1. On specific commodities
    2. General sales tax
  D. Personal property taxes
    1. Exemptions
    2. Rates

Telegrams

Typing Telegrams. Telegrams are generally prepared on blanks furnished by the telegraph companies. Blocks are provided in the upper left-hand corner for the sender to indicate with a checkmark the class of service desired. When not otherwise designated, all messages are sent as full-rate telegrams.

The major classes of domestic service are: (1) Telegrams—accepted for immediate handling, with a minimum charge based on ten words, plus a reduced charge for each additional word. (2) Day Letters—deferred day service at a lower cost, with a minimum charge for 50 words, plus a proportionate charge for each additional ten words or less. (3) Night Letters—for overnight communications, with a minimum charge for 25 words, plus a progressively decreasing charge for each additional five words or less.

Messages typed by the telegraph operators are written in ALL CAPS, as their typewriters are not provided with lower-case letters. Quite frequently the stenographer, therefore, prepares the original copy in ALL CAPS, as shown in Illustration 65, page 175.

Every telegram should carry the date. The address is usually written on two lines—the name on the first line and the street, city, and state on the second line. Double-spacing is generally used. Punctuation marks and paragraphing may be included without extra charge. Five figures are counted as one word, but characters, such as the $-sign, #-sign, and the like, are each counted as one word.

174

Sentences.   Use a line of 70 strokes.

The accumulation of wealth in itself does not make for true greatness.
What a man does with his wealth is the only measure of true greatness.
Cooperation, and not competition, is the life of all profitable trade.

Timed Writing 18

Change is the order of the day in all phases of life. A wise man	66
keeps an open mind all the time. He knows how easy it is to get into	136
a rut and how hard it is to get out of it. For that reason he keeps	205
his eyes and his ears open for new ideas. He does not jump at a new	274
thing just because it is new; he holds fast to ideas that have proved	344
their worth. It is a fact that most good things are old things; they	414
have stood the test of time. Yet it is also true that changes are	481
going on all the while. The world moves, and we must move with it.	548

(120 Words; Stroke intensity, 4.57)

Lesson 30

Warming-up Exercise 19

Common Words.   Line of 70 strokes.   Top margin, 1½ inches.

worth would write wrong wrote years young yours youth waxen razed basis
spring stated states street strong summer Sunday supply surely taking
talked thanks things thirty though trying turned twenty unable unless
thinking thanking teaching teachers standard sometime shipping shipment

Special Characters

Exclamation Point (!).   Use the apostrophe (') and the period (.) in making the exclamation point. Depress the left shift key and strike the apostrophe. With the **Back Space Lever,** back-space once and strike the period.   When the exclamation point comes at the end of a sentence, it is always followed by *two* spaces; when occurring within a sentence, it is followed by *one* space.

Refer to the back cover or the back flyleaf and find the illustration of the machine you are using; then locate the back space lever.

Caret (_/).   Type an underscore under the last letter of the word just before the caret; then type the diagonal mark.   The caret is used to indicate omissions.   Use it, however, only when the material you are typing is double spaced.

Minus Sign (−).   Type the hyphen with a space before and after.

Division Sign (÷).   Type the colon, back-space, and strike the hyphen.

Exponents $(a \times b)^n$, **Sub-numbers** (H_2O_2), **and the Degree Sign** ($60°$).   Type the letters or figures and leave spaces for the signs.   Disengage the

Ratchet Release* (also called the Ratchet Detent and Cylinder Detent Release), turn the paper up or down as required, and then type the figures or signs. Reengage the Ratchet Release and turn the cylinder very slightly; the paper will come back to the original line of writing.   If your typewriter is not equipped with this part, use the Variable Line Spacer, but be careful in resetting to line.   (*Note:* When it is desired to write off line and return to the original line of writing, the Ratchet Release should be used.   When it is desired to set to a new line, the Variable Line Spacer should be used.)

If a typed line contains several of any one of these signs, write the entire line, omitting the signs while typing, but leaving spaces for them.   Return the carriage to the proper point, adjust the cylinder, and write in all the signs.

Multiplication Sign (x).   Type the small **x.** This **x** is also used for "by" in dimensions.   The sign may be written with or without a space before and after it, thus: 2 x 8, 56x120, 2x4.

* Consult the illustration of your machine on the back cover or on the back flyleaf.

48

nished by a steel company. Justify the figures at the right-hand writing margin. Use periods, struck at alternate spaces, as leaders. Double-space. This problem will require two pages. Center the figure 2 at the top of the second page.

INDEX

Outlines

In typing outlines, the important thing is to maintain uniformity in the system of numbering and indenting. Two of the various methods of indicating the main heads and subheads are shown in Illustration 64, page 174. An indentation of five strokes is generally used for the subheads. If a phrase or a sentence in an outline requires more than one line, the carry-over (second line) is usually indented 3 strokes beyond the first line. Roman numerals may be justified on the left or on the right. When justified on the right, allowance must be made for the longest numeral. Periods may or may not be used after numerals.

Make a plan before you begin typing. To center vertically, determine the number of lines required to write the outline, including the heading. To center horizontally, examine the subheads until you find the one that extends farthest to the right. Then determine the number of strokes required, including the indentation, and set the margin stops accordingly.

factorily made on the typewriter. Insert this character with pencil as you type; later write over it with pen and ink. If the plus sign must be made on the typewriter, strike the hyphen, back-space, disengage the Ratchet Release, turn up the paper slightly, and strike the apostrophe; back-space again, turn up the paper still further, and again strike the apostrophe. Reengage the Ratchet Release and continue with your typing. (The shift for the apostrophe may be made by locking the Shift Lock in position. If your machine does not have a Ratchet Release, use the Variable Release or turn the cylinder by hand, keeping hold of the cylinder knob while striking the apostrophe.)

turn down the paper slightly, and then type the hyphen again; or type the hyphen, back-space, depress the shift key lightly, and then type the hyphen again. (Care must be taken to get the hyphens properly spaced—not too close together nor too far apart.)

Feet (') and Inches ("). Use the apostrophe for *feet* and the quotation marks for *inches*, thus: 6' 2". The space may be omitted between the feet and inches; as, 3'8".

Minutes (') and Seconds ("). *Two minutes, ten seconds* may be written thus: 2' 10".

Typing Special Characters

Use a line of 70 strokes. Make two copies, with double spacing throughout.

The warning, Stop! Look! Listen!, stood out in bold, black letters!

The temperatures yesterday were 97° maximum and 85° minimum. 10° east

There was bu_t/chance! He would take tha_t/chance! He dived/the water!

(one   one   into)

Water, H_2O, freezes at 32° Fahrenheit. H_2SO_4; H_2O_2; $CuSO_4$ 2 x 4; 2' 8".

The problem: 432 + 120 − 80 + 190 − 650 x 12 + 36 ÷ 6 − 2 − 4 + 2 = 4.

The sum of 120 + 120 = 240 − 100 ÷ 2 = 70 x 3 − 25 = 185. Add 46 and 5.

The room was exactly 10' 6" x 15' 7". The ceiling was just 9' 8".

Acceleration Drill 19

Sentences. Use a line of 60 strokes.

Next to honor, courage is the greatest quality of the mind.

Put your heart into your work and your sky will be clear.

If you would gain success, attend strictly to your business.

Timed Writing 19

Before there can be a harvest, there must be a time of planting. 66

No farmer would be so foolish as to expect a crop of wheat unless he 135

plants the seed and harrows the ground. 175

Too often a young man expects to reap almost as soon as he has 238

sown. He does not stop to think that it takes time to get an educa- 306

tion and to build up skill--that time must be spent in work and study 376

and thought. 389

The best rules to build a useful career are old and simple. 450

First, you must get knowledge. You must learn why things are as they 520

are. Next, you must get skill in applying that knowledge. You need, 590

in other words, to learn the how as well as the why. Finally, you 657

must keep ever in mind the fact that your personality, entirely apart 727

from your knowledge and your skill, is what determines the degree of 796

success you will have. 818

(159 Words; Stroke intensity, 5.14)

Application Exercise 19. Type this Contents page. Write the word *Contents* in ALL CAPS spaced out. Type the words *Part One* in ALL CAPS. Leave three single line spaces below *Part One*. Single-space, with double spacing after each section indicated by Roman numerals—I, II, III, etc. Use leaders as shown. Be sure to justify the figures at the right-hand margin.

C O N T E N T S
PART ONE

Warming-up Exercise 20

Common Words. Use a line of 70 strokes. Top margin, 1 inch.

```
wanted winter wishes within wonder writer wished lazily laxity cities
imagine include inquiry instead invoice January leaving letters looking
expense express feeling follows forward freight friends furnish further
general getting greatly haven't himself history holding however hundred
```

Punctuation Marks

The period or the comma at the end of a quotation should always precede the quotation marks. The colon or the semicolon should always follow the quotation marks.

In a sentence which ends with a quotation, the quotation marks follow the question mark or the exclamation mark if the quotation is itself the question or the exclamation.

If the sentence containing the quotation is a question or an exclamation, then the quotation marks precede the question mark or the exclamation mark.

Remember that two spaces follow all punctuation marks which end sentences. One space follows the punctuation marks , ! ? " when written within a sentence. One space follows the comma (,) and the semicolon (;). The colon (:) may be followed by one or two spaces; the general preference is for two spaces.

Typewriting Punctuation Marks. Make two copies of the following sentences just as they appear here. Always double-space for paragraphs when single spacing is used. Note carefully the placement of the punctuation marks. Use a line of 70 strokes.

```
With quiet simplicity Lincoln asked his audience, "Now, my friends,
can the country be saved on that basis?"

Do you remember the saying, "The good paymaster is lord of another
man's purse"?

Who was it that said, "I will fight it out along this line if it
takes all summer"?

"An important trait for a young man or woman to acquire," said the
lecturer, "is the habit of looking into things closely."

The professor of English made this remark about Carlyle's "French
Revolution": "It is a colorful account of an epoch—making era."
```

Acceleration Drill 20

Sentence Writing. Use a line of 70 strokes.

```
"Where Sunshine Spends the Winter" is the slogan of El Paso, Texas.
April and May are generally pleasant months in this section of Mexico.
The new novel, "This Modern Age," has a late copyright date in it.
Both of these accounts become due on the first of next September.
```

RETIREMENT MONTHLY INCOME
FOR LIFE

January 14, 19--

Present Age--44

Annual Savings--$739.00

Retirement Age--60

Monthly Income Guaranteed - - - $100.00

Increase by Dividends, 4.5% basis -   11.91

Total Monthly Income - - - - - - $111.91

At age 60 you will receive the following privileges:

1. Monthly income for Life

    Guaranteed - - - - - - - - - - - - - - $100.00

    Increase through Dividends, 4.5% basis -   11.91

    Total - - - - - - - - - - - - - - - - - - $111.91

On this basis you could expect total receipts as follows:

Guaranteed for 10 years - - - - - - - - - - - - - - - - - - - $12,000.00

Additional to cover your life expectancy from age 60 to

74.1 years -   4,920.00

Total received on life expectancy basis and expected

dividends, 14.1 years from age 60 - - - - - - - - - - - $18,935.17

Total Deposits -   11,824.00

$ 7,111.17

2. Cash Return at age 60, if monthly income is not desired:

Cash Value guaranteed - - - - - - - - - - - - - - - - - - - $14,602.64

Value of accumulated dividends, 4.5% basis - - - - - - - - -   1,739.98

$16,342.62

Total Deposits -   11,824.00

Net return over deposits on above basis - - - - - - - - - - - $ 4,518.62

Contents Pages

Application Exercise 18. Type the first line of the heading of this exercise in ALL CAPS spaced out; triple-space and write the second line in ALL CAPS underscored; double-space and write the third line in ALL CAPS; double-space and write the column headings. Double-space the lines throughout the remainder of the copy. Leave a top margin of 1 inch.

Allow 3 strokes between the first and second columns. Justify the figures in the right-hand column.

CONTENTS

BOOK FIRST

THE NATURE AND IMPORT OF SOCIOLOGY

Chapter		Page
I.	Social Life in General	3
II.	Definition and Scope of Sociology	12
III.	The Purpose and Method of Sociology	30

Illustration 63
Contents Page

No one who has never been placed in a like position can understand my feeling at this hour. For more than a quarter of a century
I have lived among you, and during all that time I have received
nothing but kindness at your hands. Here I have lived from my youth,
until now I am an old man. Here the most sacred ties of earth were
assumed. Here all my children were born; here one of them lies
buried. To you, dear friends, I owe all that I have, all that I am.

Today I leave you. I go to assume a task more difficult than
that which devolved upon Washington. Unless the great God who assisted
him shall be with me and aid me, I must fail; but if the same almighty
arm that directed and protected him shall guide and support me, I
shall not fail--I shall succeed.

Let us all pray that the God of our fathers may not forsake us
now. To Him I commend you all. With these words I must leave you,
for how long I know not.

62
131
196
266
334
398
467

529
601
672
738
771

834
902
926

—Lincoln's Farewell Address

(186 Words; Stroke intensity, 4.98)

Lesson 32
Warming-up Exercise 21

Common Words.   Use a line of 72 strokes.   Top margin, 1½ inches.

machine manager married matters meeting members mention minutes morning
nothing obliged o'clock October opening opinion ordered package payment
separate Saturday returned requests required replying remember relative
addition advising although anything approval attached building business

Punctuation Marks

The single quotation mark (') is used to enclose a quotation within a quotation.
Like the double quotation marks, the single quotation mark follows the period.

When a quotation consists of two or more paragraphs, put quotation marks at the
beginning of each paragraph, but at the end of the *last* paragraph only.   Note the
quotation marks in the article which forms Timed Writing 21, page 52.

Typewriting Punctuation Marks.   Make two copies of the following sentences.
Single-space.   Double-space for paragraphs.   Use a line of 70 strokes.

The actor said, "I saw the great Jefferson in the play, 'Rip Van
Winkle.'"

What critic is it that declares, "Hawthorne's powers of character
delineation are best shown in 'The Scarlet Letter'"?

My friend asked, "Have you seen the play, 'Rip Van Winkle'?"

Note: The titles of books, magazines, newspapers, and plays may also be underscored.   In such cases the quotation marks are not used to enclose the titles.

by Joseph H. Appel

The house of Wanamaker amassed a fortune through the vision of John Wanamaker and his sons, Rodman and Thomas. They made a store for the whole family, where all could buy at moderate prices, hear the best music, and see great works of art. With faith in this ideal the founder withstood two depressions and, through his genius in buying and selling, had built, before his death, one of the greatest stores in the world. (G. W236 A6) Macmillan.

Working with the World by Irving T. Bush

The founder of the Bush Terminal Company tells the story of his spectacular business success from the first small warehouse to the development of the gigantic Bush Terminal with its factory, labor market, and transportation facilities coordinated to put the smaller business concern on a footing with its wealthier competitors. (T54.B8) Doubleday, Doran.

Argonauts of '49 by Octavius Thorndike Howe

The history of the companies of adventurers who left Massachusetts for California in 1849 and traveled by sea through the Straits of Magellan and overland across the plains. This work has been compiled largely from records left by the Argonauts themselves in their private letters and journals. (H1865.H6) Harvard.

Leaders

"Leaders" are sometimes used to guide the eye from one column to another. They may consist of periods* or of hyphens. When used as leaders, the periods may be closed (written solid) or open (separated by spaces). Hyphens, used as leaders, should always be open. When using open leaders, be sure that each succeeding line has the same marks immediately under those in the first line. You can secure this result if you begin the second and successive lines of leaders on an odd or an even reading of the margin scale, depending on whether the first line of leaders is begun on an odd or on an even reading. Study these models. Note that the right margins are "justified."

*Be careful not to strike the period too heavily.

```
(1)   Processional........................... Edison Orchestra
(2)   Song—"The Old Refrain"—Kreisler – – – – –  Mixed Chorus
(3)   Overture . . . . . . . . . . . . . . . .Orchestra
      Invocation . . . . . . . . . . . . Reverend George C. Mason
```

Illustration 62

Application Exercise 16. Make a copy of this grocery list. Center the title of the advertisement list and write it in ALL CAPS. Use open leaders and make sure that the periods line up vertically.

CLOSE-OUT GROCERY SPECIALS

Sugar, fine granulated, 10-lb. sacks	52c
Golden West Coffee, in glass, pound	38c
Dried Choice White Figs, 2 pounds	25c
Dried Choice Black Figs, 2 pounds	25c
Dried Choice Apricots, 2 pounds	25c
Choice Seedless Raisins, pound	12c
Dried Choice Peaches, pound	15c
Heinz Ketchup, medium size	16c
Instant Postum, large size	51c
Sliced Dried Apples, pound	15c
Old Dutch Cleanser, 3 cans	19c
Carnation Milk, tall cans	10c

Sentence Writing.   Use a line of 70 strokes.

Please oblige us by giving these matters your usual prompt attention.
Your charge account is now open and ready to use at your convenience.
Have you ever read Andrew Carnegie's book, "How To Win Fortune"?
The ship, "Star of France," was built at Belfast, Ireland, in 1877.
Benjamin Franklin established "The Saturday Evening Post" in 1728.

Timed Writing 21

Type for ten minutes unless otherwise directed by your instructor.   Hereafter all
Timed Writings will be for ten minutes.

It seems that the first author to buy a typewriter was Mark	60
Twain. He tells us that as early as 1873 he saw a machine in a store	130
window and went in to look at it. But let Mark tell the story in his	200
own words.	211
"The salesman explained the machine to us, showed us samples of	275
its work, and said it could do 57 words a minute--a statement which we	346
frankly confessed that we did not believe. So he put his type-girl to	417
work, and we timed her by the watch. She actually did the 57 words in	488
60 seconds.	500
"We were partly convinced, but said it probably couldn't happen	564
again. But it did. We timed the girl over and over again, with the	633
same result always--she won out. She did her work on narrow slips of	703
paper, and we pocketed them, as fast as she turned them out, to show	772
as curiosities. The price of the machine was $125. I bought one, and	843
we went away very much excited."	876
Mark and his friend, who was with him at the time, did not look	940
closely at the slips of paper. He goes on to tell us that when they	1009
returned to their hotel, they took out the slips and were disappointed	1080
to find that they all contained the same words. The girl had econo-	1148
mized time and labor by using a formula which she knew by heart. How-	1218
ever, Mark rightly concluded that if the machine survived, experts	1285
would come to the front by and by who would double this girl's out-	1352
put. They would do 100 words a minute--his talking speed on the plat-	1422
form. That score has long ago been beaten.	1465

(284 Words; Stroke intensity, 5.16)

Lesson 33

Warming-up Exercise 22

Use a line of 70 strokes.   Top margin, 2 inches.

I have to tell he will be does as much to work on hand in your is here
he would we shall at first by which of their to place in favor on time
we shall be very glad to see you in the future do not know now if you
It has been this is the in such a way if it is as well as at this time
We shall be very glad to have you call if you have the time to do so.

A bibliography is a list of references to books or magazine articles. A bibliography should be arranged alphabetically according to authors' names. The last name of the author is written first, followed by a comma and his given name or initials. When a publication carries no author's name, the name of the organization or association issuing it is written first.

Application Exercise 14. Study this illustration; then type, with a carbon, the part of the bibliography given on this page. Use the inverted paragraph style. Follow the arrangement of the heading shown in the illustration.

Illustration 60
Bibliography

SELECT BIBLIOGRAPHY
ON THE
HISTORY OF COMMERCIAL EDUCATION

American Bankers Association. Extracts from Letters concerning Commercial Education. New York: 1892. 39 pp.

Barbour, A. H. A Contribution to the History of Commercial Education. Business Educator, May, 1903.

Committee of Ten (on Secondary School Studies). Report of, with Reports of Conferences arranged by this Committee. Washington, D. C. 1899. 249 pp.

Crissy, I. O. Evolution of Business Training. N. E. A. Proceedings, 1899.

Doggett, William E. The Commercial High School Course. N. E. A. Proceedings, 1900.

Hartog, P. J. Commercial Education in the United States. Special Reports on Educational Subjects. Vol. XI. British Education Department.

Haskins, Charles Waldo. Memorial Edition of Essays on Accountancy and Business Education. Harper & Bros., New York: 1903.

Herrick, Cheesman A. Meaning and Practice of Commercial Education. The Macmillan Company, New York: 1904.

Hinman, A. H. A History of Penmen, Early Business Education and Educators in America. Business Educator, November, 1902, following.

James, Edmund J. Commercial Education in the United States. In Education in the United States, Monographs for the Paris Exposition, 1900. American Book Company, New York: 1910.

Johnson, Joseph F. Commercial Education. In Cyclopedia of Education. Vol. II. The Macmillan Company, New York: 1911.

Application Exercise 15. Type the following annotated **library list** with a carbon. In this manuscript the side heads are written on separate lines. Study the illustration. Center the heading accurately. Leave *three* spaces above the title of each book. If you make mistakes and are allowed to erase, follow the directions you have been given for erasing.

Illustration 61
Library List

RECENT ACCESSIONS
WARDMAN PARK LIBRARY

Leaders and Periods of American Finance by Theodore J. Grayson

A biographical approach to American financial history from the first Secretary of the Treasury to Elbert H. Gary. There is an interesting chapter on the picturesque methods of Colonial and Revolutionary finance. (TK 181.G7) Wiley.

@ ¢

Illustration 37

The ;-finger making the stroke to the ¢-key.
The @-sign is the shift of the ¢-key.

$\frac{1}{2}$ $\frac{1}{4}$

Illustration 38

The ;-finger making the stroke to the $\frac{1}{2}$-key.
The $\frac{1}{4}$ is the shift of the $\frac{1}{2}$-key.

Use a line of 65 strokes. Type each line three times, with single spacing.

jjj j;j ;;; ;¢; ;¢; ;¢; ¢¢¢ j;¢ j;@ ;@; ;@; ;@; @@@ 34¢ 23¢ 65¢

;;; ;p; ;p$\frac{1}{2}$;$\frac{1}{2}$; ;$\frac{1}{2}$; ;$\frac{1}{2}$; $\frac{1}{2}\frac{1}{2}\frac{1}{2}$ j;$\frac{1}{2}$;$\frac{1}{2}\frac{1}{4}$;$\frac{1}{4}$; ;$\frac{1}{4}$; ;$\frac{1}{4}$; $\frac{1}{4}\frac{1}{4}\frac{1}{4}$ 5$\frac{1}{2}$¢ 3$\frac{1}{4}$¢ 2$\frac{1}{2}$¢

We now have for sale 23,150 tons of lump coal @ $5.00 a ton.

In sentences, always write out one-fourth ($\frac{1}{4}$) and one-half ($\frac{1}{2}$).

Acceleration Drill 22

Use a line of 70 strokes.

Please send us at once your new mail order catalog of spring goods.
We understand that your insurance money is due about September 30.
I regret that these new conditions prevent us from shipping promptly.
Do not fail to call on Brown & Co. at 40 West Broadway, New York City.
Office desk #683B56 can be furnished at $180.60 delivered at Boston.

Timed Writing 22

Do you think? 14

Can you pick up an article on some current event, and in Bacon's 79
immortal lines, "Read not to contradict and confute, nor to believe 147
and take for granted, but to weigh and consider"? 197

There is so much superstition and dogmatic knowledge in the world 263
that we must never take anything for granted. If Galileo had taken it 334
for granted that a heavy weight would descend faster than a light one, 405
would there have been a revolution overnight in the world's thinking? 475

If the Wrights had not persisted in their attempt to prove that 539
man could fly, would we today be flying the air? Many people today 607

(*Continued on page 54*)

following restaurant menu. Write across the 6½″ width of the sheet. Use the current day and date instead of those shown.

Wednesday   November 6, 19—

SONORA INN COFFEE SHOP
D I N N E R

Choice of One:

    Julienne Soup
    Cream of Celery Soup
    Consomme with Rice
    Celery—Olives—Smoked Salmon
    Chilled Tomato Juice
    Fruit and Melon Cocktail
    Tuna Fish Cocktail
    Smoked Salmon

Salads:

    Hearts of Lettuce—French Dressing
    Bohemian Salad

½ Doz. Eastern Oysters, Bacon	.90
Broiled Salmon Steak, Lemon Butter	.75
Filet of Sole, Tartar Sauce	.75
Sirloin Top Steak Maitre D'Hotel	.90
Broiled Lamb Chops, Soulaise	.90
Breaded Veal Cutlet, Viennoise	.80
Lamb Chops	1.00
New York Cut Sirloin Steak	1.10
Filet Mignon	1.10
Sirloin Steak a la Minute	.90
Tenderloin Steak Broiled	.90
Calves' Liver with Bacon	.80
Smoked Ox Tongue Bordelaise (Ready)	.75
Irish Stew, Dublin Style—Dumplings (Ready)	.75

Potatoes Hashed in Cream	Cauliflower Polonaise
Potatoes Cottage Fried	Timbale of Spinach

Fresh Green Apple Pie	Pineapple
Lemon Cream Pie	Raspberry Jello
Peach Melba	Lime Jello
Baked Apple	Chocolate Blanc Mange
Peaches	Ice Cream
Pears	Sherbet

Coffee	Tea	Milk	Buttermilk

SPECIAL VEGETABLE SALAD BOWL   .45

168

university, but they cannot think.   An educated man is a man who can   743
think.   750

Christ spoke volumes when he said, "Know the truth and the truth   815
shall make you free."   Know the truth and you will be free from super-   885
stition and foolish fears.   The way to discover the truth is by think-   955
ing.   Thinking is not easy to do.   That is why so few do it.   Most of   1025
us are too lazy, too weak.   1052

Have you ever concerned yourself with why the people of the world   1118
are in such a chaos today?   The reason is lack of thought.   The only   1187
way we shall ever get out of the abyss is by some good, clear thinking   1258
followed by lots of action.   1286

About five per cent of the people think, fifteen per cent think   1350
they think, and the rest don't think at all.   In just what class do   1418
you think you fall?   1437

—Jacques Quarles

(267 Words; Stroke intensity, 5.38)

Lesson 34
Warming-up Exercise 23

This exercise reviews certain difficult strokes, such as the q, z, x, p, b, and a strokes.   It also gives some shift key practice and reviews the writing of quotation marks.   Use a line of 70 strokes.   Write each line twice.   Top margin, 2 inches.

lurk murky perk able table place race daze minx lynx pick axes axle
plural singular goal raze zebra place please rack excel azure zero.
Edward Everett Hale wrote the famous book, "The Man Without a Country."
Salem, Oregon; Portland, Maine; Seattle, Washington; Denver, Colorado.

Acceleration Drill 23

Sentence Writing.   Use a line of 70 strokes.

After March, bills will be mailed promptly on the tenth of each month.
You may always expect the utmost in fashion, quality, and service.
I am sorry this delay has caused your firm such great inconvenience.
The Chamber of Commerce meets in Room 2291, October 29, at 7:20 p.m.
Loans at 4%, 5%, 6%, 6½%, and 7% were made.   The bonds paid only 4¼%.

Brief Timed Writing.   Type the following paragraph three times.   Write as much of the copy as you can in two minutes each time.   Use a line of 70 strokes.

When a series of words, all of which begin with small letters,   63
is abbreviated, no space is needed after any of the periods except   130
the last one.   When the series consists of all capital letters, space   200
after each period, thus: The c.o.d. package was sent to the Richmond   270
Y. M. C. A. building.   291

54

and letters. In making the second border under the Period, you would use the variable line spacer, turning up the paper slightly to write the lower edge of the border.

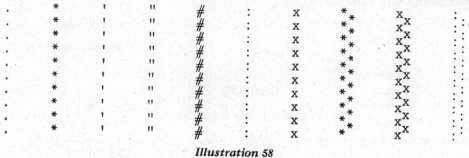

Period

. . . .

. . . .

Apostrophe

' '

Period and Apostrophe

' . ' . ' . ' . ' . ' . ' . ' . ' . ' . ' .

Illustration 57
Horizontal Borders

A few suggested side borders are also given. Use the variable line spacer and the paper release lever—to adjust the paper to the right or left—in making the second column of the characters shown in the last three borders. Practice the border you choose before you attempt to use it on a title page.

Illustration 58
Side Borders

Menus

Study Illustration 59. The design was laid out so that the top and bottom margins are each 2 inches (12 line spaces). Each side margin is 1 inch wide (10 strokes). There are 6 line spaces between the top border line and the title. The spacing below the title and below each item except the last is 5 line spaces. Between the last line and the border line are 6 spaces.

Center the lines, using the back-space or the remainder method.

Application Exercise 12. Type Illustration 59; then type the following menu with a border in the same form.

CHRISTMAS DINNER

Oysters in Green Pepper Shells

Celery   Ripe Olives

Roast Goose   Potato Stuffing   Apple Sauce

String Beans   Potato Puff

Lettuce Salad with Rice Cheese

English Plum Pudding   Bonbons

Coffee

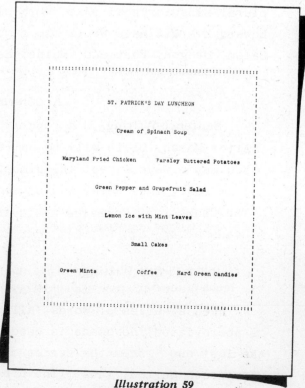

ST. PATRICK'S DAY LUNCHEON

Cream of Spinach Soup

Maryland Fried Chicken   Parsley Buttered Potatoes

Green Pepper and Grapefruit Salad

Lemon Ice with Mint Leaves

Small Cakes

Green Mints   Coffee   Hard Green Candies

Illustration 59
Menu with Border

Ten Minute Writing.   Use a line of 70 strokes.

All workers may be divided into three classes. There are, first   65
of all, the people who never have learned to work accurately. When   133
instructions are being given, they do not pay close attention; there-   202
fore, they do not know just what is wanted. Their work has to be   268
checked all the time. They make all kinds of errors, either because   337
they do not care or because they do not put their minds on their work.   408

The second class is made up of workers who do routine tasks well.   475
They have mastered their jobs, and they go ahead and do them in the   543
right way. They know that we all pay more or less for supervision;   611
the more our work has to be supervised, the more we have to pay for   679
that supervision. The workers in this class, however, lack something.   751
While they can do what they are told to do, they never seem to lift   819
their eyes above their own little jobs in an effort to find out what   888
is going on around them. They are very likely to stay in routine work   959
all their lives.   976

The workers who make up the third class--and it is a small one--   1040
have not only learned to do well the things they are told to do, but   1109
they have also learned to work on their own account. They have ini-   1177
tiative; they are self-starters. They plan ahead; they look for ways   1247
and means of increasing the value of their work. Although they can do   1318
detail work accurately, their mental activity does not cease there;   1386
their minds are creative; they are always on the alert for new ideas.   1457
It is from this third class of workers that we get our leaders in   1523
every phase of life.   1543

As you gain in experience, you will find that the two finest   1604
satisfactions that a person gets out of life are these: First, those   1674
satisfactions which grow out of the intimate relationships which are   1743
established in a happy home; second, those satisfactions which are   1810
derived from the sense of having brought a worthwhile piece of work to   1881
a successful conclusion.   1906

The formula for efficient work is really quite simple. First, you   1973
plan the piece of work which you are about to do; second, you start   2041
working and you keep on working until you have brought this particular   2112
piece of work to a conclusion; third, you forget about the work on   2179
which you have been engaged, and start all over again on another piece   2250
of work.   2259

It is a fact that the people who get things done are those who find   2327
happiness in their work. Other things being equal, the person who   2394
thoroughly enjoys his work is the one who will forge ahead into a posi-   2465
tion of leadership.   2484

(459 Words; Stroke intensity, 5.41)

55

You may occasionally be called on to typewrite poetry. Be very careful to follow the indentations of the lines shown on the copy from which you are working. In order to center the poem horizontally, count the number of strokes required to write the longest line and set the margin stops accordingly.

To center the poem on the page vertically, you will need to know the number of lines of writing and the number of lines to be left blank. A sheet of 8½ x 11 paper, as you have learned, contains 66 writing lines. When you have determined the number of lines which the poem will require, subtract that number from 66. You will then have the number of lines required for the top and bottom margins in order to center the poem on the page. Be sure to take the title into consideration.

Application Exercise 11. Write the following poem on an 8½ x 11 sheet. Center it vertically and horizontally. Leave three line spaces between the title and the first verse. Single-space your writing, with double spacing between the verses. Set a tabular stop for a 5-stroke indentation for the second, fourth, sixth, and eighth lines of each verse.

AN OFFICE

An office is a funny thing: Each morning certain men
    And certain girls and certain boys come into it again;
And hang their coats on certain pegs, their hats on certain hooks,
    And sit them down at certain desks in front of certain books.
They all have certain work to do in just a certain time,
    Concerning certain dollars for a certain fixed per diem;
And then at just a certain hour, in sunshine or in rain,
    They close their desks and hurry out to catch a certain train.

An office is a tragic thing when that is all there is,
    When each one has his certain work and certain way of his,
And wallows in a certain rut and never seems to see
    That there are certain other ones in life as well as he.
For we would find a certain fun in certain other ways,
    If we would give a word of cheer on certain busy days—
When problems vex, when certain things require a helping hand,
    Would give a certain sympathy that mortals understand.

An office is a pleasant place—at least a certain kind
    That has a certain brotherhood, where day by day you find
Some neighbor with a new idea he's glad to pass along,
    A certain sort of friendliness, a certain kind of song.
There is a certain duty that we owe to other men—
    To help them when they need a lift, to steady them again.
An office can become in time, to man and girl and boy,
    A certain kind of fellowship, and work a certain joy.

Border Designs

Border designs are sometimes typed around the matter on title pages as well as around menus, programs, and exercises for special occasions. The keynote to a good border design is *simplicity*. Careful planning is necessary to secure an attractive page.

The border design most commonly used consists of colons (:). The period (.), the quotation mark ("), the number sign (#), the dollar mark ($), the asterisk (*), and the small letters x and o are also useful in making attractive borders.

The articles in this Division are to be centered according to the directions given with each article. The Timed Writings provide supplementary material and may also be used for warming-up and drill work. If the Timed Writings are used as material for additional work in centering, the word count, given in parentheses at the end of each article, should be used.

Estimating the Number of Words. A word count is given for most of the articles in this Division. When, however, the word count is not given, it can be estimated in this way:

1. Count the number of words in three full lines of copy.

2. Divide the total word count by 3 to get the average number of words to the line.

3. Multiply that average by the number of full lines in the copy. (Group portions of short lines to make a full line.)

Example: Let us estimate the number of words in Timed Writing 25, page 59. Line 2 of the third paragraph and lines 2 and 3 of the fourth paragraph are full-length lines. They contain a total of 37 words (14 + 12 + 11). The average number of words to the line is 12 (37 ÷ 3). There are five short lines—one at the end of each paragraph. When grouped together, the five short lines will approximate two full lines. Therefore, we have a total of 12 average-length lines.

The total estimated word count is 144, obtained by multiplying the average number of words to the line (12) by the number of average-length lines (12). This count compares very favorably with the actual word count of 146 words, given at the end of the Timed Writing.

Centering a Heading. There are several methods of centering a heading. The one most frequently used is the **Back-Space Method,** which is adaptable to any typewriter. Proceed as follows:

1. Set the printing indicator at the centering point; that is, at 43 on a pica-type machine and at 51 on an elite-type machine, with the left edge of the paper inserted at 0.

2. Back-space once for every two strokes in the heading. Disregard a final odd letter.

3. Begin typing at the point at which the carriage stops when the back-spacing is completed.

Example: The heading of Article 1, page 58, *True Saving,* contains 11 strokes, including the space between the words. Therefore, back-space five times—once for *Tr,* once for *ue,* once for the space and *S,* etc. Disregard the final odd letter—*g.*

The **Centering-Scale Method** (for Underwood typewriters only) is the mechanical application of the Back-Space Method. The steps are:

1. Center the paper in the typewriter; make sure that the center of the paper is at the same point as the center of the margin scale.

2. Depress the **Marginal Stop Release Lever***, and with the thumb piece return the carriage to 0 *without removing the Margin Stops.*

3. Thumb-space the material to be centered.

4. Read the centering scale, which is the colored portion of the margin scale. If the reading is in fractions, take the next whole number.

5. Move the indicator to the number on the margin scale corresponding to the reading on the centering scale.

6. Type the heading.

Example: With the indicator at 0, strike the space bar 11 times (the number of strokes in the heading, *True Saving*). On a pica-type machine, the reading on the centering scale will be 39½; on an elite-type machine the reading will be 49½. Set the indicator at 40 if your machine has pica type; at 50 if it has elite type. You are now ready to type the heading.

Remainder or Columnar Method. This third method is of practical use only when one line (or word) is to be centered over or under another typed line or word. This method is particularly valuable for centering headings of more than one line, as, for example, columnar headings. Proceed in the following manner:

1. Set the indicator under the first letter of the "guide" line or word; for instance, under "S" of Example 1 or under "P" of Example 2 below.

2. Space, on the space bar, the new material to be centered; for example, "All Counties" in Example 1; "San Francisco County" in Example 2.

3. After spacing, find the difference between the strokes in the "guide" line and in the line to be centered.

4. Divide this difference by 2, and move the indicator either backward or forward this distance from the first letter of the "guide" line.

Example 1

STATISTICAL REPORT	STATISTICAL REPORT
(Guide Line)	ALL COUNTIES
all counties.....	*(Centered)*
(spaced on space bar)	

Example 2

PUBLIC SCHOOLS......	PUBLIC SCHOOLS
(Guide Line)	SAN FRANCISCO COUNTY
san francisco county	*(Centered)*
(spaced on space bar)	

The difference between the guide lines and the lines to be centered is 6 strokes in both examples. One-half this difference is 3. In Example 1, therefore, space forward 3 strokes from "S"; and in Example 2, back-space 3 strokes from "P" to write the second line.

* Locate this part on your machine by referring to the illustrations given on the inside back cover and on the back flyleaf of this book.

Application Exercise 10. Study the heading styles in Illustration 56, below, as well as the comments at the bottom of the page. Then type the headings on a full-size sheet just as shown in the illustration.

1   Revised Price List

2   Stewart's--The Friendly Store

3   Extract from Report on Testing of Cold-rolled Steel

4   POWER TRANSMISSION MACHINERY

5   FOREMAN TRAINING--A PRELIMINARY REPORT

6   MARKETING DATA

7   Raw Materials and Supplies

8   Sale of Electric Current

9   The Human Element

10   MAINTENANCE OF THE PLANT

11   TENSION TESTS - - ELASTIC LIMIT

12   COMMITTEE ON JOB ANALYSIS

13   TURNOVER IN INDUSTRY

14   A SUCCESSFUL PROFIT-SHARING PLAN

                BAKER TOOL COMPANY

                  JACKSON, OHIO

15   THE MUTUAL RATING SCALE

              An Interesting Development

Illustration 56
Heading Styles

Style 1. Each word begins with a capital; all the other letters are written in lower case.

Style 2. Caps and lower case. The words, but not the spaces, are underscored. Notice the dash—two hyphens.

Style 3. Caps and lower case underscored. Only the important words in a title are capitalized. Prepositions, articles, and conjunctions are written entirely in lower case. Of course, if such a word begins the title, you should write it with a capital.

Style 4. ALL CAPS.

Style 5. ALL CAPS. In writing titles of this character, remember to unlock the shift key before writing the dash; then lock it again to write the rest of the title.

Style 6. ALL CAPS underscored.

Style 7. Caps and lower case spaced out—one stroke after each letter and *three* strokes after each word.

Style 8. Caps and lower case spaced out as in Style 7; each letter underscored.

Style 9. Caps and lower case spaced out. In this style, however, the underscoring under each word is continuous.

Style 10. ALL CAPS spaced out.

Style 11. ALL CAPS spaced out. The dash is also spaced out; that is, there is one space before, after, and between the hyphens which represent the dash. It will be necessary to unlock the shift key to write the dash.

Style 12. ALL CAPS spaced out; each letter is also underscored.

Style 13. ALL CAPS spaced out. The underscoring is continuous under each word.

Style 14. ALL CAPS. This title occupies three lines.

Style 15. A two-line heading. The first line is written in ALL CAPS spaced out and *emphasized*. The typist simply types the line twice, the second time writing over the letters written the first time. The second line is written in caps and lower case; the words are *not* spaced out or emphasized.

Note: The titles shown in Illustration 56 were originally typed on a machine with pica type.

Letter-size Paper (8½″ x 11″)					**Half Sheets (8½″ x 5½″)**			
Number of Words	Line Length	To get number of lines, divide number of words in article by—			Number of Words	Line Length	To get number of lines, divide number of words in article by—	
		PICA	ELITE				PICA	ELITE
40-100...............	4 inches	7	9		40-100.............	5 inches	9	11
101-200...............	5 inches	9	11		101-200.............	6 inches	11	13
201-300...............	6 inches	11	13		201-300.............	7 inches	13	15
(Over 300 words, use two pages)								

Explanation: To use this Placement Plan, (1) note or estimate the number of words in the article you are to type and (2) decide whether it is to be written with single spacing or double spacing. If it is to be SINGLE-SPACED, subtract the number of lines of typing from the number of lines available; divide by 2, and begin on the line represented by the quotient. If it is to be DOUBLE-SPACED, multiply the number of lines of typing by 2, subtract from the number of lines available, divide by 2, and begin on the line represented by the quotient.

Example: Let us say that you wish to center an article of 146 words on letter-size paper. The procedure is as follows:

	Single-Spaced		Double-Spaced	
	Pica	Elite	Pica	Elite
Line Length, 5 inches (pica or elite)...............				
Lines available (11″ x 6)......................	66	66	66	66
Lines of typing (146 ÷ 9 for pica; 146 ÷ 11 for elite)	16	13		
Multiplied by 2 for double spacing..............			32	26
Subtract; remaining for margins..................	50	53	34	40
Divide remainder by 2 and begin on line number.....	25	26	17	20

Technically, you should begin on the next line after dividing the remainder by 2, in order to get a full-width top margin. For example, to leave a top margin of 25 line spaces, the first line of typing should begin on line 26. However, by beginning on line 25, the top margin is narrowed by one line, as there are only 24 line spaces above the first line. This practice is desirable because it automatically provides for placing the article in the "optical center."[*]

The same principle applies to double spacing: 10 lines double-spaced require only 19 line spaces for the typing, as the space below the last line becomes part of the bottom margin. In order to make provision automatically for placing the article in the optical center of the page, the procedure already explained is recommended.

Provision may be made for the heading by adding the number of lines and line spaces in the heading to the estimated number of lines of typing before subtracting from the number of lines available.

[*] The optical center is not the exact center, but is slightly higher than the exact center. If the article or other typed matter is placed in the exact center of the sheet—with the top and bottom margins the same—the article may appear to be too low on the sheet. That effect can be avoided by beginning the typing two or three lines above the exact center of the sheet.

Example:		
Lines available		66
Estimated lines of typing	16	
Heading	1	
Line Spaces (between heading and article)	2	19
Subtract for margins		47
Divide by 2		23

Problems

What will be the top and bottom margins, in single line spaces, and what will be the length of the writing line in centering the following articles on 8½ x 11 sheets?

	Length	Spacing
(1)	170 words	single
(2)	95 words	double
(3)	118 words	double
(4)	260 words	single
(5)	130 words	double
(6)	148 words	double
(7)	188 words	single
(8)	187 words	double
(9)	215 words	single
(10)	96 words	double
(11)	85 words	double
(12)	160 words	double
(13)	199 words	single
(14)	150 words	single

tary be authorized to cast one ballot for the officers named.

(Motion seconded and carried.)

THE CHAIRMAN: The secretary has duly cast one ballot for the nominees as submitted by the Nominating Committee, and the members named in the report are duly elected members of the Executive Committee.

THE CHAIRMAN: The next item is new business.

MR. J. H. GARY: I move that arrangements be made by the Association by which the managing director might visit each of the local chapters at least once a year.

MANAGING DIRECTOR STANFIELD: Under the present conditions this proposal is not practicable. It can be carried out only when the Association has secured the full-time services of a managing director.

MR. K. H. HUTTON: Has the Committee on Plan and Scope any plans that would enable us to carry out what is desired in this motion?

MR. F. G. WEST: The Committee on Plan and Scope has no report to make at this time.

MR. E. R. HANSON: Mr. Chairman, I move that we suggest to the Board of Trustees that prompt consideration be given to the question of capitalizing on the advertising possibilities of the convention that is just about to close.

MR. R. L. LAWSON: I want to second that motion, but I should like to see it referred to the Membership Committee.

THE CHAIRMAN: Is that change agreeable to you, Mr. Hanson?

MR. E. R. HANSON: Yes, certainly.

THE CHAIRMAN: Is there any discussion?

MR. G. R. ROBERTS: Will the suggestion gathered from the motion be limited to the idea of using this material in an effort to enlarge the membership of the Association?

THE CHAIRMAN: I don't think so. Much of this material will have real value to thousands of business concerns who are not eligible to membership in our Association. The Membership Committee, however, will shortly make a report to the Board of Trustees on plans for enlarging the membership.

(The motion as amended was then put to a vote and carried.)

Application Exercise 9. Type Illustration 55; then type title pages from the following data:

(a) Power Transmission Machinery / Wholesale Price List / Jones & Laughlin Company / Pittsburgh, Pennsylvania

(b) Specifications of Labor and Materials / Required for Construction Work / New Power House / Syracuse State Hospital / Syracuse, New York

(c) Executives and the Educational Director / By Charles S. Olson, Personnel Director / Higginson Pump Company / Newark, New Jersey / Published by Personnel Association of America / New York

(d) Financial Reports / December 31, 19— / Stearns Signal Company / Chicago, Illinois / Prepared by / Holton, York & Redding / Certified Public Accountants / Chicago, Illinois

(e) Measuring Stenographic, Transcribing, and Typing Efficiency / Prepared by Policyholders Service Bureau / Group Insurance Division / Metropolitan Life Insurance Company

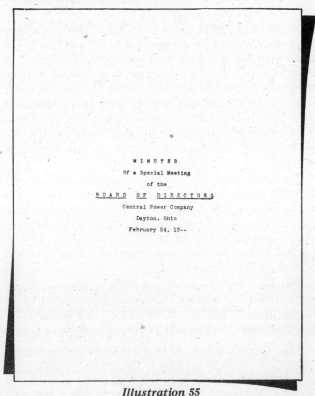

Illustration 55
Title Page

Special Instructions. You are to center each article on a full-size sheet. You are also to center each heading two or three line spaces above the article. Always make allowance for the heading line and for the line spaces between the heading and the article. Estimate the number of words when the word count is not given.

You are to type the "Timed Writing" at the beginning of the period. You will write four, five, or ten minutes as your teacher instructs.

If you complete the copy before time is called, start again at the beginning.

The work is arranged for the writing of three articles each class period. This number may be reduced or increased to meet the circumstances in your school. If your periods are very short, write two articles. If the periods are longer than average, write the three articles and any additional material that may be given you.

Budget 1

Timed Writing 24

We live in an age of speed. There is nothing wrong with speed	63
unless it robs us of a certain care and appreciation which belonged to	134
a more leisurely age of living. In our scramble for extreme accomplish-	206
ment in every line, we have lost sight of perfection in accomplishment.	279
Does it pay to demand perfection? Does it pay to be painstaking?	345
For sixteen years Palissy, the celebrated French potter, zealously	412
experimented with clay and kiln. In spite of many bitter dis-	478
couragements, he persisted until he produced a piece of pottery that	547
satisfied him.	562
Toward the end of the sixteen years, Palissy had no money for	624
fuel. He burned anything and everything he could use to heat his	690
kilns. Eventually his furniture and even the floors of his house were	761
torn up and fed into the fires.	793
But in the end Palissy produced an exquisite type of pottery that	859
met his full approval and which made him rich and famous.	916

(160 Words; Stroke intensity, 5.73)

Article 1

Special Instructions. Double-space all articles in this Budget. Consult the Placement Chart. Center the headings.

TRUE SAVING

I think that much of the advice given to young men about saving money is wrong--I never saved a cent until I was forty years old.

I invested in myself, in study, in mastering my tools, in preparation. Many a man who is putting a few dollars in the bank would do much better to put the money into himself.

—Henry Ford
(61 Words)

to a line on both sides. At least one-fifth of these stones are to be headers, reaching through the wall.

Build the piers for the iron columns, putting in the footings as in the drawings. These footing stones are to be large size, not more than two stones to one footing.

The piers are to be laid up in regular course, not less than nine inches high, with pick-dressed joints and beds. The capstone on the pier will be eighteen inches square, with pick-dressed bed and chisel-dressed top.

Build good sandstone door sills, nine inches high, fourteen inches wide, and six feet long.

Drill holes for flush bolts as directed by the carpenter.

WINDOW SILLS

All window sills will be good quality of sandstone, driven-dressed with corners perfect and surfaces straight. These sills will be four-inch build, seven-inch bed, and eight inches longer than the opening. They will all be set with a projection of two inches and will have a drip beneath.

BRICK WORK

Mortar: All brick will be laid in first-quality lime mortar, composed of one-third fresh slaked lime and two-thirds clean, sharp sand, mixed in a box and cooled five days before using.

Wetting Brick: All brick must be wet immediately before laying.

Build all walls that are colored red on the drawings to the top of the fire-wall, as shown on line on both sides, in good lime mortar; all brick must be well bedded, all joints well slushed, and brick well bonded, with headers every seventh course.

All exposed brick must be hard burned, of a uniform color.

The inside of the walls will have the joints slushed full and the joints stuck.

Fire Wall: The fire wall will be carried up as shown on the drawings and will be nine inches thick.

Build in all joists, girders, window frames, and nogging to secure tin work, as directed by the carpenter.

Window Sills: Carry up and set the window sills.

PAINTING

Kill all knots with shellac or silver lead before priming. Putty up all nail heads after priming.

Prime all door and window frames, including the backs, before they are set, and all other wood work as it goes up.

Use yellow ochre and pure linseed oil for priming.

Paint all doors and door frames, window frames, and sash three coats of such color as may be directed.

Paint the tin work one heavy coat in addition to the coating which the tinner gives it.

Use no evaporating dryer on the outside.

Convention Discussions—Dialog

When typing reports of discussions in meetings and conventions, no quotation marks are used to indicate the speakers' remarks. The names of the speakers are typed in ALL CAPS. The same practice is followed in typing the dialog in a play. The names of the characters are written in ALL CAPS, and the quotation marks are omitted in writing the speeches.

Application Exercise 8. Type the following discussion taken from a report of a convention of business men.

THE CHAIRMAN: You have heard the report of the Nominating Committee. Are there any other nominations? If not, a motion is in order to adopt the report of the Committee.

MR. DENTON: I move that the report of the Nominating Committee be adopted.

(Motion seconded and carried.)

MR. CHAIRMAN: The motion is unanimously carried. A motion is now in order that the secretary be authorized to cast one ballot for the officers as nominated. I believe that is the legal requirement.

ALGIERS

Algiers in Barbary is a large modern town with a splendid harbor, fine promenades, and gardens; and yet there still exists within its Kasbah, or native quarter, a network of narrow, crooked streets teeming with colorful animation, a walk through which will conjure up visions of the barbarous days of old. This ever-changing land, although but eight days out of New York, is a land unbelievably primitive--a land apart from all modern civilization.

*Article 2 contains every letter of the alphabet.

(72 Words)

Article 3
SERVICE THAT IS SERVICE

In France Parisians may ring up the telephone exchange and ask to be reminded, days later, of the fact that it is the wife's birthday, or that they have an appointment, or that income tax forms must be sent off. In England you can ring up to find out what the weather will be like; you can ask the exchange to be reminded of an appointment; you can arrange to be awakened at a fixed hour; by calling the exchange you can have a messenger come to take your dog--or baby--for a stroll at sixpence a mile.

—*Telephony*

Budget 2
Timed Writing 25

Two men were discussing a famous man who had gradually faded from popularity. 66 / 78

Finally one closed the conversation thus: "He has forgotten how to listen." Nothing more could be said. 143 / 184

Each one of us can take a tip from this conclusion. The art of listening is probably one of the most profitable arts, but it is also one of the least used or recognized. 248 / 322 / 355

It is not so easy as you may believe to learn to listen while another talks. The really expert listener is not over-eager in his manner. He does not always agree with the speaker, for constant agreement savors of insincerity and dullness. 417 / 485 / 550 / 596

A good listener is of a quiet manner. A good listener is casual yet alert in mind. A good listener shows appreciation and understanding. This art requires much practice. Cultivate it; it will pay you well to do so. 661 / 726 / 797 / 815

—*Liberty Magazine*
(146 Words; Stroke intensity, 5.58)

Special Instructions. Double-space all articles in Budget 2. Center the headings. Space out the letters in the heading for Article 4; that is, space once after each letter in the words of the heading; space three times after each word. The heading for Article 5 is to be emphasized. Type over the heading a second time to produce a bold-face effect. Underscore the heading of Article 6.

59

wage proportionate to his productive capacity; to prevent interference with those seeking work; to avert industrial disturbances; to harmonize differences between employers and employees, so that justice may be done to both; to uphold the law.

BY-LAWS

Article I

The name of this organization shall be "The Employers' Association of Cleveland."

Article II

Section 1. The membership shall consist of individuals, corporations, partnerships, or associations of employers employing labor in any branch of industry in northern Ohio.

Section 2. Members shall be elected by the Board of Directors on such terms and in such manner as the Board may prescribe.

Section 3. Resignation of members shall become effective after acceptance by the Board of Directors following ninety days' written request therefor filed with the Secretary.

one vote for every $100 or less annual dues paid, but no member shall have more than fifteen votes.

Article III

Section 1. The expenses of the Association shall be defrayed from dues and assessments.

Section 2. Each member shall pay annual dues equal to one dollar on each thousand dollars of payroll, computed on the basis of his payroll of the preceding year up to $500,000, and above that amount 25c on each $1,000.

A verified statement of dues payable shall be filed by each member with the Secretary of the Association on or before February 1 of each year. Dues shall be $25.00 per annum, minimum. All dues shall be payable quarterly in advance.

Section 3. In computing payrolls, expense payrolls, such as salaried officers, office help, technical staff, superintendents, general foremen, time clerks, inspectors, storekeepers, shippers, and watchmen shall be excluded.

Specifications

Application Exercise 7. Type this portion of a set of specifications with a carbon. Double-space throughout. The main heading, which you are to type, is as follows:

Specifications for a Building to be Erected for the Carter Motor Company at Orlando, Florida Prepared this   day of   , 19 , by P. R. Grant, Architect. Use today's date.

GENERAL DESCRIPTION

The building will be two stories in height. The first story will be ten feet in the clear at the lowest point, and the ceiling will rise the same slope as the roof.

The foundation will be stone.

The walls of the superstructure will be brick with stone sills.

The roof will be of tin.

LOCATION

The building will be located upon the Carter Motor Company's property as may be directed.

EXCAVATION

Excavate trenches for the walls and foundations for the columns six feet below the present grade line. The trenches must be eight inches wider than the wall.

As the walls are pointed up, fill in against them, tamping the dirt in place and grading to run all water away from the building.

Cart away from the excavation all earth not needed in grading up around the building.

FOUNDATION

All mortar used must be composed of one-third fresh slaked lime and two-thirds clean, sharp sand.

Build the walls as shown by the drawings seven feet high; that is, they will extend from six feet below the grade line to one foot above. These walls will be built of first-class rubble masonry, laid in lime mortar, using good-sized, regular-shaped sandstone, laid on natural quarry beds, and all well slushed.

Wendell Phillips once said, "How prudently most men sink into nameless graves, while now and then a few forget themselves into immortality."

Those who live only for themselves live little lives. Those who give themselves for others and for the advancement of things greater than themselves ever find a larger life than the one they surrendered.

"He that saveth his life shall lose it, and he that loseth his life for my sake shall find it," is another way of expressing the same thought. The selfish life leaves a grave marked, "Born--Died." The life of service leaves an eternal following of love and praise.

(105 Words)

Article 5

A Football Coach Speaks

"When the boys first report," wrote a famous football coach, "I call them together in a large room. There are 350 or 400 of them, and this is what I tell them: 'There are five types of boys in this room that I don't want on the football squad. I don't want them to ask for uniforms. The swelled-head who looks in the mirror and admires, and looks at his team-mates and criticizes; the complainer who whines and disorganizes; the quitter who would like to be a star and won't pay the price; the envious chap who is consumed with jealousy; and the boy with the inferiority complex.' "

(110 Words)

Article 6

Today's Job

A true story is told of a farmer who, seeking his fortune afar, sold his farm to another. One day the buyer of the farm noticed a queer black, oily film forming on the surface of the stream which ran through the farm. The former owner had placed a plank across the brook edgewise into the surface of the water. The plank, placed at sharp angles, was to throw that scum against the other bank so the cattle could drink.

Investigation led to the discovery of oil--and a fortune for the buyer of the farm whose first owner had gone far afield to seek treasure! The moral, if there be one, is that treasure most often lies in the task near at hand; it may be lost if we seek afar.

Budget 3

Timed Writing 26

The greatest enemy of us all is fear. We are afraid to make a move because we cannot see just what lies ahead of us, or because we imagine that there are dangers ahead of us--dangers which really do not exist.

A man who has had the right kind of education, obtained either in school or by himself, is in a position to look at the present and the

63

132

200

211

277

347

resourcefulness, vision, ability to discriminate between essentials and non-essentials, courage, readiness to accept responsibility, understanding of men. These qualities designate a man as an original contributor in some way to the world's progress. He gets things done.

"3. *Technique*—Technical knowledge, special experience, kinks of a trade or profession, data, formulae. These are facts acquired either from books or from experience."

To summarize these points in the reverse order, the third represents the acquired tools with which a man works; the second is his ability to use these tools; and the first is his character or, in a sense, his passport which permits him to work with the rest of us.

The majority of young men, especially those graduating from college, have the first of these qualifications and a considerable portion of the third, but two-thirds of them are lacking in the second.

---

[1] See *Proceedings* of the Sixth Annual Convention and the Seventh Annual Convention, National Personnel Association. We are also indebted to the Macmillan Company for the privilege of including in the present report certain extracts from Gowin's "The Selection and Training of the Business Executive."

Minutes

Application Exercise 5. Type these Minutes of a meeting of a Board of Directors. Use the current year date.

MINUTES
of a Special Meeting
of the
Board of Directors
Central Power Company

A special meeting of the Board of Directors of the Central Power Company was convened at the office of the company, 1241 Euclid Avenue, Dayton, Ohio, at 10 a.m., October 3, 19—. The following directors were present: Samuel F. Carlson, P. J. McLanahan, Henry F. Loeb, George W. Mason, and Charles H. Folsom.

object of the meeting, signed by all the directors, was presented. The waiver is attached and made a part of these minutes.

The president of the company, Samuel F. Carlson, presented a plan for transferring all the assets and business of the company to a corporation of the same name to be organized under the laws of the State of Pennsylvania.

After considerable discussion it was moved by Mr. P. J. McLanahan that the plan of reorganization submitted by the president be printed and copies distributed to all the stockholders of record, and that final action on the plan be deferred until the next regular annual meeting of the Board of Directors. The motion was duly seconded by Mr. George W. Mason. When it was put to a vote, the motion was carried, Mr. Folsom voting in the negative.

It was moved by Mr. Carlson and seconded by Mr. Loeb that the capital of the company be increased from $100,000.00 to $150,000.00. The motion was carried, Mr. Folsom voting in the negative.

As there was no further business, upon motion duly made by Mr. Loeb and seconded by Mr. Mason, the meeting was adjourned.

Secretary

By-Laws

Application Exercise 6. You are now asked to type, with carbon, a part of a set of by-laws of an organization of business men. Double-space, with 10-stroke paragraph indentations. Underscore all italicized words.

THE EMPLOYERS' ASSOCIATION OF CLEVELAND

Declaration of Principles and By-Laws
Adopted April 25, 19—

Objects of the Association

To secure for employers and employees freedom of contract in the matter of employment, irrespective of membership in this or kindred associations; to establish and maintain an employment bureau in the interest of both employers and employees; to oppose restrictions of output, sympathetic strikes, and boycotts; to discountenance conditions which are not just

learned how nations have met crises in their lives; he has found out
how men face and overcome dangers; he has learned facts which help
him to cast baseless fears out of his mind. For that reason he is not
taken in by the appearance of things which often create fear in the
hearts of the ignorant; he goes to the roots of a problem and studies
it from all angles; he bases his actions on facts, not on fears or
hopes. Just as the sunlight drives out darkness, so education ought
to drive out fears.

Training and education are two very different things. Training
teaches us how to do; education shows us what needs to be done.

550
621
689
759
826
895
915
979
1042

(202 Words; Stroke intensity, 5.16)

Special Instructions. Type the headings of Articles 7, 8, and 9 in upper case
(ALL CAPS). Space out the letters in the heading of Article 7 and underscore each
letter. Underscore each word in the heading of Article 8. Double-space Article 7.
Single-space Articles 8 and 9. Double-space between paragraphs.

Article 7*

V A C A T I O N

Variety is the spice of life. In order to keep up the zest of living, we
ought to mix pleasure with work. Everyone needs change, relaxation,
and recreation. Indeed, the desire for change is one of the basic facts of
human nature. As the days grow longer and summer approaches, we
begin to think of vacation and the change that it brings in our routine.
Perhaps we wend our way to the seashore, there to disport ourselves
among the waves that unceasingly roll in on the sands. Some find that
they can best relax in the shadow of mighty mountains; still others
enjoy the quiet sights and scenes of rural life--the waving fields of
wheat, the buzz of the bees, the cool running brook. When we have
communed for a while with the great outdoors, we come back to our
work with renewed vigor and a fresh zeal for our daily tasks.

(153 Words)

* Article 7 contains every letter of the alphabet.

Article 8

ACCURACY IN THE USE OF LANGUAGE

"A well-educated gentleman," wrote Ruskin, that master of English
prose, "may not know many languages--may not be able to speak any but
his own. But whatever language he knows, he knows precisely; whatever
word he pronounces, he pronounces rightly."

Accuracy in the use of language is the foundation on which all
good writing rests. Mistakes in English reflect seriously on the
writer; they are also stumbling blocks in the way of the reader.

There are many highly successful business men who did not have an
opportunity to go to college or even to high school. No matter what
may be their attitude toward education in general, they will all tell

salary or commission—not the Curtiss-Wright Company. If you want to get on to bigger things, it will pay you to be sincere in your dealings with everyone.

Understanding

In dealing with a prospect, remember that he is not the least bit interested in you or your product except insofar as you and your product or service can serve *him* and his own interests. You must form the habit of getting over on your prospect's side of the fence and looking at your product from *his* point of view. Ask yourself, "Why does he want this Private Pilot's Course?" or "Why should he want this plane?" A sympathetic understanding of a prospect's personal interest in your product will always prove an important aid in selling.

Unqualified Loyalty

We naturally like and respect the quality of loyalty in other people. We respect it in members of a family. We respect it in members of a business firm. And your prospects will respect it in you.

If you become a "yes" man and agree with the prospect who criticizes a certain policy of the company, you merely confirm what was probably only an assumption on his part that the policy in question is wrong; so he doesn't become a customer.

You may not fully agree with or understand a certain policy of the company; but when the men who are guiding its destiny decide on a policy, then make it *your* policy. Defend that policy tactfully but firmly whenever the occasion demands.

In a comparatively young industry such as ours, 100% loyalty is absolutely essential to continued success both for the individual and for the company.

You never know when a bit of disloyalty will kick back at you and cost you some profitable business, because disloyalty breeds lack of confidence in you, in your product, and in your company. In your dealings with prospects, in your contacts with the public at large, and in your conversations with friends and members of your own family, it will invariably pay you to be loyal to your company, to its policies, and to your associates in the business.

figures written slight.. above the writing line. To write figures in that way, turn back the roller about half a space. The footnotes should be written on the same page on which the reference numbers in the body of the manuscript appear. Watch your writing so that you may leave room at the bottom of the page for the footnotes. To separate the footnotes sharply from the manuscript proper, use the underscore to type a two-inch line one double space below the last line on the page. Study this illustration.

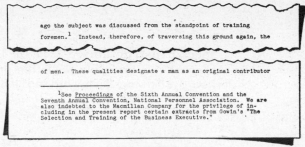

ago the subject was discussed from the standpoint of training foremen.[1] Instead, therefore, of traversing this ground again, the

of men. These qualities designate a man as an original contributor

[1] See Proceedings of the Sixth Annual Convention and the Seventh Annual Convention, National Personnel Association. We are also indebted to the Macmillan Company for the privilege of including in the present report certain extracts from Gowin's "The Selection and Training of the Business Executive."

Illustration 54
Footnote

Application Exercise 4. Type this manuscript with double spacing. Underscore all italicized words. Write the footnote, with single spacing, at the bottom of the first page of your copy.

Executive Training

The Committee on Executive Training in its report two years ago discussed the methods employed in training executives. A year ago the subject was discussed from the standpoint of training foremen.[1] Instead, therefore, of traversing this ground again, the Committee quotes a few paragraphs written on this subject recently by Mr. K. R. Harlan, whose splendid efforts in the National Association are familiar to all of us.

The particular problem Mr. Harlan describes is the development into future business leaders of relatively inexperienced young men. With reference to methods of dealing with this problem he says:

"In general, the following characteristics may be considered in selecting young men for training in any business:

"1. *Moral Fibre*—Integrity, honesty, reliability, dependability, a spirit of helpfulness, modesty, refinement, ability to work in an organization, cooperativeness, tactfulness. These qualities are those which make a man liked and trusted among his fellowmen.

in life. The young man who can express himself in clear, correct English has a decided advantage over the one who uses a plural verb with a singular subject, who writes an adjective when the context calls for an adverb, and who selects a plural pronoun when he refers to a noun that means only one person or thing.

(186 Words)

Article 9*

THE BEGINNING OF TOUCH TYPING--PART ONE

Back in the seventies typewriters were scarce in Grand Rapids, Michigan, where I was a clerk in a law office. The office boasted a No. 1 Remington--a large, awkward-looking piece of mechanism encased in tin. It sounded like a riveting machine. To depress a key, you had to hit it with a blow almost hard enough to drive a nail. No one thought of using more than the first two fingers, for the very good reason that the other fingers were not strong enough.

My employer was a mild, scholarly man of ample means, who used his office chiefly as a sanctuary from a sharp-tongued wife and an embittered sister-in-law. I had most of my time to myself. I was head clerk, office boy, janitor, and chief engineer of the big base burner coal stove--all for the princely salary of eight dollars a month. But I was a husky youth of sixteen with ambition and strong fingers. During my four years in that office I made an intensive study of law, literature, and the sciences, as well as of shorthand and typewriting. From 7 a.m. to 6 p.m., with one hour for dinner in the middle of the day--those were my office hours. A gymnasium in the back room kept me in condition, together with a long walk before breakfast and another after supper in the evening.

(236 Words)

*Written by Mr. Frank E. McGurrin, the first touch typist, especially for COLLEGE TYPING.

Budget 4

Timed Writing 27

Committing to heart each day a verse or a prose extract will train	67
the memory with surprising rapidity. An exercise that has been used	136
with good results is this: Enter a room, take a quick glance around,	206
walk out, and write down what you remember of the things that you have	277
seen. The same exercise can be applied to passing a shop window.	343
Some of us are born with the ability to memorize; for others of	407
us memory work is difficult. The speaker must have bits of prose and	477
poetry at his command; the salesman must remember names and faces; the	548
mathematician, certain formulas; everyone needs to use his memory in	617
some way. While in school, we do have the opportunity to increase our	688
ability to "learn by heart."	716

(129 Words; Stroke intensity, 5.55)

Special Instructions. Single-space all articles in this Budget. Center the headings in the styles shown.

cleaned from time to time so that it will retain its edge. An ink eraser should be used for erasing on the original, or ribbon, copy. For erasing on carbon copies, a pencil eraser may be used. A very satisfactory typewriter eraser is one which combines both a pencil and an ink eraser. For close erasing, a special celluloid erasing shield containing openings of different sizes and shapes may be used. The adjoining letter or letters will then be protected.

Before making an erasure, move the carriage to the right—or to the left—so that the particles of paper and rubber will not drop down into the bed of the typewriter. Good erasing cannot be done hurriedly. The best results will be obtained with a fast, but light, circular motion. Rub out the typed letter or word thoroughly, but be careful not to puncture the paper or to roughen it too much. Never dampen the eraser.

To make an erasure on carbon copies, turn the cylinder backward or forward as required. Insert a piece of paper back of each carbon sheet at the place where you are to erase. Make the erasure on the original sheet, remove the first piece of paper, make the erasure on the first carbon copy, remove the next piece of paper, and so on until completed. If a card is used, insert it between the original and the first carbon sheet, and make the erasure on the original; then place the card between the first carbon copy and the second carbon sheet; erase; and so on. Do not use too thick a card because of its tendency to shift the various sheets out of alignment.

When the erasing has been completed, bring the paper back into writing position and type the correction lightly, so that the impression of the retyped material will not be heavier than that of the unerased words. If necessary, restrike the letter or letters to bring about evenness of shading.

Application Exercise 3. Type this manuscript with a carbon. Center the subheads. Underscore all italicized words. The copy is adapted from the Sales Manual of the Curtiss-Wright Flying Service.

MAKING YOUR SALES SHOW A PROFIT

Personal success in anything is seldom an accident. Rather, it is the result of careful training and constant analytical study of the others can be developed only by studying your own work, correcting minor faults, and perfecting details of performance through practice and study.

Personal Appearance

The value of good personal appearance is obvious. Good appearance does not make sales, but it does aid in making the right approach to a sale.

Confidence

To do anything well you must have confidence in your ability to do it well. Self-confidence is largely a matter of "knowing your stuff."

Study each product, service, and activity you are selling. Know all the details, the good points, and the weaknesses if any. Knowledge of your product gives you a confidence that is hard to beat. With that knowledge your mind is left free to devote itself strictly to the job of presenting the product in the most effective way.

Courtesy

Courtesy is little more than taking a friendly interest in people. To take a friendly interest in people you must like them; and it's almost as easy to like people as not to like them, because there is something likable about almost everyone you meet. Always keep in mind the magical influence of a genuine smile.

Sincerity

In the sense that we have defined "courtesy," sincerity is closely akin to it. Take a really friendly interest in the prospective customer and in serving him to his own best advantage.

Two or three years ago a certain salesman who was selling school courses for an internationally known flying school made a phenomenal success—from a financial standpoint. He sold several hundred courses and made considerable money in commissions for himself. But he had promised everything under the sun in making his sales. It cost his employer several thousand dollars to appease dissatisfied students. The salesman lost his job. Subsequently he failed in two business ventures because he was "too good." When last heard of, he was looking for a job.

(Concluded on page 160)

The boss and I used to stage typewriting contests, in which he had rather the best of it with the two-finger method. One day I conceived the idea of using all the fingers on the keys and the thumb on the space bar, and it was not long before I developed a speed which left him far behind. That idea was the origin of what is now called the touch system. Pretty soon the Remington Company came out with the No. 2 machine, which had a lighter touch and for which my all-finger method was just the thing. I soon developed a speed of over a hundred words a minute.

At the end of my four years in that law office I was surprised to find that I could write shorthand and operate a typewriter faster than anybody else in sight. Soon I got a position as official court reporter at a salary of $3,000 a year. Going from $8 to $250 a month made me feel pretty rich; and, although I was admitted to the bar, I did not want to go back to a starvation income while building up a law practice. Within a short time I won a contest over fifteen others for the position of reporter in the United States Court at Salt Lake City.

During all this time the touch system which I had evolved enabled me to transcribe my notes at high speed and with a minimum of labor. I always made it a point to read over what I had written. When I found an error, I would write the word in which the error was made five times, in order to erase the scar from the subconscious self.

(288 Words)

Article 11

THE BEGINNING OF TOUCH TYPING--PART THREE

I learned very early that it is the subconscious mind that must do most of the speed work, but the subconscious mind must be trained by the conscious mind through diligent and attentive practice. Accuracy should always be the first consideration, because it is easier to go from slow to fast than to go from wrong to right.

Strangely enough, the touch system was practically unknown until 1886, when I won a $500 typewriting contest in Cincinnati. The test consisted of 45 minutes of typewriting from dictation and 45 minutes from copy. My work averaged 98 words a minute from dictation and 99 words a minute from copy. Of course, it was all new matter. The newspapers gave front-page space to the contest. The Remington Company then hired me to give exhibitions in all the leading cities of the country. My best record was made in Chicago, where I wrote from dictation 124 words, new matter, in a minute without an error.

The money I made in shorthand and typewriting enabled me to go into the banking business, which I followed for thirty years. And now, at 73, having retired from active business, I look back with the greatest affection to my shorthand and typewriting experience. It taught me the value of persistence and was the basis of whatever success I have had.

(224 Words)

Manuscripts

The typing of manuscripts of various kinds is an important phase of secretarial work. Manuscripts are generally typed on 8½ x 11 paper. The typing should always be in double spacing. Only one side of the paper should be used. The paragraphs are usually indented 5 strokes.

If the manuscript is to be left unbound, the top margin of the first page should be at least 1½ inches, with the side and bottom margins not less than 1 inch. The first line of each succeeding page should begin 1 inch from the top of the sheet.

If the manuscript is to be bound at the top, leave an extra top margin of 1 inch for this purpose; if it is to be bound on the side, leave an extra margin of 1 inch on the left side.

The pages of the manuscript, other than the first one, should be numbered. The figure representing the number of the page may be centered one-half inch from the top or one-half inch from the bottom of the page.

Application Exercise 1. Type the following article. Follow the instructions you have just read. Underscore all italicized words.

CARE OF THE TYPEWRITER

As with any other machine or piece of equipment, the typewriter requires reasonable care to give good service.

Dusting. Try to keep the typewriter as free from dust as possible. Cover it at nights or when standing long unused. Dust the frame and other outside parts frequently with a chemical dust cloth or slightly oiled rag. Dust the inside exposed parts with a long-handled brush which has fairly long bristles. A painter's small, round sash tool is suitable for this purpose. The parts under the carriage may be more easily reached with the brush if the keys are carefully depressed so as to raise the type bars.

Cleaning. Clean the type daily with a brush (one similar to a toothbrush, but wider) which has short, stiff bristles. If this cleaning is neg-lected, blurred and untidy typing will be produced. Be sure to brush parallel with the type face (forward and backward), and not across the face from left to right. The letters *a*, *e*, *o*, *s*, *d*, *b*, and *m* are particularly susceptible to clogging. Should the type faces become clogged, it may be necessary to clean them with a sharp-pointed stick (avoid using a pin or other metal) or with a good cleaning fluid.

If alcohol is used, be careful not to get it on the enamel of the machine, as it tends to dull the finish. Also be careful not to spill alcohol on the typewriter table; it will eat into the varnish and leave a scar or blemish in the finish. Do not allow the cleaning fluid to run down the type bars into the segment slots; place a blotter or absorbent tissue under the type bars to absorb the excess fluid. Cover the keyboard to prevent the keys from getting splattered. Clean the platen and the feed rolls occasionally with alcohol. If a special preparation is used for cleaning the type, follow the directions of the manufacturer.

Oiling. Apply oil sparingly. A very small drop at a time on any part is sufficient for proper lubrication. Any excess oil should be wiped off immediately; otherwise, the part may gum up with dust and dirt. The carriage ways (rods or bars on which the carriage runs) should be oiled weekly. The other rods or friction parts need to be oiled only once a month. If you have an Instruction Book for your typewriter, follow the directions given in it for oiling the machine.

Application Exercise 2. Type this article.

ERASING

Erasing, particularly during the learning period, should be resorted to as little as possible. Frequent use of the eraser will tend to weaken your typing power.

There is a knack in skillful erasing as in everything else. Good tools are essential if the erasing is to be done rapidly and efficiently. The

WISDOM IN CONVERSATION
By the Duke De La Rochefoucauld

The reason why so few people are agreeable in conversation is that everyone thinks more of what he wishes to say than of what others say. We should listen to those who speak if we would be listened to by them; we should allow them to make themselves understood and even to say pointless things.

Instead of contradicting or interrupting them, as we often do, we ought, on the contrary, to enter into their minds and their tastes, show that we understand them, praise what they say so far as it deserves to be praised, and make them see that it is from choice rather than from courtesy that we praise them.

We should avoid disputing about indifferent things, seldom ask questions (which are almost always useless), never let them think that we pretend to more sense than others, and easily concede the advantage of deciding a question.

We ought to talk of things naturally, easily, and more or less seriously, according to the temper and inclinations of the persons we entertain; never press them to approve what we say, nor even to reply to it. When we have thus complied with the duties of politeness, we may express our opinions, without prejudice or obstinacy, in making it appear that we seek to support them with the opinions of those who are listening.

We should avoid talking much of ourselves and often giving ourselves as examples. We cannot take too much care to understand the bent and the compass of those we are talking with, in order to link ourselves to the mind of him whose mind is most highly endowed; and to add his thoughts to our own, while making him think so far as possible that it is from him we take them.

(296 Words)

Brief Timed Writing

Reading good books and associating with educated people	56
will increase your vocabulary, broaden your mind, and give you	119
many new ideas which will help you to become a more efficient	181
man or woman. Many people use faulty, slipshod language simply	245
through carelessness. It is just as easy to be careful as to	307
be careless. Some people, however, do not even try to express	391
themselves correctly.	

(65 Words; Stroke intensity, 6.01)

REFILLING
(six)

Refilling shall be made in layers *cap* not more than 6 inches in thickness. ~~and~~ each layer, *shall be* thoroughly consolidated by rolling *and tamping* before the succeeding layer is put in place.

LOOSE ROCK OR SHALE
(one)

Loose rock or shale excavation shall include all lose masses of rock containing more than 10 *(ten)* cubic feet and less than 1 cubic yard, ~~and~~ *together with* all shale rock which ~~occurs~~ *is found* in large masses.

This excavation shall be paid for by the cubic yard.

ROCK

Rock excavation shall include masses of rock which require blasting. ~~This~~ *Such* excavation shall *also* be paid for by the cubic yard.

SHAPEING SUB-GRADE

Before the foundation here~~in~~*in*after dïscribed is laid, the Roadbed shall be shaped to a true surface in accordance with lines and points given by the Engineer and shown in plans. The sub-grade surface shall be thoroughly rolled with a steam *cap* roller, weighing not less than 10 *(ten)* tons, all resulting depressions, *shall then be* filled with material ~~suitable to~~ *earth approved by* the Engineer, and the ~~surface~~ again rolled until an even, compact surface is obtained.

as specified below

DRAINAGE OF SUB-GRADE

If, after the excavation for the sub-grade has been finished, the soil is of such character that it requires under-drainage, the Contractor ~~will~~ lay lines of Porous or Farm Tile, *3' to 4' deep,* which shall drain into the Catch-Basins. This tile pipe must be uniform~~al~~ly burned, straight, round in cross section, and have the ends cut off square. *These drains shall be paid for per foot in place.*

Foundations

Upon the sub-grade so prepared, a foundation of width shown in cross sections shall be laid according to the method hereinafter described. All stone in foundation shall be sound, hard, durable, frost-proof, native stone of quality to be approved by the Engineer.

Division 4—Drill Period Copy

There is no substitute for persistent, conscientious drill, if you really wish to attain accuracy with high speed. The material in this Division may be used for special drill in addition to your regular class practice.

Choose the particular drill you need to improve your typewriting. Write each line or each paragraph once, twice, or three times according to your own individual needs.

Contents

1. Single-stroke Mastery Drills

Each two lines of drill will make a single line when typed without spaces after the letters. These drills are to be typed slowly. Make as quick a finger movement as you can in stroking the proper key; then relax between this stroke and the next.

Model Line—60 strokes

fahdlgkslfahdk;jsdasg;lhkgljdfshkj;lgdhfkgj;fj;gslfdaksfjahl

(Line 1 Guide Row)

f a h d l g k s l f a h d k ; j s d a s g ; l h k g l j d f

s h k j ; l g d h f k g j ; f j ; g s l f d a k s f j a h l

(Line 2 Upper Row)

f r a q d e ; p s w h y g t j u l o k i s w j u f r a q ; p

d e l o g t k i h y e d o l q a u j w s p ; r f i k t f y j

(Line 3 Lower Row)

f v s x a z h n d c g b ; / k , l . j m ; / g b a z h n l .

j m s x d c f v n z b x . o m v , / b z n . x m / c , v m b

2. Balanced Drills

The following single-stroke exercises can be used effectively as warming-up drills. These drills introduce opposite strokes with alternate left- and right-hand fingers. Their purpose is to aid in overcoming confused letter responses, such as *i* for *e*, *g* for *h*, *v* for *b*, etc. Line of 65 strokes. Do not space after the letters.

(Line 1 Guide Row)

a j s k d l f ; g h f ; d l s k   (Repeat 3 times to complete the line.)

(Line 2 Upper Row)

p r o e i w u q y t u q i w o e   (Repeat 3 times.)

(Line 3 Lower Row)

z m x , c . v / b n v / c . x , z m b n   (Repeat 2 times.)

65

approved

Before any materials are used, samples thereof shall be furnished the Engineer; said samples,
if ~~passed~~ by the Engineer, shall remain in the
Engineer's Office and be used as the Standard with
like which all materials furnished under these specifications ~~shall~~ agree.

When the word "Engineer" is used in these
specifications, it shall understood to mean the
Engineer or his authorized representative. Wherever
the word "Contractor" is used in these specifications, it shall be understood to mean the person,
persons, association, or corporation that have let
the contract to do this work, or their representa-
tives.

TOP SOIL ————————————→ (center)

All Top Soil shall be removed from the lines
of the Avenues and stored in Spoil Banks.

EXCAVATION FOR AVENUES ————————→

After removal of Top Soil, the Sub-Soil shall
be excavated to an even sub-grade, as called for.
The Contractor shall excavate to the lines given
by the Engineer. The price for ~~earth~~ excavation
~~will~~ cover ~~this item, also cover~~ the spreading of
~~it~~ in the new location, *as well as the excavation itself.*

Excavation shall be paid for by the cubic yard.

LIMIT OF EXCAVATION ————————→

No allowance shall be made for any excavation
outside of the lines indicated in the sections.

UNSUITABLE MATERIAL IN SUB-GRADE ————————→

Should the material composing the sub-grade
at any point be, in the opinion of the Engineer or
his representative, unfit for the foundation ~~of the~~
pavement to rest, ~~on.~~ ~~Such~~ material shall be taken
out to such depth as the Engineer may order ~~and~~
the excavation so made refilled to sub-grade.
shall then be

(Continued on page 157)

156

These drills consist of like finger strokes with alternate left and right hands. Their function is to aid in the development of rapid finger reaction and acceleration. Line of 60 strokes. Do not space after the letters.

(Line 1
Guide Row)   a ; s l d k f j g h   (Repeat 5 times to complete the line.)

(Line 2
Upper Row)   a ; q p s l w o d k e i f j r u g h t y   (Repeat 2 times.)

(Line 3
Lower Row)   a ; z / s l x . d k c , f j v m g h b n   (Repeat 2 times.)

(Line 4
Mixed Rows)   a ; q p z / s l w o x . d k e i c , f j r u v m g h t y b n   (Repeat.)

4. Substitution Drills

Certain letter strokes are often confused in typewriting. These drills will help you to avoid or to correct the tendency to substitute one stroke for another. Line of 75 strokes.

(*a* for *e*
e for *a*)   kga eba xla wia qua soy exa zoa eio gel mew tex pre bea jet que yes ear
an am all sal task they liked each great agent queer razors adequately
The amazed agent saw a great aeroplane suddenly appear in the hazy sky.

(*a* for *s*
s for *a*)   aqa awl laj zam axa has zea bay sts wis sea sxs fsg asz nas aqu sas sak
so is us at as ask lash pass since scale sloop affair various scratched
Before the storm finally passed it lashed the waters into a foaming sea.

(*b* for *g*
g for *b*)   gbg fbf bja skb bpb abe aen rbt mbg gbd gaj gix cyg age gpr big gsn bug
bat bay dug give bets boxes began debut doubtless telegraph balbriggan
The big bay tug boat again began to back the damaged barge into a berth.

(*b* for *v*
v for *b*)   fvd prv cav niv dov ewv jav quv xev gbd bga kob qub biz xen reb cam aba
by but big gave vapor every ebony evenly beginning individual symbolizes
The vision of the beautiful valley village became obscured by a wet fog.

(*c* for *d*
d for *c*)   acf kic clo con jec sci byc pac dcd ogd end cid qud dix day mud lod ksd
can cot act cat cots cite code dice cold could clouds combined distances
The distinguished character actor decided to accept the contract offered.

(*c* for *v*
v for *c*)   fca oce wlc zgc dcd nbc abc anc civ zov quv idv vox fvg kev rav vem vac
cam cad lac cab cave vivid cover evince survey craved vacuums vacation
The vagabond—a victim of the chilling air—craved very heavy covering.

(*d* for *e*
e for *d*)   dfd jil dcd kds nbr txd lod diz ded oei fuj coe doe udq fed wed tye ebd
had dry lad led set day keep does ready beheld prized combined evidently
Immediate independence held the democratic minds of the destined leaders.

66

This problem consists of a part of a set of specifications. Use ruled legal paper if it is available. Write the specifications with double spacing.

If ruled legal paper (paper with vertical rulings at the left and at the right side of the sheet) is used, set the margin stops so that all the typewritten lines will begin and end *not less than* one stroke inside the ruled lines. Type the second and third page numbers one-half inch from the lower edge. Leave a 2-inch top margin and a 1-inch bottom margin.

S P E C I F I C A T I O N S

Covering

THE BUILDING OF AVENUES AND THE SURFACE DRAINAGE SYSTEM, MANHOLES, LAMP-HOLES, CATCH-BASINS, AND SEWERING on Estate of Henry W. Coughlin, Pittsburgh, Pa.

-o-

GENERAL REQUIRMENTS

The work is to be performed according to the following specifications and is to conform to any or all grades and lines furnished by the Engineer.

It must be expressly understood by the contractor that the ommision from Drawings or Specifications of any detail reasonably necessary, or proper to the complete performance of the work shall not constute a claim for extra charges, but the work or material or both shall be furnished to the satisfaction of the Engineer as no extras will be allowed on this work.

The Contractor shall give his personal attention to the work. The Contractor shall supply all labor, teams, tools, and utensils necessary for completing the work, and all material not found on the estate.

The Contractor is not to sub-let the work under any consideration without written permission from the Engineer.

The quanities given are approximate and may be decreased or increased at the option of the Engineer, and all lines, and grades shall be subject to such modifications as he may suggest.

The Engineer shall furnish cross sections, profiles, and plans, showing the nature, character, and extent of the work intended.

(Continued on page 156)

add aid fad fade field staff finds fierce feazed defied differed confound
The field staff failed to follow the Indians' fierce and defiant foray.

(*d for k*
k for d) fdf jud rod dem ide yed ady pad dak kas okx quk kiv drk lak ned kud had
do ado ask find dark back drink khaki jockey looked Denmark acknowledge
"Dirk" Van Dyke frankly acknowledged that Denmark looked for dark days.

(*d for s*
s for d) ode dug ark bid dfc duq esj his isl mas dns spd tds wps vos dox dys adz
as sky sad used desk respond comrades understood dissatisfied distinguish
The distinguished soldier showed dissatisfaction over his comrade's deeds.

(*e for i*
i for e) adf ced kek roc sel aut her bei twi oie ciz kui bie jsi iap six giy qui
set net ewe did bit exists immortal incentives distribution embroidered
Increased distribution furnished the incentive for the foreign fishermen.

(*e for r*
r for e) ceo gea pre hew eyt exj ues neb mer rts rub urb fre rns crp ret zek rex
let are air nor get defer skirt trifles frequent regarding observations
Frequent observations made the shepherd determine to explore the cavern.

(*e for s*
s for e) ded del kem tre feu wei goe fid ces sas jas sec sos spe ies zes xes swo
be so sue vex best empire gesture chickens adequate expenses scheduled
Special races scheduled Wednesday seem sufficient reward for spectators.

(*e for t*
t for e) ded use sef nem keo hew gex bek det rte syt jet ezt det qui wet teo sit
toe the get cent kept cometh indirect eternally telegraphic pathetically
For real effectiveness in written discourse, determine to master rhetoric.

(*e for w*
w for e) emn equ fel big lye dij exa eop ewe wez eks iew owe hew twe swe est ewt
one doe new went where weight whenever bewilder typewriting newspapers
We interviewed the few Northwestern newspaper workers who were Westerners.

(*f for g*
g for f) fuf dfj cfo foq jcf afu fpb zfh dfg tgb qua ygt fgb vnb gey gpr gcg big
of if foe fog life gift fatigue justify frightened significant submerged
Frightened and fatigued, the gray fox fled from the dogs into a soft field.

(*f for r*
r for f) cuf qui tif fak fla lvt for fyb ifg frt rid hor zar oxf kre ner frt qur
fag far arc for from awful frieze frequent Frederick frugality grapefruit
Frederick's frugality forbids frequent orders for fresh Florida grapefruit.

(*g for b*
b for g) gif arg gaz qug gat eig bys bak bov jib gmb wob cub pub dgh bax lug nay
dug get hug dog beg born boxes globe gables sagebrush organized prescribed
The beggar observed the gabled box-like barn before the gale began to blow.

(*g for h*
h for g) tgf jhg gbi vgs ngk qua eyg hgz goh hlp hom nbh bzh hir xmh jke the hou
go he get goes might highly bought hearsay Plutarch sagebrush something
Through "Plutarch's Lives" we are brought into another world of long ago.

67

Our company is a self-insurer, and handles ~~through its legal department~~ all ~~of the~~ accidents resulting in injury to our employees.

which is in charge of our own physi...   *our Legal Department by which is specified*

When one of our employees is injured, ~~they are~~ *he* *is* given first aid and sent immediately to the company's medical department. If the case is a serious one, the patient is taken to one of the local hospitals. We have made arrangement*s* with practically all the hospitals ~~for one~~ surgeon ~~to~~ handle our cases. ¶We allow a man his full salary from the time of his accident ~~until~~ *to* the date of his recovery, ~~Unless~~ *he* our investigation discloses some unusual circumstances which made it advisable to abide by the strict letter of the law. ¶Accidents are reported through our Legal Department to the State Industrial Accident commission ~~and an~~ *Cap. k* award made, whereupon a final settlement receipt is obtained from the employee and filed with the commission. ¶No distinction is made between salaried men and day laborers, so far as handling accident cases is concerned, ~~and~~ both classes receiv~~ing~~ *e* *Cap* their full (renumeration) as above stated.

is then   *B*

Yours very truly,

Eastern Shore Power Company) ALL CAPS

misspelled

Legal Department

Problem 9

This message is to be written on paper cut to postal card size—5½ x 3¼ inches.

Note: With paper and cards, the width is given first.

Spell out (Notice) *All caps*

The annual meeting of the stock-holders of
l.c. the Stewart Publishing Company will be held
at 2 (P.M.) (Jan.) 22~~nd~~ at the office of the company, Bidwell (Bldg), Dayton, (O.) The committee on the consolidation of subsidiary companies, appointed at last meeting, will ~~be~~   *l.c.*
present ~~their~~ *the* Report.
~~We hope you will be present.~~

Ohio
annual
2 spaces

its   *l.c.*   *the*   Yours truly,
                        Secretary

154

... ... ght tre vit wot toy mag que tag tif

go to tug gate gaze agates grapes through segments eventide registration
At eventide the tired traders came treading lightly through the old gates.

(h for j
j for h)
fjm jlv ujn jab kyj gsj pej jzr quj joh axh his cha dah thy whj hej dch
joy ajar had aha John hope jail jelly heroic journey Japanese adjoining
John's heroic journey was almost prohibited by the Japanese champion.

(h for n
n for h)
has ghy reh mhy orh quh agh xhg hin nmy vns rno nda ngh mhi nex jnk haz
he had how and hind chunk hunters elephant champion fishing authorization
The authorization of the champion's manager had never been required before.

(i for e
e for i)
aer kea oze ben tem ext cid fig ihl ios jib qui epi vie ewi yew ive cei
be pet the yet ivy his well this weigh invite heroic hostile civilization
They climbed the precipitous mountain trails that led to dizzy heights.

(i for o
o for i)
pai ihy gil isj iec kin biv min oir owx zod fot quo oil osi oni tio ody
icy bit one own omit look with would region contain unanimous revolution
Within the region of the revolution the noise of cannon fire was heard.

(i for u
u for i)
oil iwf lit yhi seg eir biz iny iku riu ryu eij qui soi bix hut ubi sue
it in up lip rub quit under circus fatigue curious stimulus unconscious
The curious circus clown found the unconscious juggler under the sofa.

(l for o
o for l)
lih cly rle plz liv blm xil aln clj lot quo wod log hlf klo sol lon olo
own oar lop low long block folio follow apologize locomotion duplication
The school bookroom held many duplications of world-known original novels.

(l for s
s for l)
alk lot ;lm led elb que oln zil vlt csl frs gls hej kls psl vas wlx yls
all oil sty sox pulp less lesson spoiled assembly exaltation conclusion
Through his telescope Al beheld the swimmer vigorously battle the seas.

(m for n
n for m)
jmw ktm lmu arm com smi mvh kem man hum fyn znb gnu nix pon qum rum men
am an sum son then them stone Norman surname minister firmament smartness
The astronomer's contemplation of the firmament constantly inspired him.

(r for e
e for r)
ort ran jur rqu ham ral beg ceg dex fen ick pre ers avy rwe ery erb ire
run urn few new rue azure oxygen memorize frequent environment observation
After frequent returns to the cavern the observant explorer found the urn.

(w for e
e for w)
sez jex the oen vie web cew dwg maw few seg hew ker wax peq yaw web ewe
he she way were waxed waves jewels bestowed powdered overwhelm deliberate
Everywhere jewels shone in the walls of this newly discovered wonderland.

5. Period-Space-Shift Combination

Backward. It grew rapidly. Kerosene burns clear. Quick actions.
Sail the seas. Heavy reinforcements. Very true. Yellow fish are
caught in the tropics. The X-ray was used. Idle hours had gone.

Study the corrections in this rough draft; then set it up as a two-page letter.   For the reference line on the second page, use the last style given on page 2 of Style Letter 8, page 112.   Date the letter November 26, 19—.

Union Electric Co.,
8792 Euclid Ave.
Cleveland, Ohio

Attention Mr. J. M. Mitchell, Vice-President

Gentlemen:

Your letter of November 21 relative to the method of handling accidents ~~which~~ results in injuries to employees of the Eastern Shore Power Company has been refered to me.

Since November 1, 1924, there has been in force in Maryland a workingmen's compensation Act, which provides for compulsory insurance against accident or the death of workmen engaged in extra hazardous employment; ~~and~~ abolishes the defenses of Contributory Negligence and Negligence of Fellow-Servants. Under the terms of the Act employers engaged in extra hazardous ~~employment~~ are compeled to insure ~~there~~ employees against accidents or death ~~by~~ one of the following three methods:

1. By insurance in the State Accident fund.

2. By insurance in an authorized Insurance Company.

3. Self-Insurance ~~by~~ furnishing proof to the Insurance Commission of ability to pay compensation.

When an employee is injured as a result of an accident, he is entitled to compensation regardless of the manner in which the accident occured, unless the injury was caused while the employee was in an intoxicated condition, was contributed to by his own willful misconduct, or was intentionaly inflicted. No compensation is allowed during the first two weeks of disability. Beginning with the fifteenth day, the employee is entitled to compensation at the rate of ½ of his average weekly wages during the continuance of the remainder of his disability, with a minimum allowance of five dollars ($5.00) and a maximum allowance of twelve dollars ($12.00) per week.

(Continued on page 154)

(1) season seasons seasoned seasoner seasonal seasoning seasonings
desperate desperado desperately desperation desperateness despair
negotiate negotiates negotiated negotiable negotiating negotiation
carpet carpets carpeted carpeting carpetbag carpenter carpentry

(2) point points pointed pointer pointers pointing pointed pointedly
back backs backed backer backing backslide backward backwardly
water waters watery waterer watered watering waterfall watercress
invite invites invited inviting invitation invitations invitingly

7. Common Letter Combinations

Use a line of 72 strokes.

(1) int dvi eiv ide ext ine att cho giv fro ein ego far eci dly dit glo buy
abl any ice mat how but the put led her has one hat let did lit man and
art com adv ban glo com ese jus eau ain uch com ade our nte ust ssi tiv

(2) war own lot fun but act add was pay low buy fur age can get wan red way
tha oun ten ore ies thi ous ame ber emb ing ord ion sed ely ily kin hav
emb ord rde one res sol eir ith fin don cho app att rit rig lea tcd pri

(3) pro pre pla ove mor pos num rew que res qui ber ame quo her ego lik ank
nam man ide ore tiv use kno not our col eci dly ide abl ese efa las amp
uni ont due you can the its did wit kin pre ext eze ith ame ber tio giv

8. Word Building

Use a line of 73 strokes.

(1) abbre abbre abbre via via via tion tion tion abbreviation abbreviation
abbreviation achieve achieve achieve ment ment ment achievement achievement achievement attain attain attain ment ment ment attainment attainment attainment ban ban ban quet quet quet banquet banquet banqueting

(2) bene bene bene fac fac fac tor tor tor benefactor benefactor benefactor
calen calen calen dar dar dar calendar calendar calendar cam cam cam
paign paign paign campaign campaign campaign dawn dawn dawn ing ing ing
dawning dawning dawning de de de vote vote vote devote devote devote

(3) equi equi equi nox nox nox equinox equinox equinox essen essen essen
tials tials tials essentials essentials essentials fare fare fare well
well well farewell farewell farewell dis dis dis guise guise guise disguise disguise disguise equal equal equal ize ize ize equalize equalize

Double-space this Agreement.   Insert the current month and year in the blanks
in the first two lines.   In the blanks at the end of the second paragraph, insert the
date of three months from today.   Use legal-size paper (8½ x 13), if available.   If
you do not have ruled legal paper, use plain paper.   Set the margin stops for a left
margin of 1½ inches and a right margin of ½ inch.   At the end type two ruled lines
for the signatures to the Agreement.   At the end of each line type (SEAL).   Leave two
double spaces between the lines.   (SEAL) should line up with the right writing margin.

ARTICLES OF AGREEMENT ← *3 spaces*

This AGREEMENT made th*is*   day of   nineteen
hundred and   , by and between Charles Winston Dunn,
/Cap. of the City of Sacramento, ~~in the~~ State of California, *party*
of the first part, and Henry Anderson, of the City of   *ALL CAPS*
Salem, ~~in the~~ State of Oregon, (witnesseth) as follows:

as set out below,
First, that the said party of the first part, for
and in consideration of the payments to be made by the
party of the second part, agrees to construct in good and
Spell out workman like manner for the party of the second part, on
a lot belonging to said party of the second part, known
as 477 Fulton St., in the City of Salem, one brick *Oregon,*
veneered dwelling house in accordance with *the* plans and *and finish*
specifications drawn by Robert L. Mason, Architect, and
here to annex as a part of this agreement, the building
is→ to be constructed of good materials in accordance with
said architect's specifications and to be ready for
A occupancy before the   day of *is* , one thousand
nine hundred and   .   *and substantial*

ready for occupancy
Second, that the party of the first part agrees
(further) that in the event of his failure to complete the
building by the above specified date, he will pay to the
party of the second part Ten Dollars ($10.00) as liqui-
dated damages for every day that the full completion of
this contract is delayed, *beyond the date specified.*

Third, that the party of the second part, in consideration thereof, agrees to pay to the said party of
the first part the sum of Twelve Thousand Dollars   */Cap*
($12,000.00) in lawful money of the United States, in
the following payment: (1) Two Thousand Dollars
($2,000.00) when the foundation, cellar, basement, and *are*
cement work ~~is~~ completed; (2) Two Thousand Dollars
C ($2,000.00) when the super structure is roofed, ~~and~~
terraced, (3) Two Thousand Dollars ($2,000.00) when the
glazing has been completed and approved by the Architect;   *and inclosed;*
and (4) the balance of Six Thousand Dollars ($6,000.00)
when the building ~~is~~ fully completed in accordance with
the plans. *ALL CAPS*   *has been*   *and plastering have*

hereunto (In witness thereof), the parties to these presents
have set their hands and seals the day and year first
above written.   *and specifications as provided herein.*

WITNESSES:

152

g in gravi gener ator ator ator generator generator generator gravi
gravi gravi tate tate tate gravitate gravitate gravitate holly holly
holly hock hock hock hollyhock hollyhock hollyhock in in in augu augu
augu rate rate rate inaugurate inaugurate inaugurate inauguration

(5) inci inci inci dent dent dent incident incident incident jani jani jani
tor tor tor janitor janitor janitor jubi jubi jubi lee lee lee jubilee
jubilee jubilee keep keep keep sake sake sake keepsake keepsake keepsake kinder kinder kinder garten garten garten kindergarten kindergarten

(6) pul pul pul ver ver ver ize ize ize pulverize pulverize pulverize quo
quo quo ta ta ta tion tion tion quotation quotation quotation radi radi
radi cal cal cal radical radical radical right right right ful ful ful
rightful rightful rightful sad sad sad dle dle dle saddle saddle saddle

9. Special Finger Drills

First Finger Words.   Use a line of 70 strokes.

for fine find fond found fourth doctor foreign finally efforts folding
ration legion running getting singing religion everything registration
rain main raise remain restrain railroad complaint entertain mountains

Second Finger Words.

ere here were there where merely serene therefore sincerely references
dock rose dose acid rock lock cock edit kite diet tied vied died cider
editor scheme inches caused excite docile eleven dances priced schemed

Third Finger Words.

loss pass list lest boss aster press lesson session possible associate
took watt supply sudden summon support witness written suppose lowered
extra except expect extreme expense exports express examine experience

Fourth Finger Words.

maps quip play pale pans ants hazy pall poll park quad papa opal quiz
braze zone squat space quasi razes hazel Japan heaps pails panel quaff
pots hopper pop potter pot pepper sipped zip quaint equips quail roped

10. Left-hand and Right-hand Words

Left-hand Words.

brass bears braces braggart bread brevet bracer bedded beast best beef
caste cafe cartage career cages carves cases caw cab casts cadets card
deeds debate detracts decades detects Dexter drew desecrate devastates

Right-hand Words.

in on pin ohm ply pop pulp plum poppy pinon opium pinion polyp opinion
upon union nun jolly Jill Polk Johnny pumpkin moon Hilo Lulu Honolulu
pull pump pink puppy Phillippi pip pippin plop poky pompon pool poplin

This problem consists of the first part of a manuscript. Study the corrections carefully; then write the manuscript with double spacing—not with single spacing. Leave a margin of 1½ inches at the top and sides and a margin of 1 inch at the bottom. Number the second page; place the notation –2– in the center about ½ inch from the bottom of the sheet.

Promotion and How It is Won (center)

~~Are you looking for PROMOTION?~~

There are three things that a business man *[or not]* takes into account in deciding whether, a worker should be promoted. Those three things are the *(1.)* accuracy with which the person does his work, the *(2)* amount of work he turns out, and *(3)* his general attitude. ¶ In business, a piece of work is either right or wrong. The worker is judged by ~~the~~ results ~~of his work~~. It is not a question of how hard he tries, *[it is taken by someone else]* In school, we may be given credit for effort, but in business, effort that does not bring results has no value. ¶ When you think you should have an increase in salary, ask yourself whether the work you do is accurate. ~~When our work must be checked all the time, we have to pay for that checking.~~ When every word that a typist writes must be checked, she is bound to get less pay for her services than the one who ~~has taught herself to~~ checks her own work before it leaves her. *[is given to]* *[always]* *(Have you taught yourself to check your own work?)*

Accuracy, however, is not the whole story. *[can]* you must be able to turn out work in volume. Business is done for a profit. The business that does not make a profit can not long endure. The company that sold the ~~machine~~ *[typewriter]* on which you are writing did so because it ~~wanted~~ to make a profit on the sale. Businessmen expect to make a profit on the service of their workers, as well as on the products ~~that~~ they sell. It is the person who can turn out accurate work in sufficient volume to make his services profitable who is ~~entitled to receive~~ *[selected for]* promotion. That work must be done right the first time. A letter which has to be written over ~~results in~~ *[causes]* waste of time and paper. ¶ The third ~~matter~~ *[factor]* you need to bear in mind is your attitude toward your work, ~~and~~ toward the other ~~people~~ *[Employees]* in the office. The people who do good work are the people who enjoy their work. If you look forward to each days work, you may be *[eagerly]* sure that you are on the right road. *However, If* you face your daily tasks with dread, resolve to change your mental attitude or seek some other kind of work ~~where~~ *[in which]* you can find joy. *[and toward the public.]*

151

craters uphill cabbages pill beeswax onlook berates plum caves poppy
drawers plum creeds pool cascades onion breezes oil caterer pony crab
olio beater Ohio cataracts pump caresses pomp crazed union cares hymn

11. Capital Letters

Line of 65 strokes.

(1)   Africa Hawaii Bulgaria Indiana Czechoslovakia Japan Denmark Iowa
Kentucky Europe Latvia Florida Manchukuo Germany Nebraska Rumania
Quebec Ontario Saskatchewan Utah Texas Yugoslavia Virgin Islands
West Indies Connecticut Oklahoma Estonia Mexico Switzerland Idaho

(2)   Here are odd names of actual towns within our own United States:
Tombstone, Arizona; Angel's Camp, California; Joy, Nebraska; Blondy,
Tennessee; Chilly, Idaho; Persist, Oregon; and Nanty Glo, Pennsylvania.

(3)   More Odd Names: Cure All, Missouri; Two Dot, Montana; Cathlamet,
Washington; Turkey, North Carolina; Straw, Montana; Mode, Illinois;
Happyland, Minnesota; Finger, Tennessee; Lingo, Missouri; Silverstreet,
South Carolina; and Nankipooh, Georgia.

12. Double Letter Combinations

Line of 70 strokes.

(1)   errs abbe wood lees will yell zoom bass till root seep doom fees ally
jolly scoff tarry cress whoop yucca Aaron abbot affix baggy banns
jenny joggle matted mellow noodle obsess occupy ratter sienna babble
hassock immense slipper nominee offense pennate quitter raccoon immerse
arrogate confetti galleons quarrels terrible vignette yearbook rattling

(2)   The immediate appointment of a receiver is recommended so that the
assets may not be dissipated. Misstatements and exaggerations already
current merely add to the difficulties and embarrass the management.
The collateral supplied when the accommodation notes were issued has
appreciated in value.

(3)   In our discussions we found that the irregularities were confined
to the Connecticut and Massachusetts territory. Additional evidence
of the effect of the new tariff rates, which was suppressed on former
occasions, has been accumulated. The receivers can carry on the
business without interruption until the necessary reorganization has
been effected.

Dear Sir:

It appears that a large proportion of the drafts received at this point for collection are drawn "with collection charges," ~~and~~ exchange and and the parties on whom these drafts are drawn refuse almost invariably to pay their exchange or collection charge. We are thus forced to return at least three-fourths of all drafts received unpaid at our own expense thereby causing a loss ~~aggregating amounting to~~ hundreds of dollars each year. We can see no good reason why we should be obliged to act as collection agents for wholesale merchants of the trading centers in helping them to collect their ~~passed~~ past due accounts at a loss to ourselves and without just compensation for our services. We have, therefore, adopted the following rules regarding collections, to which we shall strictly adhere after this date:

Rule 1.   On all items whether drawn "with exchange" or "with exchange and collection charges" or not, a collection charge of one-tenth of one per cent will be made and deducted from the remittance. Rule 2.   On items returned unpaid for any cause whatever, a charge of $.25 will be made to cover the cost of presenting, stamps, recording, etc. Rule 3.   Items sent for acceptance and return must be accompanied by a fee of $.25 for services, stationery, postage, etc.

Your careful observance of these rules in the future will be appreciated.

Respectfully yours,

Type slowly and evenly, with quick strokes; relax after each stroke. Each drill stresses a certain letter. Every letter of the alphabet is used in writing the words in each drill. Difficult letter combinations are stressed in the words. Reading and concentration play a large part in your typing. These drills will help you to keep your attention on the copy. Line of 65 strokes.

A   aerodrome aggrandize alabaster alienate amalgamation anecdote apocalypse aptitude arbitration ascertain Atlanta audaciously

B   bicarbonate blandishment boracic brazen bungalow by-product blaze bedabble bedazzle absorbent by-word debenture globule go-between

C   calcareous calculative capitalization commerce ceremonial checks connect cynical Czechoslovak consequence columns crystallizes

D   dedicated Dixie divulged dungeon disdained dwindled dynamic died declining depended disadvantages drudged divide debated deadened

E   ejaculate elderly emulsion encyclopedia epigram equilateral aces estimate estimated eucalyptus evangelist exchequer been eyelashes

F   fallibility fellowship Filipino flexible forestation fray forest fragmentary fumigate four-footed frightful fix fixation failures

G   Galilean geranium gigantic glycerin gorgeous grammatical Gresham grievous gregarious galvanize gurgle aggregating gagging grading

H   height hold humanity hydrochloric hydrometer hymnal hyssop ashes hydraulic husband hush ahead knighthood phonograph exhibitions

I   Iberian ideal idealism ignoramus ignorantly illiterate imitated immaculate inadequate infinitesimal irremediable Isthmian itemize

J   jack-o-lantern jasmine jealousy Jersey jitney journalist justice Jupiter justify jubilant juxtaposition January adjust injudicious

K   knickknack bookkeeping kodak kalsomine keeping khaki kilometers knavish linked tricky knock rink mink Nanking sinker stack back

L   lackadaisical leatherette lineage logarithm lubricate luxuriance landscape location lovely lull mull legalize excellence evolution

M   malevolence measurement metamorphosis migratory monumental music municipality mystification metaphysics pyramid mummy dump murmur

N   neutrodyne nineteen never national monkey wrench monitor portend nunnery nonsense nightingale bourn communication henna touching

O   occasion organization operations overlap October octave Olympia o'clock occupation nought notorious drool orthodox opposition

72

Read over the letter below and note all the changes; then type it in the form shown.   Use today's date instead of the date given in the letter.   Make two carbon copies.   On these copies type this notation below the identifying marks:

cc Mr. Charles Goodwin

The notation "cc" means *carbon copy*.   It is one of the Minor Parts of a business letter given in the Summary of Minor Parts and Placement, page 86, and illustrated in Instructional Letter B, page 88.

After removing the carbon copies from the typewriter, put a checkmark after the word "Goodwin" on one of the carbons.   This checkmark indicates that this carbon copy is to be mailed to Mr. Goodwin; the unchecked carbon copy is to be retained for the office files.

Address envelopes for the two outgoing letters—one to Mr. Johnson and one to Mr. Goodwin. Use the following address on Mr. Goodwin's envelope: Mr. Charles Goodwin   Tractor Sales Company   Battle Creek, Michigan.

October 14, 19--

Mr. C. F. Johnson
Bloomingdale, Michigan

Dear Sir:

We are glad to know that you are considering the

~~We beg to acknowledge receipt of~~ *Thank you for* your letter of
October 12 ~~making inquiry with regard to~~ purchasing ~~of~~
a larger size tractor than your present Model "W"
which you ~~purchased~~ *bought* three years ago.
We are ~~today~~ writing ~~to~~ *Spell out* *& Service* our distributor in your
territory, the Tractor Sales Company, Battle Creek,
Michigan ~~asking~~ Mr. ~~Chas~~ Goodwin, the manager of
that company, ~~to~~ call on you ~~and~~ discuss the matter *in detail.* *we feel sure, will* *to* *immediately*

When Mr. Goodwin ~~calls on~~ *visits* you, we ~~trust that~~ *are certain* you
will be able to make a satisfactory arrangement
~~whereby~~ you will become the owner of a late model
Cletrac *ALL CAPS* *by which*
If we can be of *further* service to you in any way, please
feel free to call on us.

mutually

Very truly yours,

CLEVELAND TRACTOR COMPANY

J. W. Mason, Sales Department

JWM:PYL

149

papyrus stop pamphlet participant parliament pronounce precarious

Q   qualify quitter quick quit quill queen quiz quadrangle quotation
Quaker lacquer liquor quarter quartermaster requisition required

R   Raphael rearrange racketeer require rarefy Rubicon romancer irate
shamrock river four reflex revere remark rubber requiem riparian

S   seasons sepsis squalls master sassy jasper isosceles isthmus sail
Israel issue restless repasts cessation administers sixty wastes

T   Tibet tutelage tzarina transatlantic tonsillitis thyroid flight
thrifty twelfth night batter tentative taxidermist taciturnity

U   injure unsound judge under ultramarine unalloyed unsuited unity
jujube utterance stumble humor humbug asunder adjust unnaturally

V   Victoria valuable vacuum valedictorian vivisect volunteer value
valvular advertise avert wavered savior Zouave lucrative vessel

W   Wolverene wrangle swift waver window wealth withdrawn waltzing
wattmeter willowy wrong aware when wreck whistle wayward wilted

X   X-ray six mix mixture xylograph extract box lax oxidized axioms
exact exert xylophone expiate exquisite examination text expend

Y   Yankee yearly yearling candy Friday Monday February July lying
youthful yuletide kindly simply Yale Yaqui scullery scythe Yates

Z   zero maze quiz zenith zigzag zealot razor blaze zephyr zone size
Zulu blizzard benzene zestful zwieback zoology glazes azure doze

14. Special Stroke Control Drills

Type these words slowly, with your attention on the "feel" of each arc stroke.
Make the stroke quickly; then relax.   Line of 70 strokes.

A   practice personally came have whereas past goal having years many was
essay explain certain insane amphibian whatever real ears stamped bad

B   better bunch desirable brushes windbags absorbing black maybe obeyed
observed debt cub hunchback bore by abase baffle baby fable vibration

C   acquittal count conception necessary across actually vicious technical
court Concord concealed caused accuse actress acquired acted concisely

D   Detroit stood develop and done board started burdens stated dart dared
word detract do devoid jaded quid odorless definite advise divide dire

E   Los Angeles shaped apple get three concerned progress achievement the
considered whether where order water anywhere foe's personal indelible

Dear Mr. Merton:

I received your good letter and confess my interest in aviation, but I am not able to consider a plane at present.

A few fellows here have asked me to find out the cost of chartering a five-place plane from Washington to Memphis about the 20th of December. While the possibilities of the trip depend very largely upon on the expense, I shall appreciate any interest you may show in the matter.

When I am next in your city, I shall hope to have the pleasure of meeting you personally.

I may   Sincerely yours,

Mr. F. H. Merton
Asst. Base Manager
Curtiss-Wright Flying Service
Baltimore, Md.

aftermath falsify rafter affectionate loaf Falstaff leafed favor fear

G-H-I yielding harbor retaining fatigue have without worthwhile either will
points higher gash inhibit engaged restraining engineer Westminster is

J-K-L speak thinking undoubtedly alone also school until animals along tell
level barrel bail look ordinarily justly judge adjust Joe jury likely

M famine met moment company America meat companies tamed aimed mammals

N imitation certain envelopes ant crown can finally young whenever anger
nunnery enemy animate annoy mansion conflicting nickel ounce shan't an

O Mayflower one those before forming long not choice of custom opponent
opposition whom environment knows out to point woman towns grown none

P-Q liquor squab lacquer aqua squalid bequest parts wiped scrap product
speed wisps expressed description apart apex sprint stamp palpitation

R Royal sure or Germany par janitor razor quire liver paper recurs other
seer general operate correct course rarer servant parked rhetoric airs

S asserts student's last surrounding pessimist possibilities shapes sty
sketches state course surroundings makes toes Communist custom duties

T tantrum attempt that action interesting short Connecticut maintain to

U-V-W few wayward mellow temperature twist knew fatigue up flaws urgent we
Sweden twill twilight valve know Grover move westward vocal availing

X-Y-Z zero luxurious you your dry busy Pizarro usualness sphinx zone extra
lazy matrix excite utilize hymn zephyr Zinnia waxed expect zest azure

15. Remedial Drills

The following lines of drills are based on letter strokes often confused.   In the
first two lines, a and s were confused in the words which form the drill.
Concentrate on your typing.   Make each stroke stand out.   Line of 68 strokes.

1 (a—s) grasp base traps paints sails says state small pass cases assists
He paints the sails of the state ship and assists with the cases.

2 (b—v) brave weaver behave behavior behoove believe beverage verb voted
It behooves all to believe in the behavior of the brave weavers.

3 (s—c) since locks comes silence consider necessary speech across cost
Since justice of speech is considered necessary, all are silenced.

4 (d—k) Dakota knuckled dark lacked disks sparked dirk curds disembarked
Dark days followed the disembarking from the dusky wrecked bark.

5 (e—i) skill edit cite emit edict brief chief tried their given either
Please write your brief letter to the newly nominated fire chief.

The handwriting in this Balance Sheet, too, is superior.   Follow the general arrangement of the copy.   If you need to review the details of the procedure, refer to Application Exercise 10, page 131.

The Todd Manufacturing Co.
Balance Sheet
December 31, 19–

Assets

Current Assets:

Cash in Bank	10200.00	
Cash in Office	200.00	10400.00
Accounts Receivable	17500.00	
Less Reserve for Uncollectible Accts	350.00	17150.00
Inventories		
Finished Goods in Stock	8420.00	
Materials in Stock	9500.00	
Materials in Process	4200.00	
Labor on Materials in Process	1750.00	
Manufacturing Expense	1480.00	25350.00
Total Current Assets		52900.00

Fixed Assets:

Store Fixtures	500.00	
Office Furniture and Fixtures	500.00	1000.00
Small Tools		1800.00
Machinery	29000.00	
Less Reserve for Dep. of Machinery	1500.00	27500.00
Total Assets		83200.00

Liabilities

Current Liabilities:

Accrued Taxes – estimated		100.00
Accrued Labor		1200.00
Accounts Payable		6000.00
Dividends Declared		
Preferred Stock $25000 at 7%	1750.00	
Common Stock $25000 at 10%	2500.00	4250.00
Total Liabilities		11550.00

Capital Stock and Surplus:

Capital Stock outstanding		
Preferred	25000.00	
Common	25000.00	
	50000.00	
Surplus (Exhibit B)	21650.00	71650.00
Total Liabilities and Capital		83200.00

Fifty different strong men fought hard for their future fortunes.

7 (g—h)   good go bought ages grate given haggard agate habit house beheld
He beheld the good gardener holding a golden-hued agate in his hand.

8 (a—i)   rain raise remain restrain railroad entertain complaint mountains
Rain in the mountains raised the streams under the railroad bridges.

9 (l—o)   royalty lowed slower pagoda almost duplication jolly journal told
Our letter ought to pull replies. It holds an appeal to women.

10 (n—o)   another separation nobility starvation nothing information nobler
Another separation of the noble companies would mean starvation.

11 (v—c)   clever captive caravan carnival cane cavalry cavity vehicle vicar
The clever vicar went to a cherry carnival in a cavalry vehicle.

12 (a—z)   Mrs. Florenz K. Jacques expected Beverly and Benjamin Azelmann to
go with her to the Philharmonic concert at the Auditorium Theatre.

13 (s—x)   experienced extra sixty. Sixty days were spent by experienced
workers in waxing the floors of these six expensive seaside homes.

14 (mb—mp) timber impassible resembles incomparable compelled example imbibed
The timber was an impassible barrier that compelled a return tramp.

15 (r—a)   awarded eradicate traits carpenter literal guarantee contract cart
The carpenter guaranteed his contract if awarded the artist's work.

16 (a—z)   The Felt & Tarrant Manufacturing Company makes the Comptometer, a
machine exceedingly beneficial to the majority of quick and zealous
office workers.

17 (c—x)   Extra care can well be exercised in boxing the many-colored wax
dripless candles which the express company will carry to Bixby.

16. Difficult Word Drills

Line of 65 strokes.

(1)   directions directed stereotyped stereopticon transferred transits
transitional dictated dictator emphasize emphasis request requiem
objectional objectives quantity quality excesses excessive action

(2)   zealous religious rebellious zeal religion rebels geographies ace
geography beauties beauty adventurous advantageous adventuresome
advantages seemed seams seem seam teems teams team gleams gleamed

(3)   discovered recovered discovering picturesque picturesqueness
rebuilding landing demand demanding builds lands simply lately
simple late later tremendous courageous tremble courage decide

(4)   deciduous decide decision explorations relations explore related
starvation starving starved pecuniary peculiar purple perplexing
parentheses parenthesis proposition preposition underscored part

Problem 1

The handwriting of this letter is superior. Type the letter in the double-spaced, indented style. Estimate or count the number of words. Make a carbon. Use the current date instead of the date shown. For the heading, type your own address above the date in the following style:

570 Broadway Terrace
Cedar Rapids, Iowa
October 5, 19--

October 5, 19—

Mr. George White, Sales Manager,
Holden Hardware Co.,
Philadelphia, Pa.

Dear Mr. White:

I am enclosing an order from the Jackson Construction Company. This order was placed by Mr. E. L. Mason, Construction Superintendent. The items listed on the order are urgently needed, and I have promised an early delivery.

Business is improving, I am glad to say, and I expect to get good orders from the Jensen Supply Company and from a number of our customers in this territory.

Very truly yours,

146

composed legible legibility developed development greater grater
signature signet grammatically grammar indelible indelibly India

(6)   acknowledge advertising application appreciated arrangements
association convenience cooperation examination informational
interesting merchandise university absolutely settlement zero

17. Common Word Drills

(1)   address advance advised against allowed already anxious arrange
carried covered catalog certain charged charges college company
expense express feeling follows forward freight friends furnish

(2)   practice promptly property purchase question received recently
Saturday separate shipment shipping somebody standard teachers
trusting vacation whatever yourself attached building approval

(3)   requested returning secretary enclosing equipment everybody
following forwarded gentlemen immediate important including
insurance knowledge mentioned afternoon answering attention

(4)   available beautiful beginning carefully certainly character
committee condition delivered September shipments wonderful
situation something sometimes statement surprised therefore

18. The Hyphen Stroke

Hyphenated Words. Line of 70 strokes.

well-read ex-governor left-handed labor-saving self-control five-ton
ten-gallon measure right-thinking self-respecting half-hearted 5-story
house follow-up letter far-reaching disease-producing self-supporting.

Word Division. Line of 70 strokes.

bene-fit capi-tal hesi-tate sepa-rate con-ven-ience privi-lege very
speci-men para-graph resi-dences com-para-tive choco-late tele-phone
medi-tate defi-cit change-able forti-eth serv-ice-able cer-tifi-cate

edi-tion ego-tism elas-tic emo-tion equal obe-di-ent uni-son amounts
bony many aban-doned able acres afraid agent eclipse eject against
apart-ment elec-tric glad-den foot-ball rai-ment rain-fall shrap-nel

19. Difficult Combinations

Quotation Marks and Capitals. Line of 70 strokes.

"Standard Transcribing Guide" "Good Housekeeping" "Zebra's Stripes"
Starting "God's Answer" "White Butterflies" "Lavender and Old Lace"

Division 7—Rough Drafts

Every typist is often called on to convert longhand into typewriting and to copy typewritten material that has been corrected or altered. Such work calls for a high degree of care and intelligence. In order to do a good job in typewriting from longhand, you must read and understand the copy you are writing. It is an unfortunate fact that much writing done by business and professional men who employ typists leaves a good deal to be desired on the score of legibility. You will do well, therefore, to familiarize yourself with handwriting written under pressure, so that you may decipher correctly any copy that is given to you to typewrite.

Typewriting in which longhand changes and corrections have been made is called "rough draft." You will need to become familiar with the marks ordinarily used in correcting typewritten copy. Without that knowledge you will be unable to typewrite rough drafts in correct form.

Marks Used in Correcting Typewritten Copy

MARK	MEANING	EXAMPLE
Cap	Use capital instead of small letter.*	correct use of the *Cap* english language
l.c.	Use small letter instead of capital.* (The letters *l. c.* are abbreviations for *lower case*.)	use of the English *l.c.* language
⌒	Close up (no space).	Some⌒times we are told
∧	Insert at the place indicated.	will∧make∧proficient
∽	Transpose; that is, write the second word first and the first word second.	have (stated already) that such have (stated already) that such
/——	Leave out. The short diagonal is struck through a single letter. A line is drawn through a long word or a series of words.	A̷ almost complete stock of
/	Leave space between words. (A long diagonal line.)	It may/be true that
⌒	Change position of the circled word as indicated.	the/purpose of this (whole) book
¶	Begin a new paragraph.	are as follows: ¶In your letter
No ¶	No paragraph at the place indicated.	No¶ All checks will be signed

*Sometimes a short diagonal line is struck through the letter in the copy, and the correct form—capital or small letter—written above.

Illustration 53
Marks Used in Correcting Typewritten Copy

145

Just then the bell tolled. Probably. Food was plentiful. Long
rendezvous. For that week they were alone. Did it. Called him.
Every man was astonished. Barren hills lay before. Henry looked

20. Alphabetic Paragraphs

Each paragraph contains every letter of the alphabet. Strive to increase your
speed and accuracy at each writing. Use a line of 70 strokes.

Paragraph 1   The warriors rode three times round the village; and as each noted   67
champion passed, the old women would scream out his name to honor   133
his bravery and to excite the emulation of the younger warriors. Little   206
urchins, not quite two years old, followed the warlike pageant with   274
glittering eyes and gazed with eager admiration at the majestic heroes   345
of their tribe.   360

Paragraph 2   Hour after hour passed away as I waited wearily and anxiously. The   68
loose bark dangling from the trunk just behind me flapped to and fro in   140
the wind, and the mosquitoes kept up their drowsy hum; but other than   210
these there was no sight or sound of life throughout the hazy, burning   281
landscape. The sun rose higher and higher, until I knew that it must   351
be very nearly noon.   371

Paragraph 3   It has been said that a certain species of ape in Africa is able to express   76
his wants and desires by means of three hundred sounds or words. It is   148
very hard for one to realize the truth of this statement. It is an equally   224
difficult task for anyone to understand why so many people get along   293
on just as few words as possible. Learn at least three new words each   364
day and learn to use them correctly.   400

Paragraph 4   Most of us depend to a great extent upon our speech—which is just a   69
name for our ability to express ourselves in words—to make our way   137
through this maze of life. Yet, knowing this fact, most of us quit the   209
study of words and self-expression very early in our education. Re-   277
member to learn at least three new words each day and learn to use   344
them intelligently.   363

21. Alphabetic Paragraph Drills

Each of these paragraphs has been specially constructed to emphasize a particular
letter stroke. Each one also contains every letter of the alphabet. Use a different
paragraph each period. Double-space. Line of 70 strokes.

A

I learned a valuable lesson in concentration from an expert   60
billiard player. I watched this player in amazement as he made many   129
long runs. It was real magic to watch those balls quickly parade   195
about that table at his command. Later I asked what made a billiard   264
player. He answered, "Practice, learning the shots and angles, and   332
greatest of all, the art of concentration." And so in whatever you   400
attempt, practice carefully, learn all you can about the particular   468
job, trade, or profession you take up, and keep your attention on what   539
you are doing.   553

When the amount of the payroll has been ascertained, the payroll clerk prepares a sheet showing the denominations of the bills and coins needed to make up the payroll envelopes.   Such a sheet is called a Cash Distribution Sheet.

Application Exercise 29.   Prepare a Cash Distribution Sheet, with a carbon, from the data given below.   Use a full-size sheet folded in half vertically, and type across the 4¼-inch width. Double-space.   Plan the 4-column tabulation before you begin work.   Use the date of Saturday of this week instead of "November 14, 19—."

Application Exercise 30.   You will now prepare a Cash Distribution Sheet based on the payroll which you prepared in Exercise 28.   Follow the directions given in Exercise 29, but use the date of last Saturday.   Begin work only after you have planned the tabulation.

LOWELL MANUFACTURING COMPANY
Lowell, Massachusetts

November 14, 19—

Number	Denom.	Dollars	Cents
	Hundreds		
	Fifties		
	Twenties		
15	Tens	150	
7	Fives	35	
	Twos		
21	Ones	21	
9	Halves	4	50
5	Quarters	1	25
13	Dimes	1	30
3	Nickels		15
25	Pennies		25
	Total	213	45

DONNELLEY MACHINE COMPANY
Newark, New Jersey

Number	Denom.	Dollars	Cents
	Hundreds		
	Fifties		
	Twenties		
13	Tens	130	
8	Fives	40	
	Twos		
15	Ones	15	
7	Halves	3	50
8	Quarters	2	
11	Dimes	1	10
5	Nickels		25
24	Pennies		24
	Total	192	9

Books probably began in the days when tribesmen laboriously inscribed characters and pictures on the bare, black cave walls, or upon tablets of stone. A later form of book-making came into being when the Hebrews inscribed the books of the Bible on sheepskin scrolls. Modern books and textbooks are the bequests of the ages. It is difficult to realize that the beautiful bindings, the durable paper, the bright pictures, and the legible type are contributions made to us just within the last few centuries.

63
134
206
277
347
414
484
510

C

It is the conclusion of the directors of great public corporations that, in considering the qualifications of applicants for clerical places or other positions in offices, character counts for very much more than any other factor. You can cram conscientiously and zealously on subjects in classes at school, yet lack the character to carry on with exceptional success in corporation offices. Education in subjects without education in character is almost completely worthless.

67
141
213
282
350
422
480

D

Far north beyond the border of the ''Land of the Midnight Sun'' has long lived an unappreciated friend. During the last decade this friend, the reindeer, has gradually received the attention justly due him. In this land of cold winds and deadly blizzards the kindly reindeer has furnished food and hides to the Eskimos. There is no more speedy runner than the reindeer. In races against dogs, reindeer have proved that dogs must step down as second raters when it comes to drawing sleds over the icy surfaces. During fogs or blinding blizzards, reindeer have a weird sense of direction. Depending upon this unexplained sense of direction, they can hold to a due course from dawn to dark, running ''blind.''

66
139
210
279
352
421
489
557
629
700
708

E

The demand for ever greater speed in these modern days is responsible for the restlessness in business life and even in the life at home. Huge steam engines are placed on side tracks to be razed or used no more because they are unable to move passenger or freight trains with sufficient speed or at low enough cost. Majestic barkentines, once believed the fastest of deep sea vessels, lie weather-beaten in the quagmire of estuaries to waste and crumble--a sacrifice to the greater speed of the steam vessel. Each year faster automobile models appear, and the slower makes are replaced. In typewriting, the average speed has risen each year, due largely to better teaching methods and greater efforts to excel through more accurate typewriting.

65
133
205
273
341
410
477
548
620
690
749

In manufacturing plants where employees are paid by the hour, it is necessary to prepare a weekly payroll. A payroll is a tabulation which gives the names of the employees, the number of hours they worked each day, the total hours for the week, the hourly rate of pay, and the total wage for the week. Payrolls are usually prepared on printed forms.

Application Exercise 27. From the following data, prepare a payroll for the Lowell Manufacturing Company, Lowell, Mass., for the week ending Saturday of this week. Single-space. Use Form 30.

Name	M	T	W	Th	F	S	Total Hours	Rate	Total Wages
Atkinson, Joseph H.	7	7	8	6	6	4	38	.47	17.86
Berman, J. W.	8	5	6	7	7	4½	37½	.47	17.63
Brighton, Henry C.	7	7	5	8	6	4½	37½	.45	16.88
Creighton, William F.	6	7	7	7	6	4½	37½	.49	18.38
Curtis, T. F.	7	7	7	7	6	3½	37½	.53	19.88
Custer, Charles	7	7	8	8	6	5	41	.53	21.73
Denton, Frederick	8	7	7	7	6	4	39	.48	18.72
Grant, Ralph H.	7	7	7	6	7	4	38	.57	21.66
Hunter, W. S.	7	7	7	7	7	4	39	.57	22.23
Jenkins, A.	7	7	7	7	7	4½	39½	.57	22.52
McMonigle, F. R.	4	6	7	4	6		27	.38	10.26
Ringwalt, Frank	7	3		5			15	.38	5.70
									213.45

Application Exercise 28. You will next prepare a payroll for the Donnelley Machine Company, Newark, New Jersey, for the week ending on Saturday of this week. Use Form 31. Single-space.

Write the surnames of the employees first, followed by their given names or initials. The letters *M, T, W, Th, F,* and *S* stand for *Monday, Tuesday, Wednesday, Thursday, Friday,* and *Saturday,* respectively. *To* stands for *Total Hours;* *R* for *Rate;* and *W* for *Total Wages.* Before you begin, type the names of the employees in alphabetical order. Use a separate sheet. Alphabetize according to the last names, and arrange the names on the payroll alphabetically.

Alfred W. Higgins: *M,* 7; *T,* 7; *W,* 7½; *Th,* 7; *F,* 5; *S,* none; *To,* 33½; *R,* .46; *W,* 15.41.

G. W. Aarons: *M,* 7; *T,* 7½; *W,* 6; *Th,* 7; *F,* 6½; *S,* 5; *To,* 39; *R,* .46; *W,* 17.94.

George W. Ransome: *M,* 7; *T,* 7½; *W,* 6; *Th,* 7; *F,* 7; *S,* 4; *To,* 38½; *R,* .38; *W,* 14.63.

R. A. Short: *M,* 7; *T,* 6; *W,* 7; *Th,* 7½; *F,* 7; *S,* 5; *To,* 39½; *R,* .44; *W,* 17.38.

T. C. Lambert: *M,* 6; *T,* 6; *W,* 7½; *Th,* 7; *F,* 7½; *S,* 4; *To,* 38; *R,* 40; *W,* 15.20.

C. E. Erickson: *M,* 6; *T,* 7; *W,* 7; *Th,* 6½; *F,* none; *S,* none; *To,* 26½; *R,* .41; *W,* 10.87.

R. T. Tremain: *M,* 7; *T,* 7; *W,* 6; *Th,* 7½; *F,* 7; *S,* 5; *To,* 39½; *R,* .43; *W,* 16.99.

H. J. McClain: *M,* 7; *T,* none; *W,* none; *Th,* 7; *F,* 7½; *S,* 5; *To,* 26½; *R,* .44; *W,* 11.66.

C. R. McReynolds: *M,* none; *T,* 7; *W,* 7½; *Th,* 7; *F,* 7; *S,* 5; *To,* 33½; *R,* .48; *W,* 16.08.

Charles W. Weldon: *M,* 7; *T,* 7½; *W,* 7; *Th,* 7½; *F,* 7; *S,* 5; *To,* 41; *R,* .47; *W,* 19.27.

Harry L. Wickersham: *M,* 7; *T,* 7; *W,* none; *Th,* 7½; *F,* 7; *S,* 5; *To,* 33½; *R,* .47; *W,* 15.75.

Harry W. Decker: *M,* 7; *T,* 7; *W,* 7½; *Th,* 7; *F,* 7½; *S,* 5; *To,* 41; *R,* .51; *W,* 20.91.

The total amount of the payroll is $192.09.

Of all nature's moods, fog is the one most feared by flyers and seafaring men alike. Facing a wall of fog afloat on the sea, or flying far above or through a floating fog curtain, the feeling is just the same--one of vague fear and helplessness. When fog fares forth above the surface of land or sea, the fastest ship or flying plane is required to slacken its pace through the haze to a safe, slow speed. Fortunately, fog is usually experienced after or during a period of gentle winds.

G

Each year our good old globe gives up to diggers for gold great sums of the golden metal. This giving of gold by the earth has gone on for ages. The experienced old "sourdough" miner still gets his "grubstake" and jogs along the roads with his good burro, heading for the great rugged hills or for the gold-bearing gulches of the desert. Along some of our rivers, dredges dig into gold-bearing gravel, finding gold in large enough quantities to give a profit. Huge quartz mines, running night and day through the years, give gold ore from ledges a mile deep in the earth. Gigantic stamp mills grind the ore, and the gold is given over to its many uses.

H

Hercules, journeying along a narrow highway, met with a hideous beast that threw up its head and threatened him. Without fear, the hero struck the beast with his extremely heavy club and thought he had frightened it away. The huge animal, however, to the astonishment of Hercules, was now three times as large as before and more threatening. Hercules thereupon hit the beast harder than before, but the harder and quicker the blows the more huge and frightful the beast grew, until it filled the highway. Pallas then appeared. "Cease your blows. The monster's name is Strife. Let him alone and he will shrink to his former small size."

I

Life insurance deserves a fixed position as an important item in your financial plans. It is a serious risk to eliminate life insurance even in periods of financial adjustment or difficulty. If life insurance premiums require considerable sacrifice at times, this same insurance will be your firmest friend in an hour of direst necessity. Fifty years ago it was the opinion that the insured must die in order that his beneficiaries might realize from his insurance. The insured believed that his insurance could never benefit him. That opinion is no longer widely held. Life insurance as it is organized today is for the living!

the first of the month, nothing. Debits: 3d, 91.76; 7th, 4.84; 14th, 27.97; 23d, 117.84; 27th, 64.55. Credits: 15th, 91.76; 23d, 32.81; 28th, 117.84. Balance, 64.55.

(4) Lamborn Transfer Service, Wilmington, Del. Owed on the first of the month, 117.88. Debits: 3d, 269.85; 7th, 461.52; 12th, 116.97; 18th, 214.44; 25th, 316.92; 26th, 97.44; 27th, 17.10; 28th, 86.42. Credits: 10th, 387.73; 20th, 571.47; 25th, 214.44. Balance, 524.90.

Credit Memorandums

When a business house allows credit to a customer for returned or damaged goods, or for any other reason, a credit memorandum is sent to the customer. The heading of a credit memorandum carries the name and address of the company issuing it, as well as spaces for the date and the name and address of the person or organization that is to receive credit. Study Illustration 52.

The lower part of a credit memorandum form is often divided into three sections to provide for (1) the quantity or number of the items for which credit is being given, (2) the catalog descriptions, and (3) the extensions. Sometimes there is a separate column for the total. Credit memorandum forms are often printed in red.

Application Exercise 25. Use the two sheets in the workbook marked Form 28 to prepare credit memorandums from the following data.

(1) *To* **Mr. L. F. Marston, 619 Marshall St., Ilion, N. Y.** *Date:* the 10th of this month.

5 Football Bladders No. RSV @ .55, 2.75; **3 Head Helmets No. 4X** @ $4.80, 14.40; **3 Footballs No. 5FV** @ $4.20, 12.60; **5 Shoulder Guards No. 21T** @ $4.45, 22.25; **4 Morrill Nose Guards No. O** @ .90, 3.60; **Total, 55.60.**

(2) *To* **Mr. R. C. Wrightson, 1116 York St., Utica, N. Y.** *Date:* the 24th of last month.

5 Baseballs No. OJ @ $1.25, 6.25; **2 Catchers' Mitts No. 41** @ $4.25, 8.50; **4 Fielders' Gloves No. ECB** @ $6.25, 25.00; **3 pr. Leg Guards No. FG** @ $6.00, 18.00; **1 Catchers' Mask No. 3M**, $2.25, 2.25; **5 Bats No. 150** @ $1.25, 6.25; **Total, 66.25.**

Application Exercise 26. On the two sheets marked Form 29, prepare credit memorandums from the following data. Use today's date.

(1) **Jacobs Electrical Supply Company, 378 Lanvale Street, Oak Park, Ill.:** 4 UX-280 Rectifier Tubes @ $2.95, 11.80; 2 #100-B Cone Speakers @ $17.50, 35.00; 3 UY-224 A. C. Screen Grid Tubes @ $3.85, 11.55; 5 UX-201-A Radiotrons @ $1.32, 6.60. Total, 64.95.

(2) **Gary Radio Products Company, 614 Willard Street, Gary, Ind.:** 2 F-2-C Electric Dynamic Speakers @ $27.25, 54.50; 1 Model #755 set 60 cycle @ $118.00; 4 CX #345 Screen Grid Tubes @ $2.37, 9.48; 7 X #380 Screen Grid Tubes @ $2.22½, 15.58. Total, 197.56.

Credit Memorandum

Lancaster Sporting Goods Company

418-422 Fulton Street
Ilion, New York

To   Mr. L. F. Marston   Date September 10, 19--
     619 Marshall St.
     Ilion, N. Y.

We have CREDITED your account as follows:

Quantity	Description	Unit Price	Amount
5	Football Bladders No. RSV	.55	2.75
3	Head Helmets No. 4X	4.80	14.40
3	Footballs No. 5FV	4.20	12.60
5	Shoulder Guards No. 21T	4.45	22.25
4	Morrill Nose Guards No. O	.90	3.60
			55.60

Illustration 52
Credit Memorandum

Jonathan Jones, a jovial farmer, journeyed to a neighboring jurist, expressing great concern for an injury which, he said, had just been done. "One of your oxen," continued he, "has just been gored by an unlucky bull of mine, and I wish to know how to make adjustment for this injury." "Thou art a just Jonathan," replied the jurist, "and I adjure thee to adjust the injury by giving me one of your oxen in return." "Thy request is just," said Jonathan, "but--it was my mistake--it was your bull that killed my ox." The jurist realized that he was caught and tried to juggle his own judgment, but the jolly Jonathan held the jurist to his own idea of justice.

68
137
208
279
351
420
490
560
630
664

K

The old log blockhouse stood on a knoll overlooking the brink of the extremely steep bank of the Snake River. The dark waters of the Snake River helped to keep back bands of attacking Indians. If attackers struck at the front of the blockhouse, skillful marksmen quickly broke down the zest of the raiders. The ability of those hardy pioneers to adjust themselves to lurking dangers and to the dark days of discomfort and sickness was truly remarkable.

65
134
198
265
337
407
455

L

Let a man talk of himself. If you are an exceptional listener, he will feel that he likes you and enjoys your company. While the man talks, you will likely learn considerable about him. It is quite impossible to learn while you are talking about yourself, unless it is to learn that you talk too much. All salesmen should learn to talk less and to avail themselves of more excellent English, so that they may tell what they do tell in simple, clear language.

64
131
195
266
335
404
462

M

One man's success may be another's failure. One man may manage a mighty business and amass amazing amounts of money. Another man might turn his face from money and business to seek joy and contentment in the quiet of a farm or country life. Another may give attention to the writing of poems or narratives. To each man in turn, the chosen position of another might mean discontent, but many men of many minds are needed to accomplish the work that the world must have done.

66
137
206
278
343
413
477

N

Old Cannon Beach in northwestern Oregon is a region rich in legends. There are romantic narratives of Spanish explorers and galleons laden with jewels and golden doubloons--galleons that put in near shore to sink the coins in chests in the tunnel that runs under towering Haystack Rock. No one quite believes it, but the legend persists in affirming that the golden treasure is still in the tunnel, and on some extremely low tide a lucky one may gain it for his own. Cannon Beach gets its name from another legend built around the finding of an ancient cannon high up on the white quartz sands of the beach.

60
129
201
274
343
414
484
549
611

In addition to bills, business houses also mail statements of account to their customers. Such statements are sent—generally on or about the first of the month—to show the customer his balance at the beginning of the preceding month, together with his charges and credits during the month. When the account is itemized in that way, the customer is able to check it with his own records.

Application Exercise 23. Study Illustration 51; then prepare four statements from the following data. Use the sheets marked Form 23, 24, 25, and 26 in the workbook.

COLLEGIATE EQUIPMENT COMPANY
1786 BROADWAY
NEW YORK, N. Y.

To Mr. C. L. Frick   Date August 1, 19--
    1214 Center St.
    Yonkers, N. Y.

Date	Debits	Credits	Amount
Balance			
7/9	87.65		
7/15	21.46		
7/20	11.75		
7/27	11.86		
7/28	5.87		
7/21		109.11	
7/27		10.00	
			19.48

Illustration 51
Statement of Account

(1) From **Collegiate Equipment Company, 1786 Broadway, New York, N. Y.** *To* **C. L. Frick, 1214 Center St., Yonkers, N. Y.** Dated the first of this month.

No balance. Debits: on the 9th of the preceding month, 87.65; on the 15th, 21.46; 20th, 11.75; 27th, 11.86; 28th, 5.87. Credits: on the 21st, 109.11; 27th, 10.00. Balance, 19.48.

(2) From **Kahn's Sport Shop, 631 Center Street, Stockton, California.** *To* **Mr. A. L. Hudson, 312 Stuart St., Stockton, Calif.** Date the statement the first of this month.

Balance at the beginning of the preceding month, 5.67. Debits: on the 4th of the preceding month, 11.87; on the 10th, 22.98; 15th, 1.41; 24th, 9.62. Credits: on the 15th, 11.87; 20th, 22.98. Balance, 16.70.

(3) From **Hillendale & Sons, 624 Fourth Ave., Wilmington, Del.** *To* **Simmons & Browning, 146 Canal St., Chester, Pa.** Dated the first of last month.

Balance on the first of the month preceding the last month, 23.78. Debits: on the 5th of the month preceding the last, 35.76; on the 8th of that month, 87.65; on the 10th, 4.89; 17th, 54.63; 25th, 111.64; 27th, 9.17. Credits: on the 15th of that month, 100.00; 20th, 28.30; 25th, 110.00. Balance, 89.22.

(4) From **Melton Publishing Company, 2678 Prairie Avenue, Chicago, Illinois.** *To* **Remington Book Store, 1416 May St., Oak Park, Ill.** Dated the first of this month.

Balance on the first of the preceding month, 42.67; on the 3d, 8.76; 7th, 2.31; 12th, 34.67; 16th, 42.02; 17th, 1.41; 18th, 6.78; 25th, 2.34. Credits: on the 10th, 53.74; 20th, 76.69. Balance, 10.53.

Application Exercise 24. On the sheets marked Form 27, prepare four statements of account from the following data. These statements are all to be dated the first of next month. The dates given are, therefore, those of the current month.

(1) **Mr. K. W. Weyforth, 147 Ocean Ave., Dover, Del.** Owed on the first of the month, nothing. Debits: 4th, 17.68; 14th, 13.48; 24th, 17.80; 25th, 19.67; 27th, 26.78. Credits: 10th, 17.68; 25th, 25.00; last day of this month, 10.00. Balance, 42.73.

(2) **Mr. C. K. Strawbridge, 786 Willard St., Wilmington, Del.** Owed on the first of the month, 35.00. Debits: 4th, 24.17; 10th, 57.78; 14th, 78.67; 21st, 3.25; 26th, 5.78. Credits: 10th, 50.00; 20th, 50.00. Balance, 104.65.

Suppose, after you complete your course in school, you work eight hours a day in an office. You do the job just well enough to hold your position. You know you could do all your work in four hours if you really got down to honest toil. Such a condition of laxity cannot continue if you hope to move forward or secure a better position. Two roads are open to you. Go out for another place in which to work, or throw yourself into the job you hold. Look for other tasks you may do to increase your value to your employer.

P

Abject poverty was never meant to be part of the ideal plan of life. The ever-present problem is the perplexing puzzle of proper distribution, so that all people may have a proper portion of this planet's plentiful production. Quickly acquired wealth presents a more dangerous problem than poverty ever does. Being ''poor'' often supplies the motive power that brings position and deserved wealth to the one who was poor earlier in life.

Q

A large quantity of square lacquered cases was trucked from the quarter deck of the ''Queen Anne'' to the quay. The quay watchman quizzed the quiet quartermaster about the squall which the ''Queen'' had encountered near the equator. As severe as the squall had been, the vessel was adequately equipped to ride out the January gale. The sixty square lacquered cases had been squeezed below the quarter-deck, and the quality of their opaque finish was unharmed.

R

There are three rules to be remembered if you're preparing to enter retail selling or any other selling position. First, be sure your product is right. Second, try to present to your customer in an interesting manner the exact reasons why it is the right product. Third, remember your first sale to a prospect presents an opportunity to repeat with other sales in the future. Never try to force a visitor to your store to purchase an article which you feel fairly sure is not the right article to answer the buyer's need.

S

The steamer ''Siletz'' left San Francisco with a brisk south wind astern. As the ship sped before seas that swept over her decks, the engines drove the propellers full speed ahead. At six the next morning the second officer of the ship sighted the lightship just off the Columbia River bar below Astoria, Oregon. In spite of high seas the officers swung the steamer straight into the channel to cross the bar. They realized that some risk attended this course; but records are records and if the ship made Astoria without stopping outside the bar several hours on account of darkness and heavy seas, a new record would be made. Five hours would be cut from the old record.

81

Account No. K-67459

Date	Items	Purchases	Mdse. Returned or Cash Paid	Pay Last Amount in This Column
	Balance Brought Forward			118.87
19—				
—* 18	Hat	3.95		
	Shade	1.59		
	Lamp	1.95		
	Crib	10.95		
	Mattress	5.95		
	2 Sheets	1.38		
	Pillow	1.50		146.14
— 22	Cash		60.00	
	Spread	3.94		90.08

*Use the name of the current month.

(3) Mrs, Charles F. Franck Fairoaks, California Account No. 6924

Date	Items	Purchases	Mdse. Returned or Cash Paid	Pay Last Amount in This Column
19—	Balance Brought Forward			138.00
— 16	Cash		33.14	
	Shoes	2.95		
	Gloves	1.25		
	Suit	8.95		
	Pants	2.95		
	Cap	.50		
	3 Shirts	2.37		
	2 "	2.00		
— 22	Varnish	1.00		
	8 Hose	2.00		
— 23	2 Gowns	1.38		
	Shoes	5.00		
	Buckles	.50		135.71

(4) Harold C. Frommer 614 Pacific Avenue Sacramento, California Account No. 3675

Date	Items	Purchases	Mdse. Returned or Cash Paid	Pay Last Amount in This Column
19—				
— 16	1 Dress Shirt	3.00		
	2 Shirts	3.30		
	1 Tie	1.50		
	2 Collars	.70		
	1 Collar	.25		
— 22	1 Tie	.35		
	1 Overcoat	38.75		
	1 Suit	40.95		88.80

64
135
208
276
345
413
483
552
624

The steamer kept straight on toward the deep water close by the jetty. All went as expected until an irresistible current of outgoing tide and a strong cross wind took the bow of the boat and quickly turned the steamer almost across the tossing, dizzily moving waters of the channel. Three breakers struck the steamer. It lay like a stricken thing, seemingly at the mercy of the tide and waters. Then, again, the unexpected happened! The stern of the steamer was almost lifted out of the water, and the bow pointed down the channel. The steamer took a straight course out to sea and stayed out until the storm abated.

U

You must utilize every moment of your hour of typewriting if you expect to be an outstanding pupil and later a successful worker. Your urge to excel in this subject must cause you to be more zealous in all your studies. Acquire the habit of checking over your finished work in typing and in every other study. Such continued checking is surely one requisite in the achievement of success.

V

As two travelers were leaving a wood, one of the travelers picked up a heavy ax which lay upon the gravel. "See," he said to his companion, "I have found an ax." "Never say, 'I have found it,' " ventured the other traveler, "but 'We have found it.' We ought to have everything together." The first traveler, however, denied the request. In just about five minutes they heard the voice of the owner of the ax raving over its loss. "We are in for it," exclaimed the traveler who had the ax. "Nay," averred the second traveler, "say, 'I am in for it!'—never 'we.' You cannot give me a share in the danger."

W

When you wind your way into the Carlsbad Caverns in New Mexico, you journey into another world, a world weird and wondrous. You wander for awesome hours in this bewitched wonderland under the world you've known. When you quit the caves and walk back into the drab world of everyday things, you prefer for a short time the overhanging ceilings of fantastic shadowy design to the azure blue of skies and the fleecy white of moving clouds. You have experienced the spell of the caverns.

X

A speed of sixty words a minute is an excellent record for the average typist. However, each extra word which you acquire above sixty should be excuse for joy and exultation on your part. You must not type an excess of copy of extra easy context. Rather, choose exercises and text material of extra complex context. Easy copy should be a luxury if you wish to excel. Stick to exercises which will help you to achieve greater accuracy. Utilize every possible means to maintain approximately perfect work as you exercise greater speed.

4600 lbs. Cylinder Castings, .10, 460.00; 1400 lbs. Cylinder Head Castings, .12½, 175.00; 1804 lbs. Main Bearing Forgings, .10, 180.40; 6427 lbs. Flywheel Castings, .08, 514.16; 360 lbs. Flywheel Hub Cap Castings, .05, 18.00; 1050 lbs. Piston Castings, .07, 73.50; 200 lbs. Piston Rings, .25, 50.00; 288 lbs. Flange Coupling Castings, .05, 14.40; 290 lbs. Flange Coupling Castings, .06, 17.40; 510 lbs. Hand Hole Plate Castings, .05½, 28.05; 270 lbs. Bottom Plate Castings, .04, 10.80; 420 lbs. Exhaust Fitting Castings, .10, 42.00; 421 lbs. Exhaust Fitting Flange Castings, .10, 42.10. Total, 1625.81.

HALL & STEWART
The Leading Department Store
SACRAMENTO, CALIF.

To Mrs. F. C. Watkins
201 Montebello Street
Sacramento, California

Date October 25, 19--
Account No. 5067

PLEASE DETACH AND RETURN WITH YOUR CHECK.　　YOUR CANCELLED CHECK IS YOUR RECEIPT.

HALL & STEWART
SACRAMENTO, CALIFORNIA

FOR CUSTOMER'S USE

Paid_____　Check No._____

Date	Items	Purchases	Mdse. Ret'd or Cash Paid	Pay Last Amount in this Column
	Balance brought forward			23.09
19-- Oct. 11	Shoes	3.95		
21	Coat	5.00		
	2 Dresses	7.76		
	Dress	5.88		
22	Rain Cape	1.00		46.68

Illustration 50
Department Store Bill

Application Exercise 21. On the two billheads marked Form 21, prepare bills from the following data. Use today's date. Terms: 2/10.

(1) No. 1879; *To* **Springdale Athletic Association, 1110 Grant St., Ann Arbor, Mich.**

4 Basket Balls No. HSB $8.75, 35.00; 3 Basket Ball Bladders No. OBC .45, 1.35; 2 pr. Basket Ball Goals No. 6 $3.85, 7.70; 2 pr. Basket Ball Goal Nets No. GN $1.00, 2.00; 9 Worsted Shirts No. 7OS $1.90, 17.10; Total, 63.15.

(2) No. 1880; *To* **University Club, 498 West Adams St., Detroit, Mich.**

8 Reach Baseballs No. OJ .90, 7.20; 3 Catchers' Mitts No. 33 $5.65, 16.95; 4 Basemen's Mitts No. 4AB $5.75, 23.00; 2 Catchers' Masks No. 4OS $2.20, 4.40; 5 Old Hickory Bats Model G $1.85, 9.25; 5 Fielders' Gloves No. 10W $1.75, 8.75; Total, 69.55.

Application Exercise 22. Study Illustration 50; then prepare four monthly department store bills. Use the four billheads in the workbook marked Form 22. Date the bills the 25th of this month. Address an envelope for each bill.

(1) **Mrs. F. C. Watkins 201 Montebello Street Sacramento, California Account No. 5067**

19—	Balance Brought Forward		23.09
— 11	Shoes	3.95	
21	Coat	5.00	
	2 Dresses	7.76	
	Dress	5.88	
22	Rain Cape	1.00	46.68

ou simply must obey the advice of the many experienced writers and speakers who constantly recommend the study of the dictionary. Acquaintance with your dictionary will steadily improve your ability to express yourself. If you will apply the rule of learning the use of three new words a day, at the end of thirty days you will have a mastery over ninety new words; in sixty days, one hundred and eighty words; and so on until your vocabulary will have become doubly rich in words. Many new words and sayings gradually make their way into our language. Just observe that the ''slangy'' speaker or the ''lazy'' speaker is generally one who lacks the words to say what he wishes to say.

132
201
270
338
407
475
547
619
685

Z

There is an amazing craze for the tales of Tarzan, that czar of African jungles. It is easier to analyze this zealous reading of novels and magazine tales about Tarzan when we realize that the author has capitalized on that tantalizing appeal of azure, equatorial skies and zigzag, hazardous trails through jungles, with the wizard Tarzan ever dazzling readers with his skillful and exceptional feats.

22. Concentration Paragraphs

Type in double-spaced form.   Line of 70 strokes.

Paragraph 1

Los monarcas espanoles se consideraban proprietarios absolutos de las tierras que sus vasallos conquistaron. Toda autoridad en las colonias emanaba, pues, de la Corona. Los virreyes, nombrados por el rey, gobernaban en su nombre, y gozaban de casi todas sus prerogativas.

Paragraph 2

Los jefes de las diversas expediciones, los gobernadores de las provincias y los empleados encargados de administrar justicia y demas funcionarios se nombran por el rey, amovibles a su voluntad y sometidos a las instrucciones de la corte.

Paragraph 3

La administracion publica es reglamentada en todos sus detalles; los colonos pierden por mucho tiempo todo sentimiento de individualidad, quedando reducidos a la inaccion politica. Este sistema de gobierno vine a ser fatal a las colonias del nuevo mundo, y determino su futura independencia.

Paragraph 4

Quibus ego confido impendere fatum aliquod et poenam iam diu improbitati, nequitiae, sceleri, libidini debitam aut instare iam plane aut certe adpropinquare. Quos si meus consulatus, quoniam sanare non potest, sustulerit, non breve nescio quod tempus, sed multa saecula propagarit rei publicae. Nulla est enim natio quam pertimescamus, nullus rex qui bellum populo Romano facere possit.

Bills are made out on printed billheads. Those billheads give the name and address of the seller, the date of the bill, the name and address of the buyer, the terms of the sale, and the number of the bill. Other items, such as the method of shipping and the order number, are sometimes included.

On printed billheads vertical lines are often used to divide the space on the lower part of the sheet into sections. The first section is for the quantity or number of the articles ordered; the second is for the catalog descriptions; and the third is for the figures representing the amounts. Those figures are called *extensions*. An extension is found by multiplying the unit price of the article by the number of articles ordered.

In Illustration 49 the unit price is a part of the catalog description. On some billheads, however, another column is provided for unit prices.

Illustration 49
Bill

Application Exercise 20. On the perforated sheet marked Form 20, make out two bills for the Wrightson Manufacturing Company, Elmira, New York, from the following data:

(1) **Order No. 8954;** *To* **Atlas Machine Tool Co., 2400 Greenspring Lane, Binghamton, N. Y.;** today's date; **Customer's Order No. 1786.** Single-space the items.

60	Starting Handles	.60	36.00
77½ lbs.	Connecting Rod Boxes	.27	20.93
58 lbs.	Connecting Rod Caps	.27	15.66
120	Main Bearing Bushings	.50	60.00
123½ lbs.	Eccentric Rods	.29	35.82
195½ lbs.	Pumps	.29	56.70
88 lbs.	Pump Plungers	.27	23.76
37½ lbs.	Pump Nuts	.27	10.13
31 lbs.	Check Valve Caps	.27	8.37
18 lbs.	Lead Ratchets	.27	4.86
60	Oil Pipe Clamps	.05	3.00
84 lbs.	Pump Discharge Pipes	.29	24.36
44½ lbs.	Ring Oilers	.27	12.02
23 lbs.	Shutter Valves	.24	5.52
			317.13

Application Exercise 19. Study the bill shown in Illustration 49; then, on the two billheads marked Form 19, prepare bills from the following data. Use today's date. The "Terms" for the two bills are "2/10," as in the bill in Illustration 49.

Note: These terms—2/10—mean that a 2% discount may be deducted from the face of the bill if it is paid within ten days.

(1) No. 1877; *To* **Mr. C. L. Foster, 110 Spruce St., Lansing, Mich.**

3 **Footballs No. 5CV** $4.20, 12.60; 2 **Footballs No. 5SR** $1.25, 2.50; 3 **Football Bladders No. RSV** .39, 1.17; 4 **Football Thumb Protectors** .90, 3.60; 14 **Shoulder Guards No. FWG** $4.45, 62.30; 14 pr. **Football Shin Guards No. 9D** $1.40, 19.60; **Total, 101.77.**

(2) No. 1878; *To* **Snyder & Watson, 416 First St., Ypsilanti, Mich.**

1 **Inflation Gauge No. DE** $1.25, 1.25; 6 **Lacing Needles No. W** .07, .42; 1 **Football Lacing Device No. MF** $5.00, 5.00; 2 **Referees' Whistles No. PW** .42, 84; 2 **Megaphones No. 1½X** $1.05, 2.10; 14 **Jerseys No. 7G** $3.30, 46.20; **Total, 55.81.**

You must develop a quick, confident stroke, free from fumbling or hesitation, in order to be able to type figures as accurately and as easily as you type letter strokes.

Important: If you have learned the standard method of fingering the figures, do not practice the optional method given on this page. If, on the other hand, you have learned the optional method, do not practice the standard method.

Standard Approach

Drill 1. s–2, d–3, f–4, f–5, j–6 controls. Line of 53 strokes.

fff frf fr4f f4f f4f f4f fff rrr 444 fr4f f4f

fff fdf ddd ded de3d d3d d3d d3d ddd eee 333 de3d d3d

fff fsf sss sws sw2s s2s s2s s2s sss www 222 sw2s s2s

fff frf fr5f f5f f5f f5f fff rrr 555 fr5f f5f

jjj jyj jy6j j6j j6j j6j jjj yyy 666 jy6j j6j

Drill 2. j–7, k–8, l–9, ;–0, ;– controls. Line of 53 strokes.

jjj juj ju7j j7j j7j j7j jjj uuu 777 ju7j j7j

jjj jkj kkk kik ki8k k8k k8k k8k kkk iii 888 ki8k k8k

jjj jlj lll lol lo91 l91 l91 l91 lll ooo 999 lo91 l91

jjj j;j ;;; ;p; ;p0; ;0; ;0; ;0; ;;; ppp 000 ;p0; ;0·

jjj j;j ;;; ;p; ;p-; ;-; ;-; ;-; ;;; ppp --- ;p-; ;-;

Drill 3. Line of 53 strokes.

3d 3d 3d 8k 8k 8k 4f 4f 4f 91 91 91 5f 5f 5f 0; 0; 0;

6j 6j 6j 2s 2s 2s 7j 7j 7j 3d 3d 3d 8k 8k 8k 5f 5f 5f

7j 7j 7j 0; 0; 0; 2s 2s 2s 6j 6j 6j 4f 4f 4f 91 91 91

Optional Approach

(See instructions above before proceeding)

Drill 1. a–2, s–3, d–4, f–5, f–6 controls. Line of 53 strokes.

fff frf fr5f f5f f5f f5f fff rrr 555 fr5f f5f

fff fdf ddd ded de4d d4d d4d d4d ddd eee 444 de4d d4d

fff fsf sss sws sw3s s3s s3s s3s sss www 333 sw3s s3s

fff faf aaa aqa aq2a a2a a2a a2a aaa qqq 222 aq2a a2a

fff ftf ft6f f6f f6f f6f fff ttt 666 ft6f f6f

Drill 2. 7–7, k–8, l–9, ;–0, ;– controls. Line of 53 strokes.

jjj juj ju7j j7j j7j j7j jjj uuu 777 ju7j j7j

jjj jkj kkk kik ki8k k8k k8k k8k kkk iii 888 ki8k k8k

jjj jlj lll lol lo91 l91 l91 l91 lll ooo 999 lo91 l91

jjj j;j ;;; ;p; ;p0; ;0; ;0; ;0; ;;; ppp 000 ;p0; ;0;

jjj j;j ;;; ;p; ;p-; ;-; ;-; ;-; ;;; ppp --- ;p-; ;-;

Drill 3. Line of 53 strokes.

4d 4d 4d 8k 8k 8k 5f 5f 5f 91 91 91 3s 3s 3s 0; 0; 0;

6f 6f 6f 2a 2a 2a 7j 7j 7j 4d 4d 4d 8k 8k 8k 5f 5f 5f

7j 7j 7j 0; 0; 0; 2a 2a 2a 6f 6f 6f 3s 3s 3s 91 91 91

INCOME FROM STOCK INVESTMENTS

No. of Shares	Cost each Share	Total Cost	Dividends each Share	Total Annual Income	Income on Investment (%)
20	$ 85.00	$1700.00	$6.00	$120.00	7.06
5	120.00	600.00	7.00	35.00	5.83
15	59.50	892.50	3.00	45.00	5.04
12	103.50	1242.00	6.00	72.00	5.80
25	37.75	943.75	2.00	50.00	5.30
10	195.25	1952.50	8.00	80.00	4.10
50	47.50	2375.00	4.00	200.00	8.42
14	154.50	2163.00	7.00	98.00	4.53
100	19.25	1925.00	1.00	100.00	5.19
75	146.50	10987.50	8.00	600.00	5.46
18	94.25	1696.50	6.00	108.00	6.37
35	62.50	2187.50	4.00	140.00	6.40
40	91.25	3650.00	5.00	200.00	5.48
65	42.75	2778.75	3.00	195.00	7.02
45	178.25	8021.25	9.00	405.00	5.05

Application Exercise 18

SCHEDULE OF PAYMENTS AND CASH MATURITY VALUES

Payments				Cash Maturity Value		
Monthly	Quarterly	Semi-Annual	Annual	15-Year	20-Year	25-Year
$ 10.00	$ 29.80	$ 59.00	$ 116.90	$ 2,500	$ 3,778	$ 5,372
15.00	44.70	88.50	174.00	3,750	5,667	8,058
20.00	59.60	118.00	232.00	5,000	7,556	10,744
25.00	74.50	147.50	290.00	6,250	9,445	13,430
30.00	89.40	177.00	348.00	7,500	11,334	16,116
35.00	104.30	206.50	406.00	8,750	13,223	18,802
40.00	119.20	236.00	464.00	10,000	15,112	21,488
50.00	149.00	295.00	580.00	12,500	18,890	26,860
60.00	178.80	354.00	696.00	15,000	22,668	32,232
70.00	208.60	413.00	812.00	17,500	26,446	37,604
75.00	223.50	442.50	870.00	18,750	28,335	40,290
80.00	238.40	472.00	928.00	20,000	30,224	42,976
100.00	298.00	590.00	1,160.00	25,000	37,780	53,720
120.00	357.60	708.00	1,392.00	30,000	45,336	64,464
150.00	447.00	885.00	1,740.00	37,500	56,670	80,580
200.00	596.00	1,180.00	2,320.00	50,000	75,560	107,440

Note: When the width between vertical lines is less than the width of a word in the column heading, the column heading will have to be divided as shown in this problem.

```
1 2 3 4 5 6 7 8 9 0 1 2 3 4 5 6 7 8 9 0 1 2 3 4 5 6 7 8 9 0 1 2 3 4
10 20 30 40 50 60 70 80 90 80 70 60 50 40 30 20 10 12 23 34 56 78 89
12 34 56 78 90 21 43 65 87 98 10 24 35 46 57 68 79 80 90 67 54 32 20
698 237 119 160 408 302 567 432 879 101 201 308 683 745 452 463 199
3847 8374 9250 2905 6611 1166 2095 5902 7755 9257 2002 3388 1616 5902
```

Drill 7.   Line of 70 strokes.

The O'Farrel & Company note (due 4/6/39) is for $3000 at 4¼% interest.
Use 1/4, 3/4, 1/2 rather than ¼, ¾, ½ when typing three carbon copies.
Confucius once rightly said, "We trip on molehills, not on mountains."
Invoice #687–B was covered by a draft for $95.43, payable September 2.

Drill 8.   Line of 70 strokes.

Please give me the total cost: 1 gross Pencils @ 50¢ a dozen; 2 dozen
Memo Pads @ 8½¢ apiece; 2 dozen reams Yellow Chemical Paper 8½ x 11 @
50¢ a ream; 50 Stenographers' Notebooks @ 6½¢ net. All items are to
be subject to a 20% discount except the 50 Stenographers' Notebooks.

24. Spacing Drills

Drill 1.   Type the copy just as given.   Line of 70 strokes.

a k d l a ; p e w v m . e q u z , x i o l c q v s d f j h g y u r t b
in an on if of to or it lo be by he we my as ze me up qu vi ty gh mn
it. home. you? them? Hurry! out! Sir: Madam: him. they? No!

Drill 2.   Abbreviations for state names.   Line of 70 strokes.

Ala., Ariz., Ark., Calif., Colo., Conn., Del., D. C., Fla., Ga., Ill.,
Ind., Kans., Ky., La., Md., Mass., Mich., Minn., Miss., Mo., Mont.,
Nebr., Nev., N. Y., N. J., N. Mex., N. C., N. Dak., Okla., Ore., Pa.,
R. I., S. C., S. Dak., Tenn., Tex., Vt., Va., Wash., Wis., W. Va.,
Wyo. Idaho, Iowa, Maine, Ohio, and Utah cannot be abbreviated.

Drill 3.   Line of 70 strokes.

Independently. On over the hill. The plains. Late enough. In time.
The western towns. I am. We have. Salem, Oregon. Always were here.
The voyagers. I shall. Went along. Over the highways. Wait for me.
Information thoughtfully. Page 57. Full–size sheet. Lines counted.

ARTICLE	COST PRICE	PER CENT MARGIN	AMOUNT OF MARGIN	SELLING PRICE
Pressure Cooker	$ 5.98	37	$2.21	$ 8.19
Radio Phones	.98	47	.46	1.44
Electric Irons	4.95	30	1.49	6.44
Albums	.75	33	.25	1.00
Velvets	2.00	40	.80	2.80
Floor Lamps	5.95	50	2.98	8.93
Table Lamps	3.95	49	1.94	5.89
Dinner set	12.50	30	3.75	16.25
Sheets	1.19	35	.42	1.61
Blankets	2.00	45	.90	2.90
Dresses	7.50	70	5.25	12.75
Hats	1.00	45	.45	1.45
Coats	29.95	25	7.49	37.44
Rugs	10.75	45	4.84	15.59
Waffle Irons	4.50	35	1.58	6.08
End Tables	1.95	50	.98	2.93
Cedar Chests	14.75	30	4.43	19.18
Hand Bags	.98	22	.22	1.20
Andirons	4.50	27	1.22	5.72
Overcoats	25.00	15	3.75	28.75
Shirts	1.29	55	.71	2.00
Socks	.25	33	.08	.33
Silk Hose	1.25	45	.56	1.81
Mirrors	8.95	28	2.51	11.46

Application Exercise 16. In this exercise there are two interlines between the first ruling and the main heading. Otherwise, the procedure is the same as for Exercise 14, except that all the rulings are made on the typewriter.

		INCOME FROM BOND INVESTMENT		
No. of Bonds	Cost each Bond	Total Cost	Total Annual Income	Income on Investment (%)
1	$ 998.75	$ 998.75	$ 50.00	5.01
2	448.75	897.50	50.00	5.57
2	996.25	1992.50	110.00	5.52
5	987.50	4937.50	225.00	4.56
3	493.75	1481.25	82.50	5.57
1	1012.50	1012.50	60.00	5.93
2	97.75	195.50	10.00	5.12
2	1043.75	2087.50	120.00	5.75
1	5137.50	5137.50	275.00	5.35
5	998.50	4992.50	250.00	5.01

The parts of a business letter fall naturally into two main classifications: (A) The Major Parts, or those which are essential to every business letter; and (B) the Minor Parts, or those which are not strictly essential but which are frequently used. These parts, together with their placement, are listed below, and in Instructional Letters A and B, pages 87 and 88.

Summaries of Major and Minor Parts and Placement

Major Parts	Line Location	Marginal Location
1 Letterhead (Printed)	2—2½ inches (12–15 Lines)	Centered (Balanced)
2 Date Line	a. Two lines below "City, State" in the Letterhead. b. Halfway between the Letterhead and the Inside Address.	(1) Center under "City, State." (2) End flush with the right margin.
3 Inside Address	Varies from the 15th to the 25th line, depending on the length of the letter.	Begin at the left margin.
4 Salutation	Two lines below the Inside Address (or Attention Phrase, when included).	Begin at the left margin.
5 Body	Two lines below the Salutation.	Begin at the left margin. Block or indent the paragraphs according to the letter style.
6 Complimentary Close	Two lines below the Body.	Varies, depending on the letter style and the Signature section.
7 Signature	Allow 3 or 4 lines for the Penwritten Signature.	Governed by the location of the Complimentary Close.
8 Identification Initials	a. Six lines below the Complimentary Close or the Typewritten Company Name. b. Two lines below the Identifying Signature or the Dictator's Title.	Begin at the left margin.

Minor Parts	Line Location	Marginal Location
Inside Address Section a. Official Title	(1) Following the name in the first line of the Inside Address. (2) At the beginning of the second line of the Inside Address.	Choice depends on which better preserves the balance of the Inside Address.
b. Attention Phrase	Two lines below the Inside Address.	(a) Begin at the left margin in the full-blocked style. (b) Indent (same as the paragraph indentation); or center.
Body Section c. Subject In re	Two lines below the Salutation. Two lines below the Salutation.	Center; or may correspond to the style of paragraph indentation.
Signature Section d. Typewritten Company Name	Two lines below the Complimentary Close.	If long, preferably end flush with the right margin.
e. Identifying Signature	Four lines below the Complimentary close or the Typewritten Company Name.	Governed by the Complimentary Close or the Typewritten Company Name.
f. Dictator's Title	(1) Same as the Identifying Signature when standing alone. (2) On the same line with, or one line below, the Identifying Signature.	Governed by the Complimetary Close or the Typewritten Company Name. Blocked, if below the Identifying Signature.
Identification Section Enclosure Notation	One or two lines below the Identification Initials.	Begin at the left margin.
h. Carbon Copy Notation (cc)	Two lines below the Identification Initials or the Enclosure Notation.	Begin at the left margin.

No.	Article	Walnut	Mahogany	Shipping Weight
120	Bed	$56.00	$67.00	185
121	Semi-Vanity	54.00	66.00	210
600	Bed	43.00	52.00	190
601	Dresser	64.00	73.00	240
602	Chifforette	52.00	60.00	210
603	Dressing Table	46.00	62.00	135
220	Bed	40.00	48.00	160
221	Dresser	59.00	68.00	200
222	Chifforette	47.00	61.00	200
223	Dressing Table	42.00	51.00	125
224	Vanity Dresser	72.00	84.00	290
225	Writing Desk	31.00	39.00	100
720	Buffet	82.00	96.00	200
721	China Cabinet	64.00	75.00	175
722	Serving Table	41.00	49.00	80
723	Dining Table	57.50	67.50	220

Application Exercise 14. The plan for this tabulation will be similar to that of the foregoing problem (Exercise 13). The entire tabulation, however, is boxed; that is, the Main Heading is included within the rulings.

CONDITION OF MOTOR VEHICLES IN ACCIDENTS RESULTING IN PERSONS KILLED AND INJURED IN ONE YEAR

Condition	Vehicles in Accidents (Total)	Vehicles in Fatal Accidents	Vehicles in Non-fatal Accidents
In apparently good condition	1,007,590	32,350	975,240
Brakes defective	17,170	840	16,330
Steering mechanism defective	4,960	220	4,740
Glaring headlights	7,020	490	6,530
One or both headlights out	1,880	90	1,790
Tail-light out or obscured	4,270	160	4,110
Other defects in equipment	2,670	250	2,420
Puncture or blowout	7,120	480	6,640
Miscellaneous	37,660	2,170	35,490
TOTAL	1,090,340	37,050	1,053,290

If there were more columns in the tabulation, the longest item would have to be taken from the main body of the tabulation and the column headings would be broken up to keep them within the allotted column widths. In this problem, however, the longest item is taken from the column headings in the last three columns. The vertical placement is determined as follows:

First ruling. 1
Interline. 2
Main heading. 2
Interline and second ruling. 1
Interline. 1
Column heading. 3
Interline and third ruling. 1
Interline. 1
                                                   ――
                                                   12

Tabulation (double-spaced). 17
Interline and fourth ruling. 1
Interline. 1
TOTAL. 1
Interline and fifth ruling. 1
                                                       ――
                                                       21

66 — 33 (12 + 21) = 33 ÷ 2 = 16, top margin. By beginning on line 16, the bottom margin will be two lines wider than the top margin. The tabulation will thus be in the optical center.

TRANSAMERICA

Airlines (1)

NEW YORK . . . LOS ANGELES

Month Date, Year (2)

Mr. ____ _____, (3)

    Street Address_____,

      City, State_____.

Dear Sir: (4)

    This letter illustrates the placement of the (5)
eight Major Parts essential to a business letter.
They are:

      (1) Letterhead (Printed)
      (2) Date Line
      (3) Inside Address
      (4) Salutation
      (5) Body
      (6) Complimentary Close
      (7) Signature
      (8) Identification Initials

    For purposes of identification, figures are
printed in the right margin of this letter. Those
figures are placed opposite the parts to which
they refer.

        Yours truly, (6)

        M. J. Jones (7)

XXX:XXX (8)

Instructional Letter A
Double-spaced; Indented; Close Punctuation

of the last column. These locations are shown by figures within brackets on the working plans.

Note: It is more convenient to use an odd number of strokes between columns rather than an even number. For that reason any extra strokes should be distributed, if possible, between the margins.

Locating the Horizontal Lines. Allow two lines for the first (double) ruling, one for the ruling, and one for the line space following. Allow one line for the line space between the column headings and the second horizontal ruling, and one line for the line space following the second horizontal ruling. Allow one line for the line space between the last items of the columns and the bottom horizontal ruling.

On the typewriter the steps would be: (1) Underscore. (2) Release the variable line spacer and turn the platen slightly forward. (3) Reengage the variable line spacer and underscore. (4) Single-space and write the column headings. (5) Single-space and underscore for the next ruling. (6) Single-space and begin the tabulation; single-space. (7) After completing the last line of the tabulation, single-space and underscore for the last ruling.

Centering Headings. Each heading should be case the rulings were made previously, set the pointer at the perpendicular line on the left and record the scale reading; move the pointer to the perpendicular line on the right and record the scale reading; add the two readings and divide by 2 to get the centering point; then center the heading in the usual manner by the back-space method.

To locate the horizontal center, set the first horizontal ruling to line (corresponding to the position of the underscore when typed), and line-space to the next horizontal ruling. Half the number of line spaces resulting is the center or writing line.

The Rulings. To make the perpendicular lines on the typewriter, use the colon (:) or the apostrophe (') or the period (.). Use the underscore (_) or the period to make the horizontal lines. Release the variable line spacer or the ratchet release (see Other Operating Parts on the back cover or back flyleaf), and turn the platen slightly forward to make the second line of the double ruling.

A simple expedient for pencil or pen ruling is to strike lightly the period at the four corners and at the top and bottom points of the inner perpendicular and horizontal rulings. Connect these points after removing the paper.

Application Exercise 13. Before you begin work, study the working plan summaries which follow.

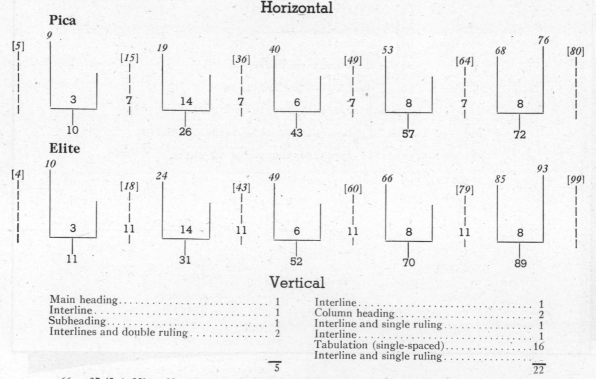

Vertical

Main heading	1
Interline	1
Subheading	1
Interlines and double ruling	2
	5

Interline	1
Column heading	2
Interline and single ruling	1
Interline	1
Tabulation (single-spaced)	16
Interline and single ruling	1
	22

$66 - 27 (5 + 22) = 39 \div 2 = 19$, top margin, or 18 for the optical center.

Note: The centering points for the column headings are the midpoints between the vertical rulings. To find these points, add the adjacent figures in brackets and divide by 2. Thus, column 2, $15 + 36 = 51 \div 2 = 25 + 1$ and $18 + 43 = 61 \div 2 = 30 + 1$. As the $ sign occurs but once in columns 3 and 4, set the tabular stop one stroke to the right, or at 41 and 53 pica or 50 and 67 elite.

Strathmore Paper Company

WEST SPRINGFIELD MILLS · WORONOCO MILLS

WEST SPRINGFIELD, MASSACHUSETTS

Month Date, Year

Company Name_____
Street Address_____
City, State_____

    Attention Mr. _____, Purchasing Agent   (a) (b)

Gentlemen:

    Subject: Minor Parts of a Business Letter   (c)

    This letter illustrates the placement of the eight Minor Parts which sometimes occur in a business letter. They are:

      (a) Attention Phrase
      (b) Official Title
      (c) Subject (In re)
      (d) Typewritten Company Name
      (e) Identifying Signature
      (f) Dictator's Title
      (g) Enclosure Notation
      (h) Carbon Copy Notation

    The use of these parts will be taken up separately in the letter styles which follow. Notice that in this letter the Official Title follows the name which is given in the Attention Phrase.

    For purposes of easy identification, letters are printed in the right margin. Those letters are placed in parentheses opposite the parts to which they refer.

                Very truly yours,

                TYPEWRITTEN COMPANY NAME   (d)

                Identifying Signature   (e)
                Dictator's Title   (f)

XXX/xxx
Enclosure   (g)

cc Mr. _____   (h)

Instructional Letter B
Single-spaced; Semi-blocked; Mixed Punctuation

columns, just as shown here. Make the intercolumn between the Assets and the Liabilities sections wider than the intercolumn between the printing and the adjacent figures. Double-space the tabulation, with single spacing for any overruns.

Condensed Statement as of March 31, 19—

WESTERN NATIONAL BANK
Member Federal Reserve System

ASSETS		LIABILITIES	
Cash in Vault	$ 693,995.80	Capital Stock	$ 750,000.00
Due from Federal Reserve Bank	2,544,798.10	Surplus and Undivided Profits	742,779.20
Exchanges for Clearing House and Due from other Banks	369,201.22	Reserve for Taxes, Interest, etc.	27,074.48
U. S. Bonds to Secure Circulation	500,000.00	National Bank Notes Outstanding	500,000.00
Other U. S. Securities	1,262,162.94	Unearned Interest, etc.	5,986.14
Stock in Federal Reserve Bank	45,000.00	Bills Payable	None
Other Bonds, Securities, etc.	1,039,287.22	DEPOSITS	7,431,289.05
Loans and Discounts	2,716,583.93		
Banking House and other Real Estate	220,135.14		
5% Redemption Fund, with U. S. Treasurer	25,000.00		
Other Assets	40,964.52		
	$9,457,128.87		$9,457,128.87

Boxed Tabulations

A boxed tabulation is one in which the columns and column headings (or the entire tabulation) are enclosed by ruled lines. Rulings for boxed tabulations may be prepared in advance with pen or pencil, or they may be made on the typewriter as part of the tabulation. They can also be put in after the paper has been removed from the typewriter.

In a boxed tabulation, the first step is to prepare a working plan of the horizontal placement. The next step is to include the locations of the perpendicular rulings. The final step is to prepare a working plan of the vertical placement, including the horizontal rulings and the accompanying interlines.

If space permits, the column heading may be used as the width of the column if it has more strokes than the longest item in the column. In the working plan for Exercise 13, page 134, only the tabulation and

column headings are boxed, and the headings *Walnut*, *Mahogany*, and *Shipping* are used as the longest items in the last three columns.

Locating the Perpendicular Lines. The perpendicular lines between columns are located midpoint of the intercolumn widths. The perpendicular lines in the margins are located outside the writing points one-half the width of the intercolumns. For instance, when the intercolumn widths are 7, as in the following pica working plan, the midpoints would be on the fourth stroke.

The locations for the perpendicular rulings in the left margin and between columns are found by subtracting one-half the intercolumn widths (4 in this instance) from the beginning points of the columns. The location of the ruling in the right margin is

133

found to be almost infallible if closely adhered to. It can be applied to transcription as well as to straight typing—whenever the number of words in the body of the letter is given or can be estimated.

The line location of the Date Line was derived after carefully measuring many letterheads, setting up letters on them in accordance with the Placement Chart, and then finding the mid-point between the Letterhead and the Inside Address. Some allowance will have to be made when non-standard or special letterhead forms are used. This section of the Placement Chart does not apply when the Date Line is located on the second line below the Letterhead.

The standard forms and styles of business letters in current use are illustrated by the Style Letters which accompany the practice assignments. No attempt has been made to include the many variations and special styles which may be peculiar to an individual business. In

ters contain information and instructions with which you should become thoroughly familiar.

General Instructions

Before proceeding with the letter practice—

(1) Study carefully the Summaries on page 86 and Instructional Letters A and B, pages 87 and 88, together with the Letter Placement Chart below.

(2) Read and study the Style Letter and the special instructions relating to each individual practice assignment.

(3) Type the Style Letter before beginning the assignment.

(4) Consult the Placement Chart to determine the length of line to be used and the line location of the Inside Address.

(5) Note that the number of words in the Body of the letter is shown in parentheses at the end of each letter.

(6) Remember that there are 10 strokes to the inch, pica type; 12 strokes to the inch, elite type.

Centering Letters

Think of the typed letter as a picture to be framed. The margins around the letter should be approximately the same with the exception of the bottom margin, which may be slightly deeper than the top margin.

The depth of the typewritten letter and the length of the lines across the page will, of course,

vary according to the number of words in the letter. The following simple Letter Placement Chart should be followed. This Chart will serve as a general guide for all the letters you type until you have developed sufficient skill and judgment to enable you to place your letters without the use of the Chart.

LETTER PLACEMENT CHART

	Short Letters	Medium-length Letters	Long Letters
Number of Words in the Body of the Letter..	0—100	100—200	200—300
Length of Line in Strokes (Pica)...	40	50	60
Length of Line in Strokes (Elite)...	48	60	72
Length of Line in Inches..	4	5	6
Start the Address on Line*...	25 to 23	22 to 19	18 to 15
Write the Date above the Address...	6 lines	5 lines	4 lines

* Do not start any letter up to 50 words higher than the 25th line.

Explanation: This Chart is to be used in centering letters written with single spacing. The number of words contained in the body of each letter you will type in this book is given at the end of the letter. Note that number of words and determine whether the letter is "short," "medium-length," or "long." Set the margin stops accordingly.

When the date is placed half way between the letterhead and the inside address, write the date above the address the number of lines indicated in the Placement Plan.

Example: Assume that you are to center a letter that contains 65 words. The length of the line will

be 4 inches. You will start the address 24 lines from the top edge of the sheet, and you will write the date 6 lines above the first line of the address. For each 25 additional words, begin the address one line space higher, thus: 75 to 100, on the 23d line; 100 to 125, on the 22d line; 125 to 150, on the 21st line; 150 to 175, on the 20th line.

Letters of more than 300 words, single-spaced, should be typed on two sheets. Plan the letter so that you will have several lines to carry over to the second sheet, in addition to the complimentary close.

ASSETS

Current Assets

Cash and Call Loans Receivable		$ 212,555.98
Accounts Receivable, Net—Schedule I		245,209.21
Installment Contracts Receivable, Net—Schedule II		73,480.25
Sundry Accounts Receivable		10,626.73
Inventory of Merchandise—Schedule III		291,296.48
Merchandise in Transit		19,940.62
Supplies Inventory		4,169.99
Miscellaneous Investments (Market Value, $12,500.00)		12,154.16
Total Current Assets		$ 869,433.42

Other Assets

Land, Building, Fixtures, and Equipment—Schedule IV		
Cost	$1,104,897.37	
Less Reserve for Depreciation	95,685.02	1,009,212.35
Prepaid Expenses		7,399.81
Good Will		1.00
Total Assets		$1,886,046.58

LIABILITIES AND CAPITAL

Current Liabilities

Accounts Payable		$ 85,108.77
Accounts Payable for Merchandise in Transit		19,940.62
Sundry Creditors		2,945.85
Accrued Salaries		5,720.05
Accrued Expenses		30,450.22
Dividends Payable		6,693.72
Reserve for Federal Income Taxes		13,000.00
Total Current Liabilities		163,859.23

Other Liabilities

Debenture Bonds 6%		515,000.00
Total Liabilities		$678,859.23

Capital

Capital Stock			
Preferred Capital Stock	$425,000.00		
Less Treasury Preferred Stock	42,500.00		
	$382,500.00		
Common Capital Stock	140,532.50		
Total Capital Stock	$523,032.50		
Earned Surplus			
Surplus, January 1, 19—*	$548,741.88		
Profit for 19—*, Exhibit B	119,687.97		
	$668,429.85		
Dividends on Preferred Stock	26,775.00	641,654.85	
Appropriated Surplus for Retirement of Preferred Stock		42,500.00	1,207,187.35
Total Liabilities and Capital			$1,886,046.58

*Last year.

132

type a letter with double spacing, multiply the actual number of words in the body of the letter by 2; then follow the directions given in the Chart for placing a letter containing the number of words found by so multiplying.

Example: Assume that you wish to center a letter of 63 words to be typed with double spacing. Multiply 63 x 2; the result is 126. The letter you are to type is, therefore, considered as a "medium-length" letter for the purposes of the Chart. By consulting the Chart, you will note that the margin stops are to be set for a line of 5 inches. The first line of the address will be typed on the 21st line from the top of

When typing on letterhead paper, the date may be written two line spaces below the printed letterhead, instead of being placed with reference to the address.

When you do not know the number of words in the letter you are to type, it will be necessary for you to estimate the number. Count the words in three full lines of the printed matter or of the shorthand notes which you are transcribing and find the average number of words in a line; then multiply by the number of lines of print or shorthand.

Assignment 1

Special Instructions. Be sure to type the Style Letter before beginning the work of the accompanying Assignment. Set up all letters according to the Letter Placement Chart. When a letter is to be double-spaced, remember to multiply the number of words by 2 before following the directions in the Chart.

In business, printed letterheads are used. In Assignments 1 and 2, however, type a letterhead (referred to as a "heading" when typed) for each letter. This practice will serve to acquaint you with that portion of a letterhead which should be typed when making a copy of an incoming letter. In addition, it will serve as a review in centering lines and headings.

The headings which you are to type are given in the instructions for writing the letters. The heading consists of the company name and the address. Begin the first line of the heading on the 7th line from the top edge of the sheet. In setting up the headings, you may use either of the styles shown below.

SERVICE ADJUSTMENT BUREAU
416 Jefferson Street
Columbus, Ohio

SERVICE ADJUSTMENT BUREAU
416 JEFFERSON STREET
COLUMBUS, OHIO

Set tabular stops for the Inside Address and the paragraph indentations. Tabular stops can also be set for the Date Line and the Complimentary Close when they begin at the same point on several letters which are to be typed. Tabulate without looking up.

When standing alone or when the parts in the Signature Section which follow are short (as in Style Letters 1, 2, and 3), the Complimentary Close is begun at the center. When the parts in the Signature Section are long, the Complimentary Close is begun to the left of the center, so that none of the parts will extend into the right margin. A very long Typewritten Company Name may be split and written on two lines, or it may be written on one line with the Complimentary Close centered above it.

A quick and entirely satisfactory method of finding the beginning point of the Date Line, when it is

placed halfway between the Letterhead and the Inside Address is to subtract 15 from the right margin stop point. In other words, if the right margin stop is set at 65, begin the date line at 50 (65 − 15 = 50). This procedure does not always place the date so that it will end flush with the right margin, but it is close enough for all practical purposes.

You are employed by the **Service Adjustment Bureau, 416 Jefferson Street, Columbus, Ohio.** Type the following letters, dictated by Mr. William C. Harden, in the form of Style Letter 1. Use Mr. Harden's initials for those of the dictator and your own initials for those of the stenographer. Date the letter the day you type it. Begin new paragraphs with the sentences preceded by (P).

Before you begin, be sure to type Style Letter 1, page 91. When you have finished, compare your work with the original.

1. **Novelty Supply Company, 1167 Mason Street, Cincinnati, Ohio. Gentlemen: Thank you for sending us the necessary papers for entering suit in your claim against George R. Young, 314 Main Street, Newark, Ohio. (P) Please make sure that your records are marked in such a way that no payment will be accepted if sent by Mr. Young to you. (P) We shall notify you promptly when suit has been filed. Very truly yours,** (*58 words*)

2. **Mr. W. R. Gross, 417 Lake Street, Sandusky, Ohio. Dear Sir: Thank you for your telegram in which you inform us that you will accept in settlement 75% of the amount owed to you by Anderson Brothers, Lima, Ohio. (P) We have instructed our attorney to close the matter without delay on that basis. As soon as collection has been made, we shall immediately send you a remittance for the proceeds. Yours truly,** (*59 words*)

hand column and the first money column; allow 2 or 3 strokes between the first and second and between the second and third money columns. Write the first line of the tabulation in ALL CAPS. Double-space and write the second line of the heading; double-space below it. Single-space the items, but leave an extra line space between the sections of the Balance Sheet. Allow one space below the underscore for the totals.

HOLMAN PROVISION COMPANY
Balance Sheet — December 31, 19—*

Assets

Cash			
In Stores	$ 465.67		
Checking Account	3,487.97		
Time Deposits	2,267.89	$ 6,221.53	
Investments		11,786.67	
Accounts Receivable			
Fifth Street Store	1,967.78		
228 Beech Street	2,767.99		
1800 Spruce Street	4,689.78	9,425.55	
Notes Receivable		250.00	
Merchandise Inventories			
Fifth Street Store	9,678.76		
228 Beech Street	7,876.61		
1800 Spruce Street	12,564.89	30,120.26	
TOTAL CURRENT ASSETS			$57 804.01
Real Estate and Buildings	14,789.78		
Less Depreciation	4,897.89	9,891.89	
Furniture and Fixtures	7,897.65		
Less Depreciation	5,884.73	2,012.92	
Automobile Trucks	2,897.76		
Less Depreciation	1,432.76	1,465.00	
TOTAL FIXED ASSETS			13,369.81
Deferred Items—			
Cash advanced et al.			176.75
TOTAL ASSETS			$71,350.57

Liabilities

Accounts Payable	23,663.13	
Notes Payable	5,000.00	
TOTAL CURRENT LIABILITIES		28,663.13
Capital Stock issued and outstanding		25,000.00
TOTAL LIABILITIES		53,663.13

Surplus

Surplus, Balance, January 1, 19—*	10,789.98	
Net Operating Profit, 19—*	6,897.46	
TOTAL SURPLUS		17,687.44
TOTAL LIABILITIES AND NET WORTH		$71,350.57

* Last year.

131

SERVICE ADJUSTMENT BUREAU

═══════ TELEPHONE, GRANT 5671 ═══════

416 JEFFERSON STREET • COLUMBUS, OHIO

Month Date, Year

Name_____,

    Street Address_____,

     City, State_____.

Dear Mr. _____:

    Most business letters are single spaced, but
a short letter is sometimes double spaced. Close
punctuation is still in use.

    The standard indentation is five spaces, but
indentations of seven or ten spaces are also used.
Tabular stops should be employed for all indentations. The use of the stops adds to facility and
speed of writing.

    The Complimentary Close, when standing alone,
is begun near the center of the typed lines in the
Body of the letter.

                       Yours truly,

XXX:XXX

(77 Words)

Style Letter 1—to accompany Assignment 1
Double-spaced; Indented; Close Punctuation

you begin work.   Make the margins and intercolumns the same width.   The columns of the tabulation are to be double spaced.   Remember that, if your typewriter
is not equipped with decimal-tabulator keys, it will be necessary to thumb-space
when writing the figures in the money columns.

DEPOSITORS' LEDGER

Depositor	Opening Balance	Deposits	Withdrawals	Closing Balance
Alt, Robert W.	$ 683.50	$116.25	$ 715.07	$ 84.68
Barker, Lee W.	529.30	20.50	543.85	5.95
Boyer, Catherine F.	1,640.22	222.55	1,750.27	112.50
Condon, Edgar P.	983.25	110.78	1,085.39	8.64
Douglas, J. Louis	756.90	505.22	1,258.87	3.25
Feldman, Bernard	84.10	80.60	138.78	25.92
Franklin, Veronica	1,246.55	111.75	1,269.85	88.45
Gifford, Leo G.	834.29	109.50	868.69	75.10
Haffner, Helen M.	756.83	222.85	878.49	101.19
Holt, Frances W.	210.90	175.25	382.90	3.45
Kent, Talbot Q.	79.56	110.26	182.04	7.78
LeBrun, Quincy C.	834.22	34.25	862.12	6.35
Mason, Mrs. Doris	596.75	9.60	595.85	10.50
Nagle, C. M.	84.29	78.56	137.60	25.25
Nichols, John H.	1,111.12	842.02	1,913.50	39.64

Application Exercise 9.   Make a copy, with carbon, of a part of Hall & Stewart's inventory as of December 31, 19—.   Prepare a suitable heading.   Make a
working plan before you begin typing.   Choose your own margin points, and center
the columns between them; or make the margins and the intercolumns the same
width.   Single-space the items of the columns.

Department		Total Amount	Reserve For Discount	Net Amount
AA	Books	46,885.13	3,911.02	42,974.11
BB	Boys' Clothing	173,880.31	5,625.02	168,255.29
CC	Candy	29,378.93	517.75	28,861.18
DD	Children's Dresses	32,437.52	900.00	31,537.52
EE	China and Glassware	3,841.95	118.75	3,723.20
FF	Coats and Suits	34,165.02	1,002.50	33,162.52
GG	Cotton Yard Goods	46,591.00	962.50	45,628.50
HH	Dresses	37,141.57	722.77	36,418.80
JJ	Furniture	35,141.87	668.75	34,473.12
KK	Furs	93,187.62	1,875.02	91,312.60
LL	Men's Furnishings	16,832.75	152.50	16,680.25
MM	Gloves	17,988.75	177.50	17,811.25
NN	Hosiery	28,490.44	323.91	28,166.53
PP	Household Goods	19,759.63	398.61	19,361.02
QQ	Jewelry	16,932.97	380.42	16,552.55
RR	Ladies' Shoes	29,007.73	677.61	28,330.12
SS	Linoleums and Rugs	19,786.97	481.85	19,305.12
TT	Men's Clothing	24,935.77	525.00	24,410.77
UU	Radios and Victrolas	22,990.30	825.00	22,165.30

Streets, Crawfordsville, Indiana. Gentlemen: Our attorney has had an interview with your debtor, Mr. K. R. Lawson, Fulton, Ohio. The debtor disputes the account and states that it is incorrect. He did not, however, have full particulars available at the time and agreed to discuss the matter with our attorney again next Tuesday. (P) Do you know on what basis the debtor might dispute your account? Very truly yours, *(61 words)*

4. **Mr. Charles G. Fuller, Industrial Building, Zanesville, Ohio. Dear Sir:** As you requested in our telephone conversation of this morning, we shall send you tomorrow an itemized statement, properly verified, together with duplicate copies of the supporting invoices. The debtor, Henry F. Grant, is doing business under the name of Central Confectionery Store at 420

promptly with the suit and keep us informed of developments. Yours very truly, *(60 words)*

5. **A. K. Wendell, Esq.,* Land Title Building, Cleveland, Ohio. Dear Sir:** We are sending you separately by registered mail our affidavit in the matter of our client's claim against Luther R. Henderson, 687 North Adams Street, Cleveland, Ohio. The affidavit has been properly executed before a Notary. We have also attached a Certificate from the County Clerk, certifying the authority of the Notary to act in this capacity. (P) Copies of all supporting invoices are also being sent to you. (P) Please proceed at once with the action. Very truly yours, *(75 words)*

*In the United States the term *Esquire* (usually abbreviated *Esq.*) is a title of office or courtesy given to lawyers and justices of the peace. It is written after the surname, and no prefixed title, such as *Mr.*, *Dr.*, etc., is used with the name.

Assignment 2

For the five letters which you will type in this Assignment, prepare letterheads from these data: **Mutual Insurance Agency, Fidelity Building, Baltimore, Maryland.** Write all three lines in ALL CAPS. The letters are dictated by Mr. George R. Terry. For the Identifying Signature you will, therefore, type **George R. Terry.** Use today's date. Continue to use tabular stops for all indentations.

Before you type these letters, write Style Letter 2, page 93.

1. **Mr. J. D. Kennedy, 145 Key Street, Frederick, Maryland. Dear Sir:** This morning I received your letter with which you enclosed an absolute assignment from Edith L. Denton to the insured under Policy No. 278,976, Denton. You also enclosed a special assignment from the insured to Eva M. Denton, his wife. (P) These papers were drawn without our assuming any responsibility for their validity. We now find that they are unsatisfactory because on each assignment the Notary failed to indicate who appeared before him to acknowledge the papers. This defect is not so important with regard to the special assignment, but in the case of the absolute assignment it is necessary for the Notary to file with us a certificate remedying the defect. Very truly yours, *(111 words)*

2. **Mr. F. C. Barrett, 786 North Avenue, Baltimore, Maryland. Dear Mr. Barrett:** I am

sorry that I am compelled to return the request which you sent us for a loan to be made on the security of your Policy No. 2,876,675. Probably through some oversight the incorrect amount was inserted. (P) As I stated in my conversation with you last week, a loan will be made for $60, not for $80, which is the amount that has been inserted in the form. (P) I shall come out to your house next Wednesday evening and bring with me another form. Mrs. Barrett, your beneficiary, and you can then execute it. Please have a competent person present as witness. (P) I shall then do everything possible to hurry along the matter. Sincerely yours, *(114 words)*

3. **Mr. E. H. Elton, 467 Center Street, Hagerstown, Maryland.** My dear Mr. Elton: I have been following with great interest the results that have been obtained in District No. 4 during this annual contest. At the end of the first three weeks I notice you had standing to your credit $12,000 of new business. That is a splendid record. (P) You have now demonstrated your selling ability. As the contest progresses, I am sure you will continue your good work, so that the close of the contest will find you in the front rank. (P) You surely have my best wishes. Please feel perfectly free to call on me whenever you think I can be of any assistance to you. Sincerely yours, *(105 words)*

In many tabulations the columns of figures contain a decimal. With a one-key tabulator, the tabular stop would be set for the longest item. The shorter items would be located by thumb-spacing from this point.

With a five-key decimal tabulator (see Illustration 33, page 29), the tabular stop would be set at the decimal point. The decimal key would be used for all items beginning with the decimal point. The units (1) key is used for items with one figure to the left of the decimal point (5.00); the tens (10) key for items with two figures to the left of the decimal point (60.97); the hundreds (100) key for items with three figures to the left of the decimal point (323.81); and the thousands (1000) key for items with four figures to the left of the decimal point (1641.78). For items with five figures to the left of the decimal point (32844.46), use the thousands key and back-space once. For the $ sign, which should be placed outside the longest item of the column (equivalent to $32844.46), use the thousands key and back-space twice.

Application Exercise 7. Prepare a working plan for the following 5-column tabulation. Write the main heading in ALL CAPS. Triple-space and write the subheading; double-space and write the first line of the column headings; single-space and write the second line of the column headings. Double-space after the column headings, and double-space after each line of the tabulation. Set up the tabulation so that the margins and the intercolumn spaces are of the same width. Center the column headings above the columns.

RESULT OF SYSTEMATIC SAVING
Interest at 3% per annum

Monthly Deposits	One Year	Five Years	Ten Years	Twenty Years
$ 1.00	$ 12.19	$ 64.70	$ 139.77	$ 328.03
5.00	60.97	323.81	699.54	1641.78
10.00	121.96	647.79	1399.60	3284.65
20.00	243.92	1295.59	2799.25	6570.15
25.00	304.89	1619.35	3498.72	8211.01
50.00	609.77	3238.81	6997.57	16422.23
100.00	1219.57	6477.65	13995.17	32844.46

Working Plan

Pica

8-(12)   22-(27)   37-(42)   52-(58)   68-(74)   77 + 8 = 5

| 7 | 7 | 8 | 7 | 8 | 7 | 9 | 7 | 9 |

11*   26*   41*   56*   72*

* Centering points for column headings.

The decimal stop points—with pica type, for example—are shown in parentheses on the working plan to the right of the beginning points of the columns.

The extra strokes resulting from the distribution of the remainder were allotted to the margins.

If your typewriter is equipped with a five-key decimal tabulator, set the stops as many places to the right of the beginning point as there are strokes to the left of the decimal point in the longest item of the column. In the second column there are 5 strokes (equivalent to $1219) to the left of the decimal; therefore, set the stop at 27 for pica type (22 + 5) and at 33 for elite type (28 + 5). If your typewriter is not equipped with sufficient stops, thumb-space from the margin point for the shorter items of column 1; otherwise, disregard the margin stop and set a tabular stop at the decimal point.

129

MUTUAL INSURANCE AGENCY

Telephone, VErnon 6457

FIDELITY BUILDING
BALTIMORE, MARYLAND

Month Date, Year

Name_____,
        Street Address_____,
            City, State_____.

My dear Mr. _____:

One Minor Part--the Identifying Signature--is included with the Major Parts in this style letter. This part consists of the typewritten name of the person who signs the letter. Its purpose is merely to identify the penwritten signature.

It is generally typed on the fourth line below the Complimentary Close or the Typewritten Company Name, when the latter is included in the signature section. In this letter it is indented to conform to the style of the letter. When an Identifying Signature is used, it is not necessary to show also the dictator's initials in the identification section. Only the stenographer's initials are typed.

Sometimes it is desired to end the Date Line exactly flush with the right-hand margin. In that case the beginning point is found by back-spacing or subtracting from the right margin point one less than the number of strokes contained in the line. If, for example, fourteen strokes are required for the Date Line, the number to back-space or subtract is thirteen.

Yours respectfully,

Identifying Signature

XXX

(170 Words)

Style Letter 2—to accompany Assignment 2
Single-spaced; Indented; Close Punctuation

which gives a list of employees, together with the positions they hold, their home addresses, and their residence telephones. Plan the tabulation before you begin. Write the second line of the heading in ALL CAPS. Leave *two* double spaces below it. The underscores indicate the longest item in each column.

Sales Division Employees
AMERICAN SMELTING COMPANY

Name	Position	Address	Telephone
Abrams, Philip J.	Salesman	157 N. Mason St.	MAnsfield 7865-J
Cadman, Elizabeth	Stenographer	6786 Fulton St.	None
Freyling, Henry W.	Correspondent	267 Jackson Place	WOlfe 7865
Gayton, Harry L.	Salesman	189 Chapman St.	MArket 7865-W
Gruber, William H.	Salesman	2467 Berkshire Ave.	GRoton 7623
Harris, Mary W.	Stenographer	1178 Rodman St.	MArket 1356
McDonnell, James K.	Salesman	567 Cherry St.	FRanklin 2675
Newton, Charles F.	Sales Manager	768 Webster St.	WEbster 8765
Preston, Farley H.	Salesman	1342 Walton St.	FRanklin 1467
Pyle, Harry F.	Correspondent	1876 Chestnut St.	GRoton 7643
Reynolds, Anna F.	Filing Clerk	1476 Adams St.	None
Rodman, Charles F.	Salesman	675 Webster St.	WEbster 765-W
Squires, Henry F.	Salesman	1765 Jefferson St.	ADams 6573-J
Timmins, Laura W.	Stenographer	2245 Adams St.	ADams 1674-W

Application Exercise 6. Insert the sheet the long way. Fold the sheet at one end and write the first five columns; then fold at the other end, reinsert, and write the sixth column.

HALL & STEWART
Treasurer's Budget
February 1, 19—, to May 31, 19—

	February	March	April	May	Total
Cash on Hand, Feb. 1, 19—	118,750				118,750
Estimated Receipts					
Collections from Customers					
Regular Retail	155,125	177,550	148,800	127,637	609,112
Installment Contracts	67,550	68,775	70,125	73,812	280,262
Cash Sales	46,250	42,562	40,000	50,105	178,917
Interest and Dividends	6,250	5,000	4,375	5,525	21,150
Total	393,925	293,887	263,300	257,079	1,208,191
Estimated Disbursements					
Payments to Creditors					
Notes for Loans	187,500	75,000	50,000		312,500
Merchandise Invoices	127,500	123,800	106,250	95,037	452,587
Sundry Items	30,050	28,750	27,500	25,000	111,300
Payrolls	38,750	35,000	35,000	32,500	141,250
Miscellaneous	7,525	31,875	5,525	3,750	48,675
Total	391,325	294,425	224,275	156,287	1,066,312
Estimated Cash on Hand, May 31, 19—					141,879

Avenue, Laurel, Maryland. Dear Mrs. Herndon: I am now able to give you the information for which you asked over the telephone. (P) At the end of the twenty-year dividend period under your policy, if you are then surviving, you will have the choice of a number of options of settlement. The statements of results under policies ending their accumulation periods next year have not yet been prepared. The profits or dividends to be apportioned to such policies will depend on our experience in such matters as lapsed policies, rates of interest, and mortality up to practically the end of this year. For that reason it is not possible to state in advance what the amount will be. (P) About thirty days before the end of the accumulation period, however, a statement of the results under your policy will be issued and mailed to you from this office. When you receive that statement, please let me know which option you decide to take. I shall then send you the necessary papers for execution. In that way the delay will be reduced to the minimum. Very truly yours, *(177 words)*

ton, Delaware. Dear Sir: We shall exchange Policy No. 267,867, Westcott, for a new $15,000 Ordinary Life contract dated December 6, 19—*, at age 60, and shall allow $344.73 in part payment of the first premium under the new policy. We shall require a regular application with full medical examination, because this policy contains the five-year exchange clause. That examination will be at the expense of the company, just as in the case of new insurance. (P) The extra premium required to make the change to a $15,000 Ordinary Life contract of original date will be $2666.45. That amount will carry the policy paid to December 8, 19—†. We shall also require a full medical examination as under Part II of the application for this change. The doctor will be paid through the Home Office in the usual way. We are charging only the net difference in reserves; therefore, we cannot allow any commission on this extra premium. (P) The total net amount at risk under all the policies on this life is $36,000. Very truly yours, *(169 words)*

*Use the current year date.
†Next year.

Assignment 3

Type these letters in the form of Style Letter 3, page 95. Use the five letterheads marked Form 5 in the Workbook of Laboratory Materials which accompanies *College Typing*. If you are not supplied with the Workbook, type the letters on plain paper; or, if your instructor directs you to do so, type letterheads, thus:

HALL & STEWART
814–824 Market Street
Sacramento, California

Use today's date. **Mr. J. W. Reynolds,** the **Merchandise Manager,** dictated the letters.

1. Mr. Henry W. Simmons 786 Grant Street Denver, Colorado My dear Mr. Simmons: I have just received a letter from Miss Mabel Lambert, who was with me for four years when I was associated with Macy's in New York. She tells me that there is a possibility that she will go to work for you in your Advertising Department. (P) In her behalf, I want to say that Miss Lambert is a capable and ambitious young lady. As a stenographer, she is accurate and always "on the job." Furthermore, she is loyal, dependable, and doesn't talk. (P) While Miss Lambert was associated with me, she had a good deal of experience in laying out display advertising. Her experience in that direction, I believe, will fit right in with your plans. I have every confidence that she will make good, if you give her a chance. (P) I hope you are about ready to launch your new enterprise and wish for you unbounded success. Sincerely yours, *(147 words)*

2. **Queen Manufacturing Company** 718 LaSalle Street Chicago, Illinois Gentlemen: We were greatly disappointed in your initial shipment of spring suits. (P) The skirt on lot 4763 was to be shirred in the back and to have patch pockets to match the coat. On lot 3675 the front and back of the coat were to have braid trimming in cluster effect, and the skirt was to be made in a straight-line model with set-in pockets. On nearly all the garments the patch pockets are

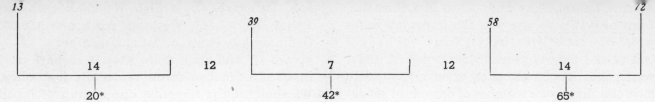

* Column heading centering points.

13 + 7 (14 ÷ 2) = 20, centering point for the first column heading.
39 + 3 (7 ÷ 2) = 42, centering point for the second column heading.
58 + 7 (14 ÷ 2) = 65, centering point for the third column heading.

Elite Type

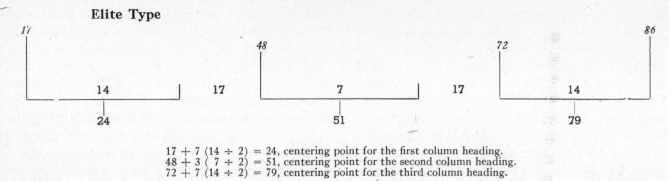

17 + 7 (14 ÷ 2) = 24, centering point for the first column heading.
48 + 3 (7 ÷ 2) = 51, centering point for the second column heading.
72 + 7 (14 ÷ 2) = 79, centering point for the third column heading.

If you will inspect your tabulation after completing it, your first impression may be that the headings of the first and last columns are not centered. This impression comes from the fact that the first two or three items in the columns are shorter in length than the longest items in the columns.

Off-centering. To make a better balanced tabulation, the column headings are often placed off-center; that is, centered on the first, or on one of the first two or three items, in the tabulation. One procedure is to leave the necessary space for the column headings and to type the first three or four items of the tabulation; then go back and fill in the headings. In the first column of Exercise 3, for instance, *State* may be centered on the word *Alabama* by back-spacing twice (once for *St* and once for *at*) from the point corresponding to the position of the letter *b* in *Alabama*. *Abbreviation* may be centered over *Ariz.* by back-spacing six times (*Ab br ev ia ti on*) from the position of the *i* in *Ariz.* To center *Capital* above *Montgomery*, back-space three times (*Ca pi ta*) from the position of the *g* in *Montgomery*.

The column heading centering points may also be found by substituting the number of strokes in the items selected for the longest items in the columns. Thus, *Alabama* contains 7 strokes; *Arizona*, 5; and *Montgomery*, 10. The centering points will be:

Pica	Elite
16 (13 + 3)	20 (17 + 3)
41 (39 + 2)	50 (48 + 2)
63 (58 + 5)	77 (72 + 5)

Application Exercise 4. When the tabulation consists of but two or three narrow columns, the intercolumn widths may be chosen arbitrarily. The width will range from 5 to 8 strokes; if the columns are very narrow, 5 will suffice; if they are wide, 7 to 8 strokes will give a better balance. Select the width of intercolumn space you are to use in this tabulation. Make up a working plan, and set up the tabulation. Single-space the items in the columns.

HALL & STEWART

Customers Whose Balances
Exceed Their Credit Limits

Name	Balance	Credit Limit
Frank Abbott	275	200
John Abell	190	150
Mary Adams	485	400
Rena Anthony	390	350
Helen Bankard	600	500
Martha Bennett	450	400
Milton Boring	395	300
Doris Bradley	955	750
Richard Brooks	625	600
Sidney Browning	450	400
Katherine Byrnes	1,900	1,500
Dorothy Carroll	3,150	3,000
Michael Carter	375	300
Richard Cassidy	980	800
Helen Chenoweth	655	500
Andrew Clagett	445	400
Miriam Clark	320	300
Nicholas Curtiss	1,175	1,000

HALL & STEWART

The Leading Department Store

Telephone: MARKET 1000

814-824 MARKET STREET
SACRAMENTO, CALIFORNIA

Month Date, Year

Name_____
Address_____
City, State_____

Gentlemen:

    The semi-blocked style, which is illustrated by
this letter, is probably the most popular business
style in use today. The lines are single-spaced, the
address and signature sections are blocked, and the
paragraphs are indented. The Inside Address is written with open punctuation, but the Salutation and the
Complimentary Close retain their punctuation marks.

    This letter also differs from Style Letter 2 in
the location of the Date Line and the use of the Dictator's Title instead of the Identifying Signature.

    The Date Line is tied in with the Letterhead by
centering it two line spaces below the printing. To
find the line location, set the "City, State" to line
by means of the Variable Line Spacer and then line-
space twice. Center the date by back-spacing from the
center of the printed line the needed number of times.

    When standing alone, the Dictator's Title is put
in the same position as the Identifying Signature.
When both are included in the letter, the Dictator's
Title may follow the Identifying Signature; or it may
be placed on the next line by itself. The choice will
depend on the appearance.

                Yours very truly,

                Dictator's Title

XXX
XXX

(191 Words)

Style Letter 3—to accompany Assignment 3
Single-spaced; Semi-blocked; Mixed Punctuation

space and write the subheading. Triple-space, move the carriage to the left margin stop, and write the first word in the first column—**begin.** Depress the tabular key and *hold it down* until the carriage stops; then write the first word in the second column—**began.** Again depress the tabular key and *hold it down* until the carriage stops; then write the first word in the third column—**begun.** Return the carriage and continue across the next line. Check to see that the line space regulator is set for single spacing.

Application Exercise 3. Prepare the following tabulation with a carbon. Write the main heading in ALL CAPS; double-space and write the subheading. Leave two interlines below the subheading and one interline below the column headings. Underscore the three column headings. Single-space the tabulation. The abbreviations for the names of the states are the ones that are recommended by the Post Office Department. Some state names should not be abbreviated. Study the list.

The asterisks and the underscores are not to be included in the tabulation. They are shown here for purposes of instruction. The asterisk is placed before the names of those states which are not abbreviated. In the second column the line should be left blank, or, better still, the omission should be indicated by three hyphen strokes, centered. The underscore indicates the longest item of each column.

In setting up the tabulation, omit the commas after the names of the states and their abbreviations.

Centering the Column Headings

In addition to a main heading and a subheading, this problem also contains a heading for each column. The column heading is generally centered with reference to the longest item in the column. When so arranged, one procedure is as follows:

(1) Divide the longest item in each column by 2 to get the center of the item.

(2) Add the resulting figure to the beginning point of the column to get the centering point for the column heading.

(3) Note the centering point on the working plan (page 127) and center the column heading by backspacing from that point once for each 2 letters in the column heading.

With Abbreviations and Capital Cities

Column headings: State   Abbreviation   Capital

Alabama, Ala., Montgomery
Arizona, Ariz., Phoenix
Arkansas, Ark., Little Rock
California, Calif., Sacramento
Colorado, Colo., Denver
Connecticut, Conn., Hartford
Delaware, Del., Dover
Florida, Fla., Tallahassee
Georgia, Ga., Atlanta
*Idaho, Boise
Illinois, Ill., Springfield
Indiana, Ind., Indianapolis
*Iowa, Des Moines
Kansas, Kans., Topeka
Kentucky, Ky., Frankfort
Louisiana, La., Baton Rouge
*Maine, Augusta
Maryland, Md., Annapolis
Massachusetts, Mass., Boston
Michigan, Mich., Lansing
Minnesota, Minn., St. Paul
Mississippi, Miss., Jackson
Missouri, Mo., Jefferson City
Montana, Mont., Helena
Nebraska, Nebr., Lincoln
Nevada, Nev., Carson City
New Hampshire, N. H., Concord
New Jersey, N. J., Trenton
New Mexico, N. Mex., Santa Fe
New York, N. Y., Albany
North Carolina, N. C., Raleigh
North Dakota, N. Dak., Bismarck
*Ohio, Columbus
Oklahoma, Okla., Oklahoma City
Oregon, Ore., Salem
Pennsylvania, Pa., Harrisburg
Rhode Island, R. I., Providence
South Carolina, S. C., Columbia
South Dakota, S. Dak., Pierre
Tennessee, Tenn., Nashville
*Texas, Austin
*Utah, Salt Lake City
Vermont, Vt., Montpelier
Virginia, Va., Richmond
Washington, Wash., Olympia
West Virginia, W. Va., Charleston
Wisconsin, Wis., Madison
Wyoming, Wyo., Cheyenne

you must have confused the specifications on our order with the specifications on some other order. These suits are certainly not made up in accordance with our copy of the order. (P) We need the suits and can use them to advantage, but not in their present condition. We shall hold them subject to instructions from you as to their disposition. Please let us have a prompt reply. Yours very truly, (*151 words*)

3. King Clothing Company 578 Pacific Street Los Angeles, California Gentlemen: We have a uniform coat here for Mr. Charles C. Madsen, "Highland Cadet Officer" pattern, which we are returning to you today. (P) If you will refer to the specifications on our Order No. 6754, you will notice that we asked for a six-button coat. You made the garment with fly front, which is not what our customer wants. The coat will, therefore, have to be changed to regular button front. Contrary to the specifications, you have placed buttons on the rear flaps of the coat. (P) Yesterday we also returned to you the coat made for Mr. T. I. Ormond, our Order No. 5432. The rear flaps on this coat should be 2" longer than at present. We have indicated by a tag the place where the lower button on the front of the coat is to be placed. (P) Please have these alterations made and the garments returned to us as soon as possible. Very truly yours, (*154 words*)

4. Mrs. William C. Davis 618 South Street Sacramento, California Dear Mrs. Davis: We are sorry that we cannot give you permission to return the hat which you purchased. It is the rule of all stores not to put back in stock merchandise of this character. You will realize, we feel sure, that the protection of our customers makes such a rule imperative. Although it deprives us of the pleasure of serving you in this it is a necessary safeguard. (P) It is a pleasure to learn of your interest in our sale of gowns, which begins next week. We shall feature a splendid collection of exclusive garments in advanced styles—garments that are truly distinctive. In the collection are magnificent dinner gowns of lace, net, and georgette from $85 to $115, as well as printed georgette frocks for afternoon wear, in attractive combinations, at $35 to $95. (P) We shall look forward with real pleasure to your visit next week. Very truly yours, (*155 words*)

5. Mr. Harry C. Taylor 2465 Weldon Street Sacramento, California Dear Mr. Taylor: Our Men's Shop has a business principle that it sticks to religiously: Not to give the least for the most, but the most for the least—and bring you back again. (P) Plenty of men are funny about buying clothes. They never return to a store if the suit they bought didn't satisfy them. Sometimes it's the dealer's fault; sometimes the manufacturer's; sometimes the customer's. (P) If any purchase you make here doesn't give you one hundred per cent satisfaction, we want to know why—and right away! Our object is to make it right—without question or quibble. (P) This is the home of good-looking clothes for men; not only good-looking, but well-wearing— made of the right stuff. There's a great difference in clothes, the men who wear them, and the dealer who sells them. (P) This store is crankier than the customer about giving him a perfect fit. We don't want the smallest cloud of discontent to hang over any purchase. (P) Our stock of live, likable styles was never before so complete; it's brimming over with new models and fabrics—for *you*! Make your selection now while you have a wide choice—don't put it off. Sincerely yours, (*197 words*)

Assignment 4

The following letters were dictated by **Mr. George A. Sawyer, Manager** of the **Columbia Radio Company.** Type the letters on the letterheads marked Form 6 in the Workbook of Laboratory Materials. First, type Style Letter 4, page 97.

1. **Mr. E. J. Jennings 719 Green Street Hammond, Indiana Dear Sir:** Our Shipping Department reports that you have returned to us a quantity of defective replacement parts which have evidently been removed from the type 30A and 30B receivers. (P) These receivers have been in service very much longer than their guarantee period; consequently, defective parts removed from such receivers are no longer eligible to no-charge replacement or credit. On January 15 of this year free replacements were discontinued, and all dealers were requested to submit

			/			
begin	began	begun	/	break	broke	broken
bring	brought	brought	/	choose	chose	chosen
eat	ate	eaten	/	forget	forgot	forgotten
go	went	gone	/	hurt	hurt	hurt
know	knew	known	/	lead	led	led
lie	lay	lain	/	lose	lost	lost
mislay	mislaid	mislaid	/	overpay	overpaid	overpaid
ride	rode	ridden	/	ring	rang	rung
see	saw	seen	/	speak	spoke	spoken
swim	swam	swum	/	throw	threw	thrown
typewrite	typewrote	typewritten	/	understand	understood	understood
undertake	undertook	undertaken	/	withdraw	withdrew	withdrawn

Planning the Tabulation

Check your working plan against the following figures, as called for in the Reference Guide for Tabulation, pages 121 and 122.

Horizontal Placement (The tabulation will have three columns.)

	Pica	Elite
Total strokes available (full width of paper)	85	102
Strokes used: Total of the longest item in each of the three columns	31	31
Strokes remaining: To be divided between the two intercolumns and the two margins	54	71

Pica: $54 \div 4 = 13 + 2$. Add one of the extra strokes to the left margin and one to the right margin, leaving 13 strokes for each of the two intercolumns.

Elite: $71 \div 4 = 18 - 1$. Subtract the extra stroke from the right margin, leaving 17 strokes for the right margin and 18 strokes for the left margin and for each of the two intercolumns.

Locating the Tabular Stops

	Pica	Elite
Set the margin stop for the first column at	14	18
Begin the second column at	37	46

Pica: $14 + 10$ (longest item in the first column) $+ 13$ (strokes between the columns) $= 37$

Elite: $18 + 10 + 18 = 46$

Begin the third column at	60	74

Pica: $37 + 10 + 13 = 60$

Elite: $46 + 10 + 18 = 74$

Proof: Pica: 60 (beginning point of the third column) $+ 11$ (longest item in the third column) $=$ 71 (ending point of the third column) $+ 14$ (width of right margin) $= 85$

Elite: $74 + 11 = 85 + 17 = 102$

Vertical Placement

Lines available on an 8½ x 11 sheet	66
Lines used:	
Heading plus 1 interline (blank space) 2	
Subheading plus 2 interlines (blank spaces)	3
Number of lines in tabulation	24
Total lines used	29
Lines remaining for top and bottom margins	37

$37 \div 2 = 18 + 1$, or 19 line spaces for the bottom margin and 18 line spaces for the top margin. (When the division is unequal, add the extra line to the bottom margin.)

Proof: 18 (top margin) + 29 (headings and tabulation) + 19 (bottom margin) = 66, total lines available on the sheet.

Centering the Headings

The main heading requires 27 strokes. Set the carriage at 43 with pica type and at 51 with elite type, and back-space once for each 2 strokes in the heading. Disregard the extra letter in the back-spacing.

If the figures on your working plan check with those given here, you are ready to begin work. Insert the sheet into your machine and space down 18 single line spaces from the top edge.

COLUMBIA RADIO COMPANY

648-652 LIBERTY STREET · CHICAGO, ILLINOIS

Month Date, Year

Name_____
Address_____
City, State_____

Dear Madam:

This letter takes up the Typewritten Company Name--another of the Minor Parts--which is frequently included in the signature section.

The Typewritten Company Name is usually written in upper case (ALL CAPS), and should contain the same wording as that given in the Letterhead. It may be blocked, indented, or centered two line spaces below the Complimentary Close, depending on the style of the letter and the length of the Company Name.

An acceptable form with a very long Typewritten Company Name is to end it flush with the right margin. The beginning point may be ascertained by either back-spacing or subtracting from the right marginal point one stroke less than the number of strokes which the name contains. Sometimes the Company Name is split and written on two lines; sometimes it is written on one line with the Complimentary Close centered above it.

In this letter the Typewritten Company Name is short; the closing and signature sections are, there-fore, begun near the center. Tabular stops should be set for all these parts, as well as for the paragraph indentations.

Very truly yours,

TYPEWRITTEN COMPANY NAME

Diotator's Title

XXX/xxx

(182 Words)

Style Letter 4—to accompany Assignment 4
Single-spaced; Semi-blocked; Mixed Punctuation

The same information may be illustrated graphically by a working plan made with pencil on paper as follows:

⌐ ¬
| |
| |
⌐__⌐ indicates the columns of the tabulation.

The figures within the brackets indicate the longest item in each column.

The figures between the brackets indicate the space between the columns.

Horizontal Placement

Pica Type

The figures 23 and 63 represent the margin stop points.

The figures 32, 41, 50, and 60 represent the beginning points and, in this problem, the tabular stop points of the last four columns.

Elite Type

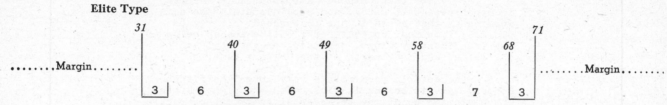

31 and 71 represent the margin stop points; 40, 49, 58, and 68 represent the beginning and the tabular stop points of the last four columns.

Vertical Placement

Main Heading.	1 line space
Interlines.	2 line spaces
Lines in the tabulation.	12 line spaces
Spaces between the horizontal lines of the tabulation.	11 line spaces
Total lines used.	26

66 — 26 lines used leaves 40 lines for the top and bottom margins.

40 ÷ 2 = 20. Write the main heading on the 20th, or on the 18th, line.

Application Exercise 2. You are to prepare a working plan for the following 3-column tabulation. Type the main heading in ALL CAPS. Double-space and write the subheading; then triple-space and begin the tabulation. Single-space the tabulation. This time, instead of using a 40-stroke line, *set up the columns so that the margins and the intercolumn spaces will be the same width.*

Remember that when the margins are given, **the** remainder (the difference between the strokes available and the strokes used) is divided by the number of columns less 1, as in Exercise 1. When the margins are to be made the same width as the intercolumns, divide by the number of columns plus 1, as in this problem. See page 122.

When typing the tabulation, read across the lines. The material is set up in this manner so that you can determine, without loss of time, the longest item in each column.

needed for service work. (P) The defective parts are without value to us. To return the parts to you will cost about $5.50. We have set aside the material until you have had an opportunity to write us about its disposition. Very truly yours, (*121 words*)

2. **Downey Radio Company 418 Twelfth Street Gary, Indiana Gentlemen:** We are sorry that we are unable to allow you the discount of $14.61 which you deducted when making remittance in payment of your account. (P) The discount that we allow on bills paid by the tenth of the month is made possible by the fact that we are thus able to use the money in discounting some of our own bills. The manufacturers allow us the same discount; we then turn around and pass on the amount to our customers. Unfortunately your check reached us too late in the month to permit us to use the money in taking advantage of the factory discount. (P) There is also an inadvertent error of $1.30 in subtraction. We have, therefore, marked your account "short paid $15.91." This amount will be shown on your next statement. If you find that we are correct, we shall be grateful to you for including that amount in your remittance to cover your purchases to date. Very truly yours, (*158 words*)

3. **Mr. Arthur J. Kaylor 718 Franklin Street Lansing, Michigan Dear Mr. Kaylor:** Since we received your recent letter, we have had an opportunity to review our previous correspondence and have noted that you are using an antenna some 400 feet long. An aerial of this length is not at all suited to modern broadcasting conditions and is even less suited to short wave reception. (P) For your purpose we suggest an antenna with a total length not to exceed 60 feet, including the lead-in. This antenna should be well elevated and free from surrounding objects. The employment of a longer aerial will merely increase the noise level of your set and broaden the instrument without appreciably increasing the sensitivity. We suggest that you alter your aerial by shortening the antenna; then tell us what results you get. (P) We are always interested in seeing that all users of our products obtain the satisfaction which they have a right to expect. Please be sure that we shall be glad to aid you in any way we can. Very truly yours, (*163 words*)

are sorry indeed to learn that you have been having trouble with your 489 AC Superheterodyne. (P) From the information you have given us in your letter, we believe that the trouble is caused by a short circuit in the B supply end of the receiver. This short circuit could be in a defective power tube, could be caused by the wiring in shorting against the chassis, or could be the result of a broken-down condenser bank. (P) We suggest that you check over the receiver according to Data Sheet No. 27 in the book we sent with your original order. If you find any parts which you believe to be defective, we shall be glad to have you return those parts to us for adjustment, shipping charges prepaid. Please return also this letter as authorization for the return. (P) If we can be of further assistance to you in any way, please do not hesitate to call on us. Remember that we are sincerely anxious that you obtain satisfactory service from your set. Very truly yours, (*173 words*)

5. **Mr. R. L. Kenneth 942 Summer Street Whitewater, Wisconsin Dear Sir:** This letter will authorize you to return your Zenith instrument for inspection and repair, shipping charges prepaid. If you do not have the original container, it would be well to confer with the agents of the transportation company about the proper method of packing. It is not possible to sustain a claim for damage if the method of packing does not conform to the transportation company's specifications. We ask you also to notify us at the time of shipment so that we may know when to expect it. (P) Repairs will be made free of charge if the receiver is still within the guarantee period and if our inspection indicates that there are actual defects in material or workmanship. (P) As you can readily understand, we do not find it possible to rebuild old instruments to make them conform to the specifications of late models. We can, however, completely overhaul them and put them in first-class condition. (P) All the instruments we repair go through the same series of rigid tests under actual operating conditions that are applied to new instruments. (P) As soon as we receive the instrument you are returning, we shall write you again. Very truly yours, (*194 words*)

(1) Number of columns to be used............................... 5

(2) Longest item of each column............................... 3 3 3 3 3

(3) Add the longest items; total............................... 15

(4) Deduct this total from strokes available.................... 40 − 15 = 25

(5) Divide by the number of intercolumns
(5 columns − 1)............................... 25 ÷ 4 = 6, with 1 over

The first three intercolumns will be 6 strokes wide, and the last intercolumn 7 strokes wide. (The 1 stroke left over is added to 6.)

Locating the Tabular Stops

Pica Type

(1) Left margin stop location for the first column = 23 (using 43 as the centering point).

(2) 23 + 3 (longest item in column 1) + 6 (intercolumn space) = 32 (the tabular stop point for the second column).

(3) 32 + 3 (longest item in column 2) + 6 (intercolumn space) = 41 (the tabular stop point for the third column).

(4) 41 + 3 (longest item in column 3) + 6 (intercolumn space) = 50 (the tabular stop point for the fourth column).

(5) 50 + 3 (longest item in column 4) + 7 (intercolumn space) = 60 (the tabular stop point for the fifth column).

Proof: 60 + 3 (longest item in column 5) = 63 (the right margin stop location).

Elite Type

(1) Left margin stop location for the first column = 31 (using 51 as the centering point).

(2) 31 + 3 (longest item in column 1) + 6 (intercolumn space) = 40 (the tabular stop point for the second column).

(3) 40 + 3 (longest item in column 2) + 6 (intercolumn space) = 49 (the tabular stop point for the third column).

(4) 49 + 3 (longest item in column 3) + 6 (intercolumn space) = 58 (the tabular stop point for the fourth column).

(5) 58 + 3 (longest item in column 4) + 7 (intercolumn space) = 68 (the tabular stop point for the fifth column).

Proof: 68 + 3 (longest item in column 5) = 71 (the right margin stop location).

Vertical Placement

(1) Main heading, one line............................... 1

Lines between main heading and columns............................... 2

Lines in the tabulation............................... 12

Interlines (space between tabulation lines)............................... 11

Total lines used............................... 26

(2) 66 (total lines available on 11-inch paper) − 26 (total lines used) = 40 (unused lines to be divided between the top and bottom margins).

(3) 40 (remaining lines) ÷ 2 = 20, or the width of the top and bottom margins. If you wish to allow for the optical center, begin the main heading on the 18th line.

123

The five letters in this Assignment were dictated by **Mr. Charles W. Sadler, First Vice-President** of the **Central Trust Company.** Type the letters in the form of Style Letter 5; place the Official Title on the first or second line of the Inside Address—whichever gives the better balance. Use the five letterheads marked Form 7.

First, type Style Letter 5, page 100.

1. **Treadway Printing Company 718 Kent Street Muncie, Indiana Attention Mr. J. U. Olds, Vice-President Gentlemen** We note with pleasure your recent purchase of certain securities from us, and we want to assure you of our appreciation of the opportunity you have given us to serve you. (P) It is our purpose and desire to render our customers efficient service not only in investment matters but in all phases of banking. Please make full use of our facilities. (P) We are also glad to give you what little information we have about the gentleman about whom you made inquiry in your letter of January 14. He opened an account with us about two months ago. All our transactions with him have been perfectly satisfactory. He is the manager of the Adams Confectionery at 1786 Boone Street and lives at 754 North Medford Avenue. (P) At the time he opened the account with us, he did not give us a financial statement or provide us with any information about his personal financial affairs; consequently, we are unable to give you any information in that direction which would be helpful to you. (P) If you would like us to do so, we shall gladly have an investigation made and send you a detailed statement. **Very truly yours** (*192 words*)

2. **Mr. J. C. Cahill, President Rutgers Manufacturing Company 786 Southworth Street Newark, New Jersey Dear Sir** Thank you for your letter in which you ask us to confirm our collection terms and, if possible, quote a more favorable rate. (P) On February 14 we wrote you offering a choice of two arrangements. You replied on February 20 and indicated your acceptance of the plan we proposed to remit your Chicago items by our draft at par the day they are received. (P) Should you wish to send us items on other points in this Federal Reserve District, we shall be pleased to remit at par for the totals of such items three days after receipt. It would, of course, be necessary for us to deduct the actual cost to us on items not collected at par through the Federal Reserve Bank. Please tell us whether the plan we have outlined is acceptable. (P) It is a pleasure, we assure you, to place your name on our list to receive our statements as they are published each half year. **Very truly yours** (*159 words*)

3. **Mr. George Wellington Hatton President, Western Mills Company 785 Central Avenue Minneapolis, Minnesota Dear Mr. Hatton** Thank you for your letter of February 14 with which you enclosed your note for $18,000, dated March 1, payable six months after date, with collateral as listed. The securities offered are quite satisfactory. We have, therefore, placed the amount of the note to the credit of the Hamilton Trust Company, Chicago, as deposited by you. A memorandum of deposit is being sent to you separately by registered mail. (P) In the same envelope we are also returning two certificates of Hampton Coal Company stock for indorsement by your company. Please indorse the stock, have the signatures of the president and the treasurer witnessed, and return the certificates to us. (P) As you have put us on notice that the certificates are the property of the Hatton Coal Company, our attorney advises us that we should obtain from that company a letter addressed to us setting forth that the stock has been assigned to the Western Mills Company for the purpose of permitting your company to place it with us as collateral on the note for $18,000. Please arrange to have such a letter sent to us. **Very truly yours** (*185 words*)

4. **O'Neill Construction Company Tenth and Jackson Streets Indianapolis, Indiana Attention Mr. C. K. Lee, Treasurer Gentlemen** The Legislature of North Carolina has recently passed a bill entitled "An Act to Promote the Solvency of State Banks." This bill authorizes state banks to deduct a collection charge when remitting for checks sent to them; and, if the checks are presented through an express company, a post office, or a Federal Reserve Bank, to refuse payment in cash and instead tender exchange in settlement, even though the check be presented by an agent in person at the counter of the drawee bank. The Act also prohibits any notary public from protesting a check

column tabulation, three intercolumns, etc. If the full width of the sheet is to be used and the margins are to be the same width as that of the intercolumns, the dividing number would be ONE MORE THAN THE NUMBER OF COLUMNS. For a three-column tabulation, the dividing number would be 4; for a four-column tabulation, the dividing number would be 5, etc.

Setting the Tabular Stops

(1) Set the left margin stop for the first column.

(2) To this number add (a) the number of strokes in the longest item of the first column and (b) the number of strokes allowed for the intercolumn space. This total will represent the point at which the tabular stop will be set for the second column.

(3) Proceed from column 2 in the same manner to find the point at which the tabular stop will be set for column 3; and from column 3 to find the tabular stop setting for column 4, etc.

If your typewriter is equipped with a decimal tabulator, the tabular stops should be set to correspond to the decimal point in those columns containing decimals.

work on the sheet so that the top and bottom margins will be of approximately the same width. When you plan the vertical placement, you must make allowance for the main heading as well as for the subheadings and the column headings, when included. If the column headings are long, it may be necessary to break them up into two or three lines. Allowance must be made for these extra lines. Proceed as follows:

(1) Count the number of lines required for the entire tabulation. Include in this count all extra lines for headings and all lines between headings, subheadings, etc.

(2) Subtract the total found in (1) from total lines available on the sheet.

(3) Divide the remainder found in (2) by 2.

The result of this division will give you the number of line spaces to be allowed for the top and bottom margins.

If you wish to allow for the optical center, start the first line of the tabulation 2 or 3 lines higher on the paper so that the bottom margin will be slightly wider than the top margin. (See the note on page 57.)

Application Exercises

The exercises which you will now work out have been carefully constructed to help you acquire the art of arranging tabulations attractively. You will be shown in detail just how the Reference Guide operates, and how you can apply its principles to any kind of tabulating work you may be called on to do. Study carefully the explanations which are given for Exercises 1 and 2.

Be sure to make a pencil working plan as illustrated on page 124 before beginning to type. By following such a plan, the placement will be more accurate, and considerable time will be saved.

Application Exercise 1. The problem consists of making a 5-column tabulation of the 3-

letter words given in the following list. Write the main heading in ALL CAPS; then triple-space and begin the first line of the columns. Write the tabulation with double spacing. Use an 8½ x 11 sheet. Set the margin stops for a 40-stroke line. Read *across* the lines of the copy as given here.

SELECTED THREE-LETTER WORDS

pad pod pig pip pop / pan pen pin pun pay
pat pet pit pot put / pup pug peg pea pie
fad fed fay fly fry / few fan fen fin fun
fat far for fur fro / fix fox fib fob fag
fit you are not who / and him the has can
yes was our sir may / did add get see all

Planning the Tabulation

We shall now go through the steps as called for in the Reference Guide for Tabulation, pages 121 and 122.

CENTRAL TRUST COMPANY

• Resources of More Than $100,000,000

Fourth and Wood Streets   Indianapolis, Ind.

Month Date, Year

Company Name_____
Address_____
City, State_____

Attention Mr. _____ _____, Vice-President

Gentlemen

The full-blocked, open punctuation style illustrated by this
letter is gaining in popularity because of its simplicity and
time-saving features. The paragraphs are indicated by double
spacing; therefore, this style does not easily lend itself to
double-spaced writing.

The two new Minor Parts taken up in this letter are the Official Title and the Attention Phrase.

The Official Title may follow the name in the first line of
the address, or it may be made a part of the second line preceding the company name or the department to which it relates.
The choice is that of the writer and depends upon which gives
the better balance to the Inside Address. Both placements are
shown below.

Mr. _____, Manager   Mr. _____
Texicana Plantation Company, Inc. President, Lee Coal Company
City, State   City, State

The word Attention need not be followed by of. The Attention
Phrase is placed between the Inside Address and the Salutation.
It may be blocked or indented to conform to the letter style.
No period follows the Attention Phrase.

Note that the Official Title may also be a part of the Attention Phrase, as illustrated in this letter. This use of the
Official Title is an expression of courtesy.

Sincerely yours

TYPEWRITTEN COMPANY NAME

Dictator's Title
Xx

(203 Words)

Style Letter 5—to accompany Assignment 5
Single-spaced; Full-blocked; Open Punctuation

A **tabulation** is the arrangement of information in the form of a table. Material so arranged is much more easily read and understood than when put in paragraph form. Every tabulation is an individual problem; hence, the placement of its several parts is the most important phase of the work.

The blank space between lines (for example, between the Main Heading and the Subheading, between the Subheading and the Column Headings, etc.) is called the **Interline**. The blank space between the columns of a tabulation is called the **Intercolumn**.

The typewritten parts which make up a tabulation are:

```
              MAIN HEADING
               Subheading
Column         Column         Column
Heading        Heading        Heading
Tabulation     Tabulation     Tabulation
 (Column)       (Column)       (Column)
```

Each or all of these parts, or a combination of them, may be included in a tabulation. For instance, Application Exercise 1, page 122, contains a main heading and five columns. Exercise 2, page 124, introduces the subheading, and Exercise 3, page 126, includes column headings.

Different spacings may be employed to separate the various parts. It is, therefore, quite important that the correct interpretation be given to the spacing directions. Keep in mind that with single-spaced typing there is no interline (line space) between two lines of typing; with double-spacing there is one interline; and with triple-spacing there are two interlines. The following statements, therefore, carry the same meaning:

"Double-space between the Main Heading and the Subheading."

"Type the Main Heading; then triple-space and type the Subheading."

Each statement means that there are to be two interlines (line spaces) between the main heading and the subheading.

Reference Guide for Tabulation

Before you start typing, you should make a plan for both the horizontal and the vertical placement of the tabulation.

Horizontal Placement includes (1) the centering of the main heading and the subheading across the sheet, (2) the centering of the column headings above the columns, and (3) the setting up of the columns; that is, determining the width of the side margins and of the intercolumns. The width of the intercolumns depends on the width of the columns, as well as on the number of columns which the tabulation is to contain. The main heading and the subheading may be centered by the Back-Space or the Centering-Scale Method. The placement of column headings will be taken up in Exercise 3, page 126.

After determining the dimensions of the paper and the size of the type on your typewriter, the procedure for locating the columns is as follows:

(1) Decide on the number of columns to be set up in the tabulation.

(2) Count the number of strokes in the longest item of each column. (As you make the calculations, put down the figures with a pencil.)

(3) Add together the figures which represent the number of strokes required to write the longest item in each column.

(4) Deduct the total found in Step (3) from the total strokes available. If the tabulation is to occupy the entire line across the page, there will be available 85 pica strokes or 102 elite strokes. If the line length is given, the difference between the figures representing the margin stop locations will give the total strokes available. Thus, with the margin stops set at 13 and 73, there will be 60 (73 — 13) strokes available.

(5) Divide the remainder found in Step (4) by the number of intercolumns (or intercolumns and margins) to find the width of this space. If the division does not come out even, the odd stroke may be added to or subtracted from one of the margins or intercolumn spaces.

If the columns are to be kept within a given length, say between 13 and 73, the number of intercolumns will be ONE LESS THAN THE NUMBER OF COLUMNS. A three-column

tenders exchange. (By exchange is meant the drawee bank's check on another financial institution.) (P) We have received a list of sixty-nine banking institutions that have entered into an injunction suit against the Reserve Bank seeking to restrain the collection of checks on these banks unless they are permitted to deduct a collection charge. (P) It is impossible to foresee how many banks in North Carolina may attempt to take advantage of this law. To provide for the fullest protection of our depositors and correspondents, we are compelled to inform you that until further notice we will not receive on deposit or for collection checks or drafts drawn on any of these banks. We shall receive, as heretofore, items drawn on national banks in North Carolina and on all state institutions that will pay their checks at par to the Federal Reserve Bank. Very truly yours *(246 words)*

5. **Mr. F. C. Raleigh, Treasurer Millbank Manufacturing Company 897 Fulton Street Indianapolis, Indiana Dear Mr. Raleigh One of our depositors has informed us that you are thinking of changing your banking connection. This letter extends to you our cordial invitation to open an account with us. (P) Our capital, surplus, and profits aggregate more than $6,400,000.** resources. (P) Our officers are experienced men well known in financial circles, and our board of directors is composed of active business men of high standing. Our equipment is thoroughly modern, and our employees are courteous and accommodating to everyone. (P) On many occasions this bank has had the privilege of being a real factor in the growth of leading business concerns in our community. We are always glad to extend reasonable accommodation to our depositors. (P) On individual savings accounts we pay 2% interest and allow withdrawals without the usual notice. We do not restrict our depositors in any way; they may deposit or withdraw large or small sums as they desire. (P) Our safe deposit boxes are housed in fire-proof vaults and are protected by every known safety device. The rentals are extremely modest and range from $1.50 per annum upward. (P) Separately we are sending you six copies of our last annual statement. It shows an increase in our deposits during the last year of more than $700,000. We shall appreciate your bringing the statements to the attention of your officers and board of directors. (P) Please be sure that we shall be happy to be of service to you in any way. Yours very truly *(251 words)*

Envelope Addressing

The face of the envelope may be divided into four sections:

1. The **Return Address** section is the upper left part.

This section may be printed for business correspondence or typed for personal correspondence. When typing the return address, the blocked form is used, and a margin of about a quarter of an inch is left at the top and left sides.

2. The **Stamp** section is the upper right part.

Stamps should be firmly applied not less than one-eighth of an inch from the corner to prevent the possibility of their being torn loose by the canceling machine.

3. The **Miscellaneous** section is the lower left part.

This section may be used for such notations as "Personal," "In care of ——," "Attention——," "Introducing——," etc.; or for the street address or the room number of a building.

4. The **Outside Address** section is the lower right part.

The four sections are shown by number in the outlines—Illustrations 39 and 40, page 102.

Always use a high degree of care in addressing envelopes. In all ordinary cases the envelope address should agree with the inside address of the letter. Check the spelling of all names in the address. If you are replying to a letter from a company, use the name of the company in the exact form printed on the letterhead, both for the inside address and for the envelope address. Make sure that you type the correct state name. There are many cities and towns of the same name in different states.

"Because of carelessness in addressing and preparing matter for mailing," says the United States Official Postal Guide, "or the failure of the sender to place his name and address on it, millions of letters and other pieces of mail which cannot be delivered or returned to the sender are each year sent to the Division of Dead Letters."

In order to simplify the sorting and delivering of mail, the tendency is toward writing out all state names in full in envelope addresses, even though, for the sake of balance, the state name in the inside address may have been abbreviated. It is also good practice to write out official titles, as well as such words as *Street*, *Avenue*, and *Building*.

the country. Our figures are in such shape that I can readily prepare charts which I believe will be of practical value and interest to the members. (P) Thank you for the invitation and rest assured that I will do my best. Cordially yours,

(161 words)

Type the following letter in the Single-spaced, Semi-blocked Style. The letter has a postscript, which is to be typed below the Identification Initials. Use Form 18. Study Illustration 47. When typing a letter with a carbon copy notation or with a postscript, raise the Inside Address two or more lines to allow space for the carbon copy notation or the postscript.

In ordinary business letters postscripts should usually be avoided. In sales letters, however, postscripts are often successfully used to call attention to a special offer which is made in the letter.

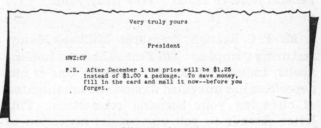

Illustration 47

Illustration 46

Illustration 46 shows a letter written in a personal or semi-business style. This style is suitable for use in writing letters of application, which should always be typed on plain paper.

Type the letter on plain paper. For the heading use your own address and the current date. Next, type the letter again; this time use the letterhead marked Form 17 and type the address below the letter as shown in Illustration 45, page 119.

2. **Mr. Clarence C. Hooper   International Association of Milk Dealers   516 Prairie Avenue   Kansas City, Missouri   Dear Mr. Hooper:** I was very glad to hear from you again and to know that you still have pleasant recollections of the day you spent with us nearly a year ago. I am sorry indeed that your stay was so short. When you come this way again, by all means plan your trip so that you can spend several days with us. (P) I accept your invitation to address the convention on the subject, "What the Product Cost Statement Revealed to our Company." We have now had almost three years' experience with the fine uniform cost system established by the Association. I think it is in many respects the greatest contribution the Association

3. **Mrs. George W. Lander   817 Creston Street   Springfield, Illinois   Dear Madam:** Great news for you this morning! I have just received permission from the Government to ship my **OLD TYME** delicacies outside of the State of Wisconsin. (P) My father and I have made and sold sausage in Milwaukee for more than thirty years; now for the first time it is available to you. (P) And what sausage—what a flavor—made of a secret formula known only to me—of pure fresh meats—the purest of spices—in a spotlessly clean shop—by sausage-makers who learned their trade in the old country. (P) We want your permission to send a trial shipment to you—at no risk on your part. Just fill in the enclosed card telling me what you want. I shall make shipment at once, postpaid. (P) Thank you! Very truly yours President P. S. After December 1 the price will be $1.25 instead of $1.00 a package. To save money, fill in the card and mail it now—before you forget. *(155 words)*

```
┌─────────────────────────┬─────────────────────────┐
│          (1)            │          (2)            │
│                         │          ┌─────────┐    │
│  ---1/3 Envelope        │          │ ╱╲╱╲╱╲╱ │    │
│       Width----         │          │         │    │
│                         │          │         │    │
│      (Center)           │          │         │    │
│                         │          └─────────┘    │
│               Name_____     │
│          (3)  Address_____     (4)     │
│                City_____                │
│               State_____               │
│                         │                         │
└─────────────────────────┴─────────────────────────┘
```

Illustration 39
Double-spaced, Indented Style
Names of city and state on separate lines

```
┌─────────────────────────┬─────────────────────────┐
│ Name_____          │          ┌─────────┐    │
│ Address_____       │          │ ╱╲╱╲╱╲╱ │    │
│ City, State_____     │          │         │    │
│                    (Center)        │         │    │
│          (1)            │   (2)    └─────────┘    │
│                         │                         │
│       (Center)          │                         │
│               Name_____     │
│          (3)  Address_____     (4)    │
│               City, State_____          │
│                         │                         │
│ Room 324, Administration Building                 │
└─────────────────────────┴─────────────────────────┘
```

Illustration 40
Single-spaced, Blocked Style
Typed Return Address.   Miscellaneous section used.

will be yours. Sincerely yours, *Ann Fenning* Manager (*174 words*)

2. **Mr. James Wallace Reardon** 991 North Washington Street Jersey City, New Jersey Dear Mr. Reardon: For many years you have been compelled to attend to the detail of winding, oiling, and regulating your clocks. (P) Now for the first time we offer an electric clock that has been perfected and designed expressly for use on electric current which is supplied to your home. The Hammond Electric Clock, described in the enclosed circular, may be put into service by simply inserting the plug into any convenient outlet. (P) You set the hands to the correct time in the usual manner and start the clock. When you have done so, you will be sure to get dependable time. (P) Notice especially the description of the Hammond Calendar Clock that tells the day and date automatically, as well as the time. The price of this model is only $22.50.

charge account when buying a Hammond Electric Clock. Sincerely yours, *W. C. Hampton* Sales Manager (*145 words*)

3. **Mr. John C. McHenry,** President United Construction & Development Company 581 Monterey Street Paterson, New Jersey Dear Mr. McHenry: Our Executive Committee has requested me to extend to you a cordial invitation to become a member of the Covina Aviation Country Club. (P) Covina will be one of the most modern clubs on the Atlantic Coast. Located at the east entrance to Bear Valley, the property provides one of the most beautiful sites for the purpose to be found anywhere. (P) Furthermore, Covina is being developed under the direction of men who have had practical and successful experience in aviation and club organization and development. (P) I hope that we may have the honor of including your name in our list of charter members. Sincerely yours, *C. W. Martin*, Managing Director (*102 words*)

Assignment 11

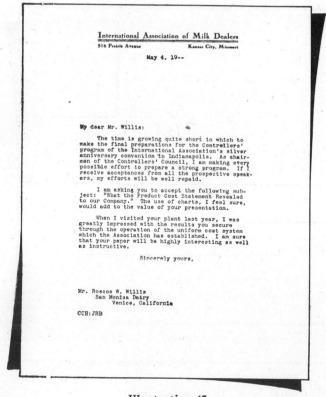

Illustration 45
Style Letter 11

Illustration 45 is that of an informal or personal letter. Note that the Inside Address is typed six lines below the Complimentary Close. Begin the Salutation on the same line that you would begin the Inside Address according to the Letter Placement Chart. Study Illustration 45; then type Letter 1 on the letterhead marked Form 16.

1. **My dear Mr. Willis:** The time is growing quite short in which to make the final preparations for the Controllers' program of the International Association's silver anniversary convention in Indianapolis. As chairman of the Controllers' Council, I am making every possible effort to prepare a strong program. If I receive acceptances from all the prospective speakers, my efforts will be well repaid. (P) I am asking you to accept the following subject: "What the Product Cost Statement Revealed to our Company." The use of charts, I feel sure, would add to the value of your presentation. (P) When I visited your plant last year, I was greatly impressed with the results you secure through the operation of the uniform cost system which the Association has established. I am sure that your paper will be highly interesting as well as instructive. Sincerely yours, Mr. Roscoe W. Willis San Monica Dairy Venice, California (*134 words*)

As a general rule, the Outside Address should be so typed that it will not consist of more than four lines; further necessary information should be placed in the Miscellaneous Section.

Four address styles are in general use:

1. Double-spaced, indented (Style 1, Illustration 41, page 104)
2. Single-spaced, indented (Style 2)
3. Double-spaced, blocked (Style 3)
4. Single-spaced, blocked (Style 4)

The *line* location of the Outside Address is one line space below the horizontal center. On a 6¾ envelope the first line would begin two inches, or twelve line spaces, from the top; that is, approximately one line below center.

The *beginning point* of the first line will depend on the address style used and the width of the envelope.

When using the indented style on a No. 6¾ envelope, begin about one-third the width of the envelope from the left side. See Illustration 39.

With the blocked style, begin slightly to the left of the center of the envelope as shown in Illustration 40.

When using legal size envelopes (No. 10), begin slightly to the left of center in the indented style and slightly to the right of center in the blocked style. Examples of addresses typed on No. 10 envelopes are shown in Styles 5 and 6, Illustration 41, page 104.

Double-spaced envelope addresses are preferred to single-spaced addresses because double-spaced addresses are more quickly and easily read.

Both close and open punctuation are acceptable, although open punctuation is now the more widely used. If the names of the city and the state are written on the same line, they should be separated by a comma.

Assignment

Refer to Illustrations 39 and 40, page 102, as a guide for placing the several parts of the address on a No. 6¾ envelope. If No. 6¾ envelopes are not available, cut paper to envelope size—6½″ wide by 3⅝″ deep.

A. Type the Outside Address shown in Style 1, Illustration 41, page 104; then type the following addresses in the same style. Use your own name and home address for the Return Address.

1. **Alpha Printing Company   789 Market Street San Antonio   Texas**
2. **Mr. Samuel C. Rutherford   278 Spring Street Kansas City   Kansas**
3. **Dr. H. W. Harrington   128 Eighth Avenue Louisville   Kentucky**
4. **Miss Carrie W. Weatherford   The Severn Baltimore   Maryland**
5. **Charles L. Springer, Esq.   416 Professional Building   Los Angeles   California**

B. Type Style 2, Illustration 41; then type these addresses in the same style.

1. **Messrs. Handy & Winters   1897 Green Street Portland, Oregon**
2. **Julius W. Tremont & Sons   Arch and Madison Streets   Easton, Pennsylvania**
3. **Mrs. Elizabeth Y. Towne   416 Spruce Street Cincinnati, Ohio**
4. **Mr. C. J. Green   1140 West 56th Street Cleveland, Ohio**
5. **Roberts Stationery Company   619 Lincoln Avenue   Denver, Colorado**

C. Type Style 3, Illustration 41; then type these addresses in the same style.

1. **Mr. P. C. Paulson   35 D Street, N. W.   Washington, D. C.**
2. **Miss Laura W. Jenkins   915 St. Paul Place Milwaukee, Wisconsin**
3. **Messrs. Wilson, Madison & Hall   914 Ransome Street   Pittsburgh, Pennsylvania**
4. **Art Motal Company   Fourth and Mason Streets   Wheeling, West Virginia**
5. **Henry W. Higginson, Esq.   Monadnock Building   San Francisco, California**

D. Type Style 4, Illustration 41; then type these addresses in the same form.

1. **Messrs. Hayden, Scott, Myers & Wells   217 Fidelity Trust Building   Omaha, Nebraska   Introducing Mr. Charles C. Gray**
2. **Gail-Kenyon Company   Fourth and Harris Streets   Salt Lake City, Utah   Attention Mr. J. L. Kenyon**
3. **Dr. H. T. Jacobson   1786 River Drive   Los Angeles, California   Please forward**
4. **Mr. C. R. Ayres   718 Amsterdam Street Albany, New York   Personal**
5. **Miss Elizabeth H. Kenyon   416 Severn Avenue Baltimore, Maryland   Personal**

COHAN & McCANN DIRECT MAIL Advertising

COMMERCIAL BANK BUILDING

February
18
19--

CLEVELAND·OHIO

Mr. Samuel L. Nicholson
President, Art Metal Company
1178 Higginson Street
Indianapolis, Indiana

Dear Mr. Nicholson:

Has it ever occurred to you that successful sales
letters must be built and not written--if they
are to secure real results?

In our last "Achievement Letter" we told you about
a letter that pulled 26% replies on a mailing
of 178,000, and that replies were still being
received twelve months after the letters had
been mailed. We told you also about another
three-page letter that secured 11% orders.

Why were these letters so successful?

Because they were built according to a definite
plan. There is a plan for the construction
of a successful sales letter--a plan which is
just as exact as that for the erection of a
skyscraper. We use such a plan--an actual
"Letter Building Plan," written on one sheet
of paper.

If you will fill in the enclosed card and mail it
to us, we'll gladly send you a copy of our
"Letter Building Plan."

                    Sincerely yours,

                    CW Bruns

                    Manager

CWBruns--XXX

Enclosure

(153 Words)

Style Letter 10
Single-spaced; Inverted Style; Mixed Punctuation

118

given in Style 3 below; then type the following addresses in the same style. Consult page 103 for the placement of the Outside Address on No. 10 envelopes. If No. 10 envelopes are not available, cut paper to size—9½″ wide by 4⅛″ deep.

1. **Mr. B. K. Green** 519 South River Street Harrisburg Pennsylvania

2. **Mr. Hamilton C. Gray** Commonwealth Trust Building Providence Rhode Island

3. **Miss Katherine W. Walters** 1941 Calhoun Avenue Nashville Tennessee

then type the following addresses in that form.

1. **Messrs. Raymond, Whitaker & Jenks** Professional Arts Building Main and Chestnut Streets Newark, New Jersey Introducing Mr. Daniel F. Reyburn

2. **The F. G. French Company** South Street and Park Avenue Springfield, Illinois Accounting Department

3. **The Evening Journal** Journal Square Syracuse, New York Attention Miss Laura C. Caldwell

Illustration 41
Common Envelope Address Styles

Data Sheet 12540 of the Central Freight Association authorizes a rate of $1 a gross ton on pyrites ore cinder from the Cleveland District to Mahoning and Shenango Valley, which would be the basis to Sharpsville, Pa. (P) The General Chemical Company, located on our Newburg Branch, .8 mile from Newburg Junction, makes regular shipments of this commodity to Sharpsville. We can secure this traffic provided we publish the Cleveland District rate of $1. (P) Please let me know whether I have your authority to arrange accordingly with the Traffic Department. L. O. Lewis, Freight Agent (*84 words*)

5. **Mr. L. R. Breyer** I am turning over to you the following papers in the Beckman vs. Gessford matter: (1) Draft of decree, (2) Court files, (3) Office file, (4) Transcript of testimony, and (5) Master's report and copy. (P) The changes you suggested when transmitting the file to me have been made. Mr. Oxnam suggests that there should be an amendment setting up the changes in the personnel of the Bondholders' Committee. I thoroughly concur in this suggestal character and should be set out in a supplemental bill rather than as an amendment. (P) There might well be included in the supplemental bill, as a matter of amendment, a correction in the amended supplemental bill which now sets out, as does the original bill, that the six $500.00 notes were dated February 28. They were actually dated April 28, and the Master has so found. (P) I note also that Mrs. Grant did not answer and is in default. This fact is not material, as she appears to have deposited her notes and no longer has any interest in the subject-matter of the suit. (P) The same thing seems to be true of several other defendants. The letter of the Fulton Title & Trust Company calls for an explanation of the reason for making that Company a defendant. It might be advisable, in connection with the supplemental bill, to set out that the Trust Company was originally a noteholder but has since deposited the notes which it held. (P) When the decree was drawn, I indicated that the supplemental bill was already on file. J. K. Trewin (*264 words*)

Assignment 10

Type Style Letter 10, page 118, on the letterhead, Form 12. Next, type the following letters in the same style on the letterheads marked Form 13, Form 14, and Form 15, respectively.

After writing the address, the salutation, and the first line of a letter to be typed in the inverted style, reset the margin stop at the point where the second and succeeding lines of each paragraph are to begin. When writing the first line of each new paragraph, use the margin release and move the carriage to 0. Set the first tabular stop at the point at which the first line is to begin, and tabulate from 0 to this point.

The inverted style is often used in sales letters, or when an unusual effect is sought. It is not practical for ordinary letters.

There are many possible variations of the inverted style. The address of the letter, for example, may be typed in the indented style instead of in the blocked style. The second and succeeding lines of the paragraphs may be indented ten strokes instead of five strokes, as is done in Style Letter 10. Another interesting variation is obtained by beginning the second and succeeding lines of each paragraph at the midpoint of the first line of the paragraph. In a letter written in that way the complimentary close, the company name, and the identifying signature may be lined up with the indented lines. Sometimes, too, the lines in the address and the conclusion are typed flush with the left-hand margin, and all the lines which make up the paragraphs are indented ten strokes from that margin.

1. **Miss Harriet W. Springman 4897 Walnut Street Newark, New Jersey Dear Miss Springman:** I was a stenographer once, and I know very well how much you and our sister stenographers like to have well-groomed, good-looking hands. (P) A stenographer's hands attract attention, and all the stenographers I have ever known were proud girls who always tried to present a good appearance. (P) I have studied stenographers. I have studied hands and nails. The result is a little manicure kit for stenographers. It contains nail polish that is refined and natural-looking, yet bright and glossy. It also has a nail polish remover, an orange wood stick, and a compact pencil of nail white. It is a handy little kit that fits into one's handbag or into a corner of a girl's desk drawer or dressing table. (P) It is made by a stenographer for stenographers. The name of it is "Gloria's Kit." The price is ridiculously low—fifty cents, the price of a couple of nut sundaes. A coin card is enclosed. Mail it today, in the enclosed

Illustration 42 shows the steps to be followed in folding a letter which is to be enclosed in a No. 6¾ envelope. Always follow this procedure; then, when the letter is taken out of the envelope, it can easily be opened and spread out.

A letter which is to be put into a No. 10 envelope is creased twice only. Fold from the bottom edge about one-third of the length of the sheet. Crease the fold. Then bring down the upper third of the sheet to within one-quarter inch of the fold. Crease this second fold also. Make sure that you fold and crease the paper neatly and evenly. The sheet is inserted in the envelope with the last fold toward you. When the envelope is opened, the letter may then be conveniently unfolded.

Practice the folding of 8½ x 11 sheets to be inserted in No. 6¾ envelopes; then refold the sheets for insertion in No. 10 envelopes. Do not leave this detail until you have mastered it.

Here is another way of folding letter sheets, which is used by some mailing clerks: (1) Fold over the lower part of the sheet within one-half inch of the top edge. Crease the fold evenly. (2) Fold over the sheet from the left edge about one-third of its width. Crease the fold evenly. (3) Fold over the right edge so that it extends about one-quarter of an inch beyond the fold made in Step Two. Crease this fold evenly. (4) Insert the folded letter in the envelope in such a way that the crease made in Step Three will be at the bottom of the envelope. When the letter is removed from the envelope, pick up the sheet by the upper right-hand corner and shake open the letter. It will then be right side up in position to read.

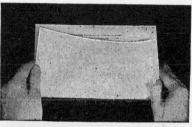

Step One

Fold over the lower part of the sheet so as to bring the bottom edge within one-half inch of the top edge. Crease the fold evenly. Step One shows the letter in the process of being folded.

Step Two

Fold over the sheet from the right edge about one-third of its width. Crease the fold evenly.

Step Three

Fold over the left edge to within one-fourth of an inch of the fold made in Step Two. Crease this fold evenly.

Step Four

Hold the folded letter as shown in the illustration at the left. Insert it in the envelope in such a way that the crease made in Step Three will be at the bottom of the envelope.

Illustration 42
Steps in Folding a Letter

CURTISS-WRIGHT FLYING SERVICE

INTER-DEPARTMENTAL COMMUNICATION

Date:

From:

To:

Subject: Inter-Departmental and Inter-Office Correspondence

    This is the Army style of inter-departmental communications. It has been adopted, with many variations, by business firms.

    Both plain paper and letterhead paper in full letter-size and half sheets are used. The heading--Date, To, From, Subject--may or may not be printed. The arrangement and the location of this heading vary with different companies to meet their specific needs or requirements.

Style Letter 9A
To accompany Assignment 9

MEMORANDUM

Month Date, Year

Name_____

    The Memorandum is a common form of inter-office communication from one department to another or from a department head to his subordinates.

    Short Memorandums are generally written on half-size plain paper. The major parts of the business letter not shown in this Memorandum are usually omitted.

    Carbon copies of inter-departmental and inter-office corre-spondence are usually made on full letter-size "second" sheets to permit greater facility in filing.

Typed Signature

Style Letter 9B
To accompany Assignment 9

bills, statements, and other business papers, are often mailed in window envelopes. A window envelope has a cut-out in which a piece of transparent paper is sometimes inserted. On the letter or other paper to be inserted in a window envelope, there is often printed a guide (⌐) to show just where the address is to be typed. The sheet must then be folded in

cut-out. To insert an 8½x11 sheet into a No. 10 window envelope, fold up the sheet from the bottom about one-third; then fold back the proper distance so that the address will be visible through the cut-out. Study Illustrations 43 and 44.

Window envelopes save time—the address is not typed on the envelope. Furthermore, they reduce the possibility of error because the address is typed once only.

Note the style in which the address, which shows through the "window" of the envelope, is typed. The first three lines are single spaced. The state name is set off by double spacing to make it stand out clearly.

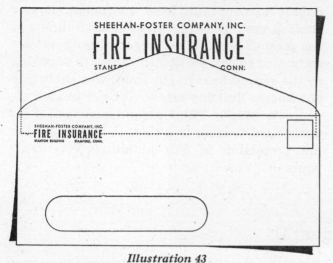

Illustration 43

Illustration 44

Assignment 6

The following letters were dictated by **H. J. Sloan** of the **Woodlawn Homes Realty Corporation.** Type the letters, with carbons, in the form of Style Letter 6. Address a No. 6¾ envelope for each letter. Be sure to make the proper Enclosure Notation for each letter. Use the five letterheads marked Form 8. Study and type Style Letter 6, page 107.

To prepare carbon paper for insertion, first lay the second sheet on the table; next, lay the carbon paper on this sheet with the glazed or carbon side down; then lay the letterhead on top of the carbon paper. Insert in the machine according to the directions given on page 7 for inserting paper (Letter Writing or Carbon Copy Method).

In case several copies are to be made, the upper edges of the sheets may be kept even by slipping them inside the crease of a folded piece of paper or under the flap of an envelope. It may be necessary to disengage the Paper Release in order to get the paper started.

1. **Mr. Charles G. West 854 Walnut Street Aurora, Illinois Dear Sir:** We have leased your farm near Niles, Michigan, to Mr. Samuel J. Cook for a yearly cash rental of $600. We have made a number of inquiries about Mr. Cook in Niles, where he has lived for several years. He is, we believe, a competent and reliable man and will prove to be a desirable tenant. **(P)** Here is our check for $88, which is the amount of the

first quarter's rent after deducting our commission of 2% on the first year's rent and also the amount of $50 which we paid for the repair work done by Mr. A. L. Johnson as authorized by you. Mr. Johnson's receipted bill is also enclosed. Very truly yours, *(112 words)*

2. **Mr. A. F. Kingsley 517 Queen Street Evanston, Illinois Dear Mr. Kingsley:** Some time ago you asked us to bring to your attention properties in the Fenwick section which might be listed with us. **(P)** You will be interested, we believe, in the property at 540 Chestnut Hill Boulevard, which was placed on our list yesterday. A copy of this new list is enclosed. **(P)** The lot is 75′ x 150′ and is improved with a handsome eleven-room, brownstone-front dwelling with garage in the rear. These buildings were erected three years ago, and no expense was spared in their construction. **(P)** The property was owned by the late Judge Walter Wilkins, and his executors are required to dispose of it in the settlement of his estate. **(P)** We believe you will want to inspect this splendid property. Will you let us know when it will be convenient for you to do so? We shall gladly have one of our men accompany you. Very truly yours, *(148 words)*

cials object to incurring any expense for this work; but in view of the fact that the protection is required for our cable runs and not particularly in view of our status as tenants of the building, I recommend that further protection be installed at our expense. (P) An item not covered by Mr. Jennison's letter is the entrance to the freight elevator shaft at the northwest corner of the building. This shaft opens right into the boiler room and is without protection of any description. The window casings and doors throughout the length of the shaft are composed of wood and seem to present a risk. We have requested the Bourse officials to provide a suitable fire door for this opening, but they object to doing the work because of the sary. I therefore recommend that this door be sheathed at our expense. (P) The work which I recommend that we do at our own expense consists of the following: (P) Sheathe the door from the pipe shaft on the second floor to the rooms of the Board of Trade. (P) Sheathe the double doors opening from the freight elevator shaft at the northwest corner of the building at the seventh floor. The foregoing two items are estimated to cost $67.50. (P) Close the opening at the second floor in the southwest shaft into the Bourse Building offices. The estimated expense is $22.50. (P) I recommend that I be authorized to incur this expense to increase the fire protection in this building. Very truly yours *(742 words)*

Assignment 9

First, type Style Letters 9A and 9B, page 116; then write Memorandums No. 1 and No. 2 in the form of Style Letter 9A. Use the two Inter-office letterheads marked Form 11. The Letter Placement Chart does not apply to half sheets; hence, you will need to use your own judgment in setting up these memorandums.

Next, type on plain paper Memorandums 3, 4, and 5 in the form of Style Letter 9B. A full-size sheet will be required for No. 5. Center the word **MEMORANDUM** on each sheet. Use today's date.

1. **From: C. W. Herrick, Base Manager To: J. R. Haggerty, General Manager Subject: Additional Personnel** Authority is respectfully requested to employ the following personnel: (P) Mr. G. R. Woodley as a solicitor of students for the ground school and flying school courses. We have made an arrangement with Mr. Woodley by which we shall pay him 10% commission on all sales. For the first month we have agreed to allow him a drawing account of $125. (P) Mr. H. J. Connolly as a solicitor for aerial photography. The arrangement we have made with Mr. Connolly calls for a commission of 20% on sales, with a drawing account of $20 a week for one month. (P) In both cases the solicitors will be required to stay within their drawing accounts. *(111 words)*

2. **From: H. G. Sheffield, Assistant Base Manager To: Arthur J. Denton Subject: Exhaust Valve Guides—Whirlwind 240 Engine** Please arrange to have returned to us at once the guides that were replaced in Mr. Linton's Whirlwind 240 Engine. It would appear that Mr. Linton is entitled to some adjustment. (P) From your report I cannot tell whether or not the carburetor settings in this engine have been changed. As such a change would probably do more toward reducing valve guide wear than any other change, we have already recommended that it be incorporated in all Whirlwind 240 engines as soon as possible. (P) I am writing at once to the Bendix Stromberg Company for an adjustment on the defective carburetor. *(100 words)*

3. **Mr. C. K. Taylor** I had an analysis made of the number of packages returned by customers during the past year. In February the percentage of returns was 5¼%; in April, 4½%; and in June, 5%. (P) Since that time the percentage of returns has increased considerably. In July, for example, the percentage was 7½%; in September, 7%; in October, 7¾%; in November, 7½%; in December, 8%; and in January, 9½%. (P) This upward trend shows that returns in relation to sales were continuously on the increase during the latter part of the year. Please make an investigation immediately to determine what steps we may take to minimize returns. **J. W. Mason** *(103 words)*

WOODLAWN HOMES
REALTY CORPORATION

484 MICHIGAN BOULEVARD
. . . CHICAGO, ILLINOIS

Month Date, Year

Name_____
Address_____
City, State_____

My dear Sir:

This letter includes the Minor Part, "Enclosure Notation," and discusses briefly the use of carbon paper.

When an enclosure is mentioned in a letter, a notation to that effect should be made below the Reference Initials as a secondary check for the reader and the mailing clerk. If there is only one enclosure, the word "Enclosure" will be sufficient. When there is more than one enclosure, the number is indicated by typing the appropriate figure after "Enclosure." The abbreviation "Enc." or "Encl." may be used, but many writers prefer to spell the word in full.

Carbon copies should be made of all outgoing letters. A plain sheet of paper called a "second sheet" is generally used, although the copy is sometimes made on the back of the letter being answered. Letterhead paper should not be used for carbon copies.

The carbon paper should be carefully selected according to weight and finish for the purpose for which it is to be used. The different weights are standard, light, medium, and heavy. The finishes are medium, hard, dull, bright, slightly hard, and extra hard. Special carbon paper is obtainable for billing and for use with noiseless typewriters. Carbon paper may also be obtained in various sizes and colors, depending upon the needs.

Standard letter-size ($8\frac{1}{2}$ x 11) and legal-size ($8\frac{1}{2}$ x 13) carbon sheets are in general use. If the letter-size is used, the corners should be cut to allow the carbon paper to slide out while holding the typewritten sheets by the corners.

Yours truly,

TYPEWRITTEN COMPANY NAME

XXX:XXX
Enclosures 2

(255 Words)

Style Letter 6—to accompany Assignment 6
Single-spaced; Semi-blocked; Mixed Punctuation

pected to remain covered by the insulation for some years without undergoing any change. The expense involved in tinning copper conductors to be used in the manufacture of cables would, however, add appreciably to the cost of the cables. (P) Another method of preventing reaction between the leather and the copper consists of covering the copper with a layer of unvulcanized leather to separate it from a covering of vulcanized leather which is applied subsequently. This method is not used to any appreciable extent nowadays because of the greater advantages possessed by the tin coating. It was used, however, to a considerable extent in the early days of insulated wire manufacture. The consistency of leather changes appreciably with the ordinary ranges of outdoor temperatures. Leather becomes soft and sticky under the higher temperatures and stiff and brittle in cold weather. (P) Many leather insulating compounds are very susceptible to the action of hot paraffine. Some dissolve in hot paraffine; others swell and disintegrate. Although compounds can be selected which would show a reasonably high resistance to damage by the hot paraffine necessary for the "boiling out" of splices, the changes which leather compounds undergo in storage gradually reduce this resistance. For this reason, a splice successfully made and subsequently opened after a lapse of time would probably show sufficient deterioration of the leather compound to make "boiling out" impracticable after the work for which the splice was opened had been done. (P) In view of the foregoing facts, it is our judgment that the use of leather sleeving for insulating the wire joints in cable splices would introduce a serious hazard to the service. Very truly yours (*440 words*)

3. **Mr. W. I. Wilson, General Superintendent United Telephone Company 897 Madison Avenue New York, New York Dear Sir Subject: File No. 627855** All the defects noted in Mr. Jennison's letter to me dated January 10 have now been corrected with the exception of the following, all of which refer to the southwest shaft: (P) A. Openings from the shaft to the Bourse Building and to the Board of Trade offices on the second floor seem to be unnecessary and should be walled up. If these openings vided for them. (P) The Bourse officials consider this work unnecessary. (P) B. The opening between the two parts of the shaft on the second floor should be provided with a fire door. (P) The Bourse officials object to this work. (P) C. All fuse blocks should be cleaned up and mounted in wooden cases lined with asbestos. (P) Our request to the Bourse officials covered only the second floor. As this work has been done and as the fuses on the other floors have been put in good condition and are not now considered a risk, I believe that this item may be considered as satisfactorily finished. (P) D. Wooden ladders and staging should be replaced by iron work. (P) This work has been done except that there still remain two boards used as a passageway in the lower part of the shaft at the second floor line and a wooden extension ladder supported on two planks and located between the second floor and the exhibition floor. The Bourse officials do not consider this material as a risk and object to replacing it. (P) E. Two sprinklers should be installed in the lower part of the shaft. (P) The Bourse officials maintain that this work is unnecessary and do not care to assume the risk of false operation. (P) F. The two hose reels on the seventh floor should be replaced with modern racks, and the hose should either be tested and proved satisfactory or replaced. (P) The Bourse officials maintain that the reels are not of an obsolete type and object to replacing them. The hose has been tested and has proved satisfactory. (P) Item "C" has been satisfactorily taken care of by the work done by the Bourse officials, and I recommend that this feature be accepted as it stands. (P) On Items "E" and "F"—in view of the Bourse officials' objection to taking any further steps— I believe that the situation is satisfactory and recommend that these features be accepted as they stand. (P) On Item "D" the presence of the wooden work noted in this letter still seems to me to be objectionable; but in view of its small amount and of the objection by the Bourse officials to incurring any further expense, I recommend that this feature be accepted as it stands. (P) On Items "A" and "B" I believe that we should make further efforts to protect the shaft, especially as it is used between the exhibition floor and the second floor, and is a

velopment Company Madison, Wisconsin My dear Mr. White: I am sorry that I shall be unable to attend the meeting of the Board of Directors and of the stockholders next Saturday. Mr. Jenkins will present my report and will be glad to give whatever assistance he can. For your information I enclose a copy of that report. (P) As to the suggestion of the extra dividend, I have concluded that the letter which is to be sent to the stockholders with the regular dividend checks will be sufficient to satisfy them as to the success of the enterprise and the value of their investment. (P) The right policy, I believe, is to conserve the resources of the company at this time. Later on, when the fixed charges are lowered through a reduction in the mortgage indebtedness, we can pay regularly an additional 1% on the stock without adding much to the financial burden of the company. I am, therefore, not in favor of any extra distribution of profits at this time. (P) You may rely on my continued cooperation at all times. Sincerely yours, (171 words)

4. Mr. J. W. Samuels 843 South 45th Street Chicago, Illinois Dear Sir: Thank you for your letter about your lot No. 61 in the Hollingsworth Plot. A receipt is enclosed for the balance on the account. (P) In order to issue the deed in the name of your wife, it will be necessary to make an examination and transfer of title, which will cost you $4.50. We can, however, have the deed drawn to you and your wife jointly without any extra cost. (P) If you wish a policy of title insurance on your property, the Title Guaranty Company will issue one to you for $25. We do not issue an abstract with your deed, but we shall be glad to arrange the matter for you through the Title Guaranty Company if you wish us to do so. (P) The specifications for a number of bungalows to be erected on this Plot

specifications will be available by the time you are ready to build. The sewerage system has already been completed, and the paving of the streets is well under way. Building operations will be started soon. Very truly yours, (180 words)

5. Mrs. Mary W. Landis 7865 Cadillac Avenue Oak Park, Illinois Dear Mrs. Landis: Have you just moved? If you have, you know that moving is hard on the nerves! It involves plenty of work and worry. (P) Moving is expensive, too. Curtains, rugs, and many other things must be bought, in addition to the actual cost of the hauling. (P) If you moved from one rented house to another, have you really bettered yourself? Aren't there some things about your new location that you would not put up with in a home of your own? (P) You may be living in a better neighborhood, but you have really gained nothing—if you are still paying rent. The only person who has gained is your new landlord. (P) Deep down in your heart you want a home of your own some day. Why not bring that day nearer? We can help you. (P) If you are still renting, the chances are that you don't know just how easy it is to own your own home. We have developed a plan that will enable you to move into your own home sooner than you might think possible. It is a brand new plan—a plan that you can start NOW—with little or no sacrifice on your part. We have shown this new plan to many other people, and the grateful letters they have written us show that they have really been benefited and helped to achieve their ambition. (P) Will you let us explain the plan to you without any obligation whatever on your part? Just use the card that comes with this letter, and our experienced real estate counselor will call on you promptly to help you in any way he can. Very truly yours, (274 words)

Assignment 7

Type these five letters in the form of Style Letter 7. Use the letterheads marked Form 9. The letters were dictated by Mr. O. A. Adamson, General Superintendent of the Turner Construction Company. First, type Style Letter 7, page 109.

1. Consolidated Gas Company 1706 West Sixth Street Cleveland, Ohio Gentlemen: Subject: Proposed Branch Plant In a short time we shall begin the construction of a branch plant in or

Mr. John Brown--2--April 2, 19--

8. Do not use letterhead paper for the second and subsequent pages.

One style of reference in use is shown above; other styles are given below:

Mr. John Brown--Page 2--April 2, 19--

Mr. John Brown--Page Two--April 2, 19--

Mr. John Brown
Page Two
April 2, 19--

Mr. John Brown   Page 2   April 2, 19--

Mr. John Brown   2   April 2, 19--

Some typists use the back of the first carbon copy for the carbon copy of the second page. This practice effects a saving in paper and filing space, but makes the copy harder to read. It is better practice to use a separate sheet for each copy.

To erase when using carbons, insert a strip of paper in back of each carbon sheet, or use a thin celluloid shield. Place the shield in back of the sheet being erased and in front of the carbon sheet. Do not let the particles lodge between the sheets.

                        Yours very truly

                        TYPEWRITTEN COMPANY NAME

                        Identifying Signature
                        Dictator's Title

XXX/xxx

TURNER CONSTRUCTION COMPANY ⚹ ENGINEERS & CONTRACTORS

EXECUTIVE OFFICES ⚹ SECOND NATIONAL BANK BUILDING

ST. LOUIS, MISSOURI

Month Date, Year

TELEPHONE
MAIN 4396

Name_____
  Address_____
  City, State_____

Dear Sir:

    Subject: Additional Minor Part

  The Minor Part, "Subject," is shown in this
letter. There is also a variation in the placement of the Identifying Signature, which is incorporated in the reference section instead of in the
signature section.

  The Subject line may be either blocked or centered, depending upon the style of the letter. As
in the case of the Attention Phrase, the Subject
line is to be considered as a manuscript title and
therefore does not require a period at the end.

  "In re" is a Latin expression which means "in
the matter of." It is sometimes found in insurance
and legal letters. In such letters it takes the
place of the subject, and its placement follows the
style of the letter. If the phrase which begins
with "In re" is quite long, it may be considered
as the first paragraph of the letter and indented
or blocked accordingly.

      Very truly yours,

       Dictator's Title

Dictator's Name:XXX

(150 Words)

Style Letter 7—to accompany Assignment 7
Single-spaced; Indented; Mixed Punctuation

UNITED TELEPHONE COMPANY

≈≈≈≈≈≈≈≈≈≈≈≈≈≈≈≈≈≈≈≈≈≈≈≈

829 BROAD STREET ● PHILADELPHIA, PA

K. L. SLOAN
Division Traffic Superintendent

Month Date, Year

Name_____
Address_____
City, State_____

Dear Sir:

The first page of a two-page letter follows the placement of
a long letter, as given in the Letter Placement Chart at the
beginning of this Division. The second page carries the remaining part of the Body and the closing, the signature, and
the reference sections.

Care must be exercised to preserve the balance of a two-page
letter. The following information will serve as a guide in
this respect:

1. If a paragraph breaks at the bottom of the first page, do
not have less than two lines on the first page, nor less than
three lines on the second page. A four-line paragraph, therefore, should be placed entirely on the first page or entirely
on the second page.

2. If it is possible, do not end the first page of a broken
paragraph with a period. The period may give the impression
that the letter is finished.

3. When it can be avoided, do not end the first page of the
letter with a hyphen. Either complete the word on the first
page, or carry the entire word over to the second page.

4. Never change the side margins when writing the second and
subsequent pages of a letter.

5. Begin the first line on the second page far enough down on
the sheet so that the top margin will be the same width as the
left margin.

6. The first line of the second page is a reference line. It
may be written in one of the several ways illustrated on the
next page.

7. Begin the first paragraph of the second page on the second
or the third line below the reference.

(442 Words)

recommended as a desirable site because of its natural gas supply. (P) We recognize, of course, the greater heat value and lower price of natural gas as compared with the manufactured product, but we should like to get definite information about the quality of your gas and its availability. (P) We shall be grateful if you will send us such data as, in your judgment and experience, would be of value to us in arriving at a conclusion on the proper location of our new plant. Very truly yours, (*110 words*)

2. **Mr. W. C. Kenton, Secretary   United Athletic Association   Jefferson, Missouri   Dear Sir:** In re Excavation of Athletic Field This letter confirms our telephone quotation of thirty-three cents (.33) a cubic yard for the proposed excavation of your new ball field. We understand that the material is to be deposited in accordance with the plan explained to us by Mr. Jackson. This bid does not include any landscaping, but covers only the simple excavation and deposit of material according to your plans. (P) We have a steam shovel close at hand, with a complete outfit consisting of locomotive, cars, etc., which could be put on this work within 48 hours if time is any object. (P) We shall be glad to have you tell us whether this figure is satisfactory. Should you award the contract to us, you will be assured of a first-class excavation job. Very truly yours, (*133 words*)

3. **Mr. Charles W. Duke   Central Trust Company   Second and Pine Streets   St. Louis, Missouri   Dear Sir:** In re Triangle Building Mr. Hull has referred to me your letter of August 28, in which you express the belief that the bill in the amount of $23.21 for covering the sidewalk on the Boone Street side of the Triangle Building is excessive. I want to explain that, in accordance with our previous custom, we simply mounted the subcontractor's bill on our billhead and sent it to you after the bill had received the approval of our office. (P) We have investigated the matter further and have found that it was necessary for the subcontractor—the Simpson Paving Company—to cut away the sidewalk and renew the waterproofing around the walk lights. The job required two separate operations. That fact accounts for the apparently excessive bill for such a small area of

of the subcontractor for this work and shall appreciate your having a check for the amount sent to us. Yours very truly, (*158 words*)

4. **Carter Realty Company   Ninth and Green Streets   St. Louis, Missouri   Gentlemen:** Subject: Sand-blasting Union Trust Company Building We have now had an opportunity to examine in detail the bids of the Acme Sand-blasting Company and the Jamison Construction Company for doing the required work on the Union Trust Company building. (P) We have decided to accept the bid of the Acme Company. The amount of the bid, as you know, is $667.00. It covers the sand-blasting of the lower stone work on all three sides of the building from the pavement to the second story. We have investigated the company to some extent by communicating with people who have used its facilities. We suggest, however, that you make additional inquiries. (P) We do not consider it necessary to accept the Acme proposal for painting the windows on the ground floor and on the second floor of the building. Our painters can do that work when the sand-blasting has been completed. (P) The bids are being returned to you separately. Please let us know as soon as you have made definite arrangements to go ahead with the work. Very truly yours, (*173 words*)

5. **Hampton Elevator Company   2800 Michigan Boulevard   Chicago, Illinois   Gentlemen:** Subject: Western Trust Company Building Alterations We are authorized by the Western Trust Company to accept your proposal dated July 28 in the amount of Three Thousand Six Hundred Forty-eight Dollars ($3,648.00) for furnishing and installing one Electric Passenger and Coin Lift for the Tenth Street Branch of the Trust Company. (P) All work is to be done in strict accordance with the plans and specifications which you have submitted and to the entire satisfaction and final acceptance of the Architect, Mr. H. Foster Wagner, and of the Trust Company's Real Estate Manager, Mr. F. W. DeMuth. (P) This acceptance is sent you at this time in order that you may begin work immediately on detailing the doors. The elevator details, however, cannot be prepared right away.

the elevator. Mr. Wagner informs us that this information will be available within a week. (P) The acceptance of your proposal is contingent upon your preparing detailed shop drawings which are to be submitted at the earliest possible date to Mr. Edward J. Herring, Assistant in charge of the Tenth Street Branch, and to Mr. H. Foster Wagner, Architect, for approval. (P) Please acknowledge receipt of this acceptance and inform us when you will be prepared to submit the shop drawings. Very truly yours, (*220 words*)

Assignment 8

Type these three letters in the form of Style Letter 8. Use one of the letterheads marked Form 10 for the first page of each letter. Use a plain sheet for the second page. The letters were dictated by **K. L. Sloan, Division Traffic Superintendent** of the **United Telephone Company.** Make a carbon copy of each letter and address a No. 10 envelope for it. Use a different reference style for the second page of each letter.

First, type Style Letter 8, pages 112 and 113.

1. **Mr. W. C. Keim, Chief Engineer United Telephone Company 897 Madison Avenue New York, New York Dear Sir** This letter is in regard to the supports for loading coils that are to be installed in connection with the Wayland cable, as recently discussed with Mr. Dixon. It is our understanding that at least four cases, each weighing approximately 5,700 pounds, will be installed at each loading point, and that there is a possibility that a fifth case may be installed. In view of these facts, we have designed a fixture suitable for a maximum of five cases and capable of supporting a load of 27,000 pounds distributed over the span. (P) I am sending you separately a copy of Drawing No. 002-X-AC, which shows the general arrangement of the support recommended for this work and the method of mounting the coil cases upon it. A copy of this drawing has already been handed to Mr. Dixon informally by Mr. Burton, so that arrangements could be made for ordering the material in advance. (P) The support consists of six 14″ x 6¾″ x ¾″ channels, each 75′ 2″ long, which are bolted to two poles spaced 17½′ between centers along the line. The channels are braced laterally by means of ⅞″ suspension clamp bolts and vertically by means of four 6″ x 7″ x ¾″ angles. Each loading coil is secured to the support by means of long ⅞″ bolts, which pass through the tops of the coil cases and which are fastened underneath the channels by means

of flat steel straps. The lengths of the ⅞″ bolts and steel straps are determined by the dimensions of the coil cases and should be specified when ordering the material. (P) As it is possible that you may experience some difficulty in obtaining channels of the exact size shown on the drawing, I have listed below two alternate sizes that may be employed, if necessary, for the main members of the support:

15″ x 3.60″ x 14″ channels—17 lbs. a foot
18″ x 2.64″ x 20″ channels—26 lbs. a foot

(P) As the angles and straps are of common commercial sizes, I do not anticipate any difficulty in obtaining them. (P) In case any additional information is desired in connection with the supporting of these loading coil cases, please inform me promptly. Very truly yours (*370 words*)

2. **Mr. Frank C. Frederick General Electric Company Schenectady, New York Dear Sir** I have been asked to reply to your letter in which you ask our views on the substitution of leather for brass sleeves to insulate the wire joints in cable splices. (P) The application to untinned copper conductors of a vulcanized leather covering is likely to result in serious damage both to the conductor and to the covering. The reaction between the copper and the leather is due to the sulphur content of the latter material; and if the reaction is allowed to proceed for any considerable period of time, either the leather covering or the conductor will be destroyed. (P) This tendency to reaction between copper and leather has been recognized ever since the manufacture of leather-covered wire was undertaken on a considerable scale. The usual means of combating the reaction is to apply a coating of tin to the copper conductor before it is insulated. Tin does not react with leather; and if the tin coating is reasonably pure and covers the

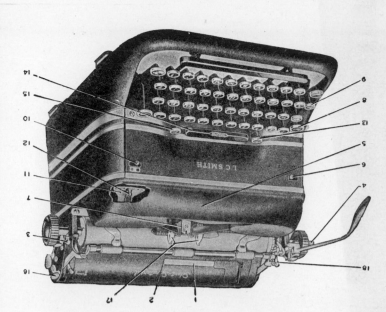

Other Operating Parts
I. C. Smith

1. Paper Gauge Scale
2. Paper Gauge Indicator
3. Platen Lock
4. Variable Control
5. Ribbon Spool Cover
6. Manual Ribbon Reverse
7. Ribbon Carrier
8. Back Space Key
9. Shift Lock Key
10. Ribbon Control
11. Touch Selector Indicator
12. Touch Selector
13. Individual Tabulator Stop Clear Key
14. Tabulator Bar
15. Tabulator Stop Set Key
16. Tabulator Stop Universal Clear Lever
17. Card and Envelope Fingers

Other Operating Parts
Woodstock

1. Tabulator Stop
2. Tabulator Bar
3. Front Scale Indicator
4. Card Holder
5. Tabular Release Key
6. Ribbon Shift Lever
7. Tabulator Key
8. Left Shift Lock
9. Right Shift Lock
10. Tabular Set Key
11. Back Space Key
12. Ribbon Reverse Rod
13. Cylinder Detent Release
14. Variable Line Spacer

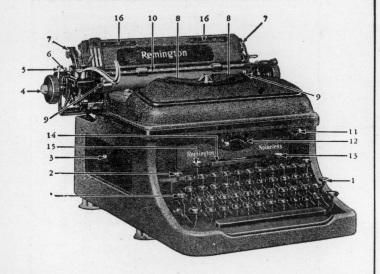

Other Operating Parts
Remington Noiseless

1. **Double Shift Lock**
2. **Back-Spacer Key**
3. **Ribbon Reverse**
4. **Variable Line Spacer**
5. **Variable Lock Lever**
6. **Ratchet Detent Lever**
7. **Removable Platen Lock**
8. **Card Holders**
9. **Paper Fingers**
10. **Paper Bail**
11. **Ribbon Color Change and Stencil Lever**
12. **Pressure Dial**
13. **Tabulator Set Key**
14. **Tabulator Bar**
15. **Tabulator Clear Key**
16. **Paper Centering Scales**

Other Operating Parts
Underwood

1. **Variable Line Spacer**
2. **Ratchet Release** (line space disengaging lever)
3. **Paper Centering Scales**
4. **Paper Holder Bail Release Lever**
5. **Envelope Holder Arm**
6. **Card Holders**
7. **Marginal Stop Release Lever**
8. **Bi-chrome Ribbon Shift** (ribbon indicator)
9. **Shift Lock**
10. **Back Space Key (Back spacer)**
11. **Tabulator Stop Set Key**
12. **Key Set Tabulator Bar**
13. **Tabulator Stop Clear Key**
14. **Carriage Frame Pointer**
15. **Touch Tuning**